C000302449

The Book of
POOLE HARBOUR

ABOVE
The Harbour's first coastguard station was a nineteenth century gunboat built to serve in the shallow waters of the Baltic. It stood high on the dunes on North Haven Point. In 1879 a new coastguard station was built, and the gunboat was sold at auction to a Poole shipbuilder, who strengthened and lengthened it and relaunched it as a three-masted schooner in the coasting trade.

FOLLOWING PAGES
An aerial view of Poole Harbour, with the Sandbanks peninsula in the foreground.

Edited by

BERNARD DYER AND TIMOTHY DARVILL

THE DOVECOTE PRESS
In association with POOLE HARBOUR HERITAGE PROJECT

The Book of
POOLE HARBOUR

The steam packet *Gannet* in 1902, flying the house flag of
H.A. Burden: attributed to C.C. Hyatt.

First published in 2010 by The Dovecote Press Ltd
Stanbridge, Wimborne Minster, Dorset BH21 4JD
in association with
Poole Harbour Heritage Project

ISBN 978-1-904-34982-2

© The Contributors and Poole Harbour Heritage Project 2010

The contributors have asserted their rights under the Copyright, Designs
and Patent Act 1988 to be identified as authors of this work

Designed by The Dovecote Press
Typeset in Sabon
Printed and bound in Singapore by KHL Printing Ltd

All papers used by The Dovecote Press are natural,
recyclable products made from wood grown in sustainable,
well-managed forests

A CIP catalogue record for this book is available
from the British Library

All rights reserved

1 3 5 7 9 8 6 4 2

Contents

The Contributors

MICHAEL A'COURT sadly died before the publication of this book. Originally from Jersey, he came to the UK to train as an Electronics Engineer, working initially with EMI and later for NatWest Credit Sevices. On retirement, he moved to Poole to pursue his love of sailing and joined Poole Maritime Trust in 1995. A founder member of Poole Harbour Heritage Project, he contributed in a major way to the initial planning of this book

IAN ANDREWS came to Poole in 1961 and was Town Clerk and Chief Executive Officer, Poole Borough Council, from 1973 until retirement in 1993 and the Hon Borough Archivist. He is currently Trustee and Hon Secretary, Poole Historical Trust; Co-Founder and Chairman, Wessex Newfoundland Society; President, Society of Poole Men; and a member of the Poole Maritime Trust and many other organisations. He is the author of several books and articles on Poole

PETER BELLAMY has been Principal Archaeologist at Terrain Archaeology since 1997. He has been a professional archaeologist for over 25 years and has worked extensively in Dorset and south-west Britain. He is particularly interested in prehistoric and Roman archaeology and the historic towns of Dorset.

GILL BROADBENT has an interest in archaeology which began over 20 years ago following her re-location to Dorset. This interest led to the completion of a degree in Archaeological Studies at Bristol University as a mature student. Gill joined Poole Harbour Heritage Project in 2005, since when she has played an active role in the Dorset Alum and Copperas Project

ALAN BROMBY was born in Poole and served in the Royal Navy in the Second World War in the Arctic and the Mediterranean seas. All his working life has been on the islands in Poole Harbour, first on Furzey Island, then Round Island and from 1962 to 1987 as Head Warden for the National trust on Brownsea Island. He is a member of Poole Harbour Heritage Project and the Dorset Wildlife Trust.

PETER BURT is a Poole Harbour Commissioner. He has been in the boat business since 1962 and Managing Director of Arthur Bray Ltd, the local boatyard, since 1970. He was Commodore of the Royal Motor Yacht Club 1995/97, and is a cruising sailor. He is the past Chairman of the Poole Harbour Watch and a member of the Wessex Marine Business Association. He is a Fellow of the Royal Society of Arts.

BEN BUXTON is honorary assistant curator of Wareham Museum, a tutor in archaeology in adult education, and a heathland ranger. He is the author of books and articles on local history in Dorset and in the Outer Hebrides.

EDWARD COOMBE was the winner of the Herbertson Memorial Prize for best undergraduate dissertation at Oxford, 1981, and a joint 1st winner of the Royal Geographical Society open UK Essay Award, 1981, and was elected Fellow. Now retired, he currently is a Consultant in Coastal Geomorphology, and a lecturer with Poole U3A.

DAVID COUSINS retired in 2002 after a career in forensic science. He became a part time student at King Alfred's College (now the University of Winchester) and gained an MA in history and archaeology in 2005. He is currently completing a research project on the Dorset monasteries in the late Middle Ages for a PhD.

ANDREW DAVID served for more than forty years in the Royal Navy, during which he took part in surveys in many parts of the world, from which several Admiralty charts have been published. Since retiring he has published numerous articles on the work of early surveyors, including three on Murdock Mackenzie, in whose work he has taken a particular interest.

BRIAN ELLIS graduated from London University in 1962 and spent thirty years teaching history. Membership of the Fortress Study Group since 1990 added to his knowledge of military archaeology. His association with Brownsea Island started in 1995 and in recent years he has devised and led 'Brownsea Island at War' walks for the National Trust.

RAYMOND FARLEIGH grew up across the border in Bournemouth but has lived in the borough of Poole for 50 years. He retired from the Lord Chancellor's Department in 1990 but had previously worked with Eldridge Pope, the Dorchester Brewer, for 30 years. He is a member of the Brewery History Society and was a founder member of the old Poole Industrial Archaeology Group.

DAVID GRANGER is a retired GP, after 40 years of practice in Poole. Previously a frequent long-distance sailor from Poole Harbour but, at 82, now happily restricted to the harbour edge.

SARAH-JANE HATHAWAY studied archaeology at Bournemouth University, where she is completing her doctoral research into the salt-making industries of southern and western England during later prehistoric and Roman times. She is currently the Historic Environment Records Officer for Kent County Council.

ANDREW HAWKES family has been associated with Poole and its Harbour since the late eighteenth century in making leather waterproof boots for fishermen. They also ran the family shoe business in Poole High Street for over 150 years. Andrew served on the Poole Lifeboat for 37½ years and is a Honorary Freeman of the Town of Poole.

ALAN HAWKINS is a retired Building Society Mortgage Manager. He has a long-standing interest in Local History and Archaeology and is a member of several local societies ,including East Dorset Antiquarian Society (since 1991) and Poole Harbour Heritage Project since it was founded in 1997 and the Alum and Copperas Project. He is a volunteer with Poole Museum Services and the History Centre.

KEITH JARVIS graduated in mathematics from Bath University. He worked at Harwell and Nuffield College, Oxford, before excavating widely in Southern England. He was the M5 motorway archaeologist for Devon and subsequently archaeologist for Christchurch. As director of the Poole Museums Archaeological Unit he was associated with many local excavations, including the Studland Bay Wreck. He is married with two daughters and lives in Wareham.

LILIAN LADLE grew up in Northumberland and has lived in Wareham since 1965. She has researched local history since the 1970s and has had had a number of books published. She is a regular contributor to *Dorset Life*. Between 1992-2005 she directed excavations at Bestwall Quarry, Wareham, and has a continuing active involvement in local archaeology.

GORDON LE PARD is a Marine Archaeologist working for Dorset County Council, where he created the Maritime element of the Historic Environment Record, listing all the known shipwrecks and other archaeological finds around the Dorset coast. He has had a long acquaintance with Poole Harbour ever since getting stuck in the mud there at the age of eight.

VINCENT MAY is Professor Emeritus of Coastal Geomorphology and Conservation at Bournemouth University. Until recently Chair of the Poole Harbour Study Group, he has investigated Poole Harbour geomorphology since the 1960s. Joint editor of 'Coastal Geomorphology of Great Britain' and 'The Ecology of Poole Harbour', he now studies coastal change in England and California.

POOLE FLYING BOATS CELEBRATION is a registered charity celebrating the illustrious history and times of the the Fying Boats and Seaplanes based in Poole belonging to the allied forces and to UK civil aviation, before, during and after the Second World War. This was a remarkable era, for Poole Harbour was the main UK civil airport during the war.

WILLIAM SHELDRICK served in the Royal Navy from 1943 to 1946, followed by studies at Durham University. After twenty-four years in the UK and overseas chemical industry he joined the World Bank in Washington in 1974 as Industry Adviser. On his return to the UK in 1989 he worked as International Industrial Consultant for clients including the World Bank, other UN Agencies and the Chinese Government until he retired in 2002. He has since worked on environmental issues such as nutrient depletion and bio-ethanol production.

ERIC STREET studied chemistry and chemical engineering at Manchester University and Imperial College. He worked in the chemical industry for 45 years, covering many different chemicals and chemical waste products. Subsequently he went on behalf of UNIDO and the BESO to Brazil, the Ukraine, Thailand and China as a process consultant. He has been developing a theory about the early formation for the earth and helping Poole Harbour Heritage Project.

JEAN SUTTON is a graduate of the London School of Economics, University of London. Inspired by accounts of the wreck of the *Halsewell*, an East Indiaman, off St Aldhelm's Head, she began researching the East India Company's shipping, leading to the publication of a general history in 1981 and a history of the Company's Maritime Service in 2010.

DAVID WATKINS is a graduate of the University of Wales and an Associate of the Institute of Field Archaeologists. He started work with Poole Museum in 1984 as an archaeologist and managed several large excavations in the Borough. For the last ten years he has managed the Poole History Centre within Poole Museum.

SARAH WELTON moved to Dorset in 1971 after graduating in Zoology from the University of Wales. She worked for Dorset Wildlife Trust as Marine Conservation Officer and Warden of the Purbeck Marine Wildlife Reserve and as an Education Officer for the Marine Conservation Society. She is a Poole Harbour Commissioner.

CHRISTINE WIDDOWSON has always had a keen interest in architectural history which led to her studying for a Master's degree at the University of Southampton. Since graduating, she has assisted the National Trust transcribing Elizabethan documents and is currently secretary of Poole Harbour Heritage Project.

EILEEN WILKES is Lecturer in Archaeology at Bournemouth University. Her research focuses on prehistoric intertidal and coastal archaeology along and across the English Channel as well as survey and interpretation of inland sites. She is currently on the Council of the Prehistoric Society and the Steering Committee of the Poole Harbour Heritage Project.

Acknowledgements

TEXT

A large number of organisations and individuals have been involved in the preparation of this book, and the editors wish to acknowledge the considerable help and support that they have received from them. Our first and greatest debt is to the contributors, all of whom have managed to research and write their chapters whilst fitting it in with the rest of their work.

Members of the Poole Maritime Trust and the Poole Harbour Heritage Project; Bernard Aston; Suzie Baverstock(BP); Malcolm R. Bowditch; Annabella Burt; Ray Cherrett; Anthony Clarke; Sheila Cox; Robin Culpan; Peter J.G. Dawson; Katie Gardiner (Poole Museum); Jim Gordon; Katie Hanks; Ken Latham; Brian Mullins; Charles Palfreeman; Robin Phipps; Eric Scoble; Ann C. Smeaton; John Smith; Peter Stebbing; Mike Tombs; Gerry Wareham; Jeremy Waters; David Watkins and his staff (Poole History Centre); Annie Willats (Poole Harbour Commissioners).

Special thanks are due to Christine Widdowson, Secretary of the Poole Harbour Heritage Project.

BERNARD DYER AND TIMOTHY DARVILL

ILLUSTRATIONS

A considerable number of people and organisations have helped provide the illustrations in this book. It may seem ungenerous to single out one source of illustrations at the expense of all the others, but it is no exaggeration to say that this book would not exist in its present form without the support of Poole Museum and Poole History Centre, and I would like to thank Michael Spender, Dai Watkins, Sue Beckett and Katie Gardiner for their help and encouragement. They have cheerfully given of their time and knowledge of Poole, and turned the task of selecting the illustrations in the Museum Collection into a pleasure.

But there are many others who merit thanking, and I am grateful to the following: Harry Alexander (Poole Flying Boats Celebration), Victor Ambrus, Katie Anderson (The Natural History Museum/NHM Image Resources), Ian Andrews, Grahame Austin (Kitchenham Photography), Lin Baldock, Suzie J. Baverstock (BP Exploration Operating Co Ltd), Mrs Margaret Bell, Peter Bellamy, Bridgeman Art Library (Joanne Hardy), Gill Broadbent, Alan Bromby, Jonathan Butler (English Heritage Photo Library), Peter and Trelawny Burt, Ben Buxton, Mrs Myrna Chave, Andy Clewer (RNLI), David Cousins, Andy Criddle and Tamsin Wenham (United Kingdom Hydrographic Office),Timothy Darvill, Andrew David, Bryan Edwards, Brian Ellis, Raymond Farleigh, Mark Forrest and Matthew Knowles (Dorset History Centre), Nick Gribble, David Harding (www.sailingscenes.co.uk), Anna Harrison (The National Trust Photo Library); Sarah-Jane Hathaway, Andrew Hawkes, Keith Jarvis, Lilian Ladle, Gemma Langridge (Sunseeker International Ltd), Gordon Le Pard, Vincent May, Yvonne Oliver and Rosanna Wilkinson (Imperial War Museum), William Sheldrick, Mrs A. Shinn, Julie Snow (Poole Borough Council), Jean Sutton, Colin and Susy Varndell, Roger Ward, Sarah Welton, Lorna Whitehead (Poole Yacht Club), Annie Willats (Poole Harbour Commissioners), John Willows, Willie Wilson and Elinor Cole (Imray Laurie Norie & Wilson Ltd)

I would also like to thank the following for allowing the inclusion of illustrations in their possession,or which they hold the copyright: Mike A'Court; 39 bottom: Victor Ambrus; 67: Ian Andrews; 38 top, 81, 84 both, 96 top, 190, 193 both, 203: Lin Baldock; 28 both, 29 both; David Bailey; 12/13, 26 top, 53, 79, 129, 175 top, 187 centre, 192, 199, 201, 202 top, 234: Bournemouth University/Poole Museum; 188: Jane Brayne; 65 top: Bridgeman Art Library/Torre Abbey, Torquay; the front cover painting by Herbert Kerr Rooke (1872-1944), *Shipping in Poole Harbour*: BP Exploration Operating Co Ltd; 121: Gill Broadbent; 109, 110 all: Alan Bromby; 100, 101: Ben Buxton; 87, 88, 123 bottom, 124 all, 211 top, 212 top right: Vanessa Constant; 60: *Daily Echo*; 134 top right: David Cousins; 126 both:

The South Haven slipway
in the 1930s.

Timothy Darvill; 61 right: Dorset History Centre; 167: Dorset History Centre/National Trust; 78, 90: English Heritage; 69: Bryan Edwards; 24 both, 25 top: Raymond Farleigh; 141, 142 top: David Harding/www.sailingscenes.co.uk; 22, 82, 159 top, 163 bottom, 184 top, 187 top, 208 bottom, 233, 234, 240 bottom, 241: Sarah-Jane Hathaway; 107 both: Andrew Hawkes; 9, 45 top, 130 top, 133, 136 bottom, 139 top, 142 bottom, 143 both, 144 top, 145 top, 146 top, 206, 207 all, 225 top, 226 top left and centre, 227 bottom, 230 bottom, 231: Imperial War Museum; 96 bottom, 97 all, 116 bottom: Imray Laurie Norie & Wilson; 170/171: Keith Jarvis; 71, 106: Kitchenham Photography; 2/3, 19, 20, 68, 77, 83, 119 top, 185 top, 215, 239: Lilian Ladle; 63, 64 all, 65 bottom: Gordon Le Pard; 36, 38, 44 both: Mike Markey/Poole Museum; 62: Vincent May; 18 bottom, 21 top: Ministry of Defence; 186 bottom: The Natural History Museum, London; 57: Pierre Pétrequin/Project JADE; 61 left: Poole Borough Council; 240: Poole Flying Boats Celebration; 216, 217 both, 218 both, 219 all, 220 bottom, 221: Poole Harbour Commssioners; 41, 45, 162 bottom right, 184 centre, bottom left, bottom right, 187 top and bottom right, 189 bottom: Poole Lifeboat Station; 208 top: Poole Museum; 10, 14/15, 32/33, 34, 37, 39 top, 40, 43, 45, 54/55, 70, 73 both, 98 centre and bottom, 99, 102/103, 113, 114, 115 both, 116 top and centre, 117, 122, 125, 127 both, 128, 131 top left, 131 all, 132, 133 top left and bottom, 134 top left, 135 top, 136 top, 137 all, 139 bottom, 140 top, 146 bottom, 147 all, 148, 149, 150 all, 151, 152 both, 153 both, 154 all, 155, 156 top, 159, 160 both, 161 both, 162 top, 164/16, 172, 173 both, 174 bottom, 175 bottom, 176 both, 177 all, 178/179, 180 both, 181 all, 182 both, 183 top, 192 bottom left, 194 both, 195 both, 197, 198 bottom, 200, 212 bottom, 214 bottom, 220 top, 222, 223, 224 both, 225 bottom, 226 bottom and top right, 227 top, 228 top, 229 top, 230 top left and centre, 232 both, 236/237: Poole Yacht Club; 229: Royal Motor Yacht Club/Peter Burt; 96 top: RNLI; 209 both: Mrs A. Shinn; 210: Graham Smith/Poole Museum; 91: William Sheldrick; 135 bottom, 140 bottom: Stoborough First School; 122 top: Sunseeker International Ltd; 157 both: Terrain Archaeology; 72 both: United Kingdom Hydrographic Office; 168, 169, 170/171: Colin Varndell; 23, 25 bottom, 26 bottom, 27 top left and top right, 27 bottom, 30, 31, 85, 214 top: Wessex Water; 51 both, 52 both: Yachting World/John Iddon/Peter Burt: 231 bottom.

I am also grateful to Peter Lightfoot of Media4 Graphix Ltd for his skill in creating the maps on pages 17, 18 top, 46/47, 49, 66, 101, 107, 118, 119 bottom, 129, 191, 213.

The Dovecote Press has made all reasonable efforts to track down holders of copyright, but would be grateful to be informed of any omissions.

DAVID BURNETT, THE DOVECOTE PRESS

The brigantine Lady of Avenal *at Town Quay,* by Arthur Bradbury (1892-1977).

Foreword

POOLE HARBOUR – reputedly (but disputably) the second largest natural harbour in the world – has a long and fascinating history that has had a determining influence not only locally but also nationally and internationally.

Many studies have, in the past, been carried out on specific aspects of its heritage, but towards the end of the 1990s it became apparent that these needed to be brought together and, where necessary, extended. Accordingly, the Poole Harbour Heritage Project (PHHP) was set up as an associate of the Poole Maritime Trust to do this and to promulgate the results of its studies to the public – especially to young people who would ultimately be inheriting this heritage.

Continuing work has shown a need for a publication that sets out the overall picture, to act both as an educational reference and as a guide towards further work. The present book attempts to fulfil these purposes and is commended to all with an interest in the past, the present, and the future of Poole Harbour.

CAPTAIN MICHAEL FULFORD-DOBSON CVO, OBE, KStJ, JP, DL,
ROYAL NAVY
Lord Lieutenant for Dorset, 1999 – 2006
Patron, Poole Harbour Heritage Project

Poole harbour has been, and continues to be, a dynamic place in all senses of the word. In geological terms its life, so far, has been relatively short but much has happened during that time. Its formation dates only from the end of the Ice Age 10,000 years ago, and its development into its present form is the story of continuing evolution that has had, in turn, a major influence on mankind's development in and around it.

Prior to the end of the Ice Age there was no Harbour as such, nor any English Channel to connect with it, but merely a river system with its origins in the depths of what we now know as Dorset. This system, formed from what are now the rivers Piddle, Frome, Corfe and Sherford, flowed in a valley coinciding broadly with the principal channels of the present Harbour until it became one river flowing in an easterly direction parallel with the present Hampshire coast through what is now the Solent. It was joined by tributaries from both north and south until it turned in a south-westerly direction east of what is now the Isle of Wight to join a Channel river flowing towards the Atlantic Ocean in the west.

Rising water levels led to the formation of the English Channel and ultimately to a breakthrough of the land between what are now the Needles and the Old Harry Rocks. Continuing increases in water levels led to the inundation of land in what is now the general area of the present Harbour, with the higher parts remaining as separate islands within it.

Long before the Harbour itself was developed in

this way, the riverbanks would have been occupied by humans, but they would necessarily have had to move back as these banks receded. Evidence of such occupation accordingly must still exist under the waters of the present Harbour, and it was this thought that prompted Teddy Neville-Jones, the then-Chairman of the Poole Maritime Trust, towards the end of the 1990s to propose that this would be worth further investigation. Unfortunately, soon after this he died but those of us remaining continued to explore the idea, as a result of which the Poole Harbour Heritage Project (PHHP) was formed as an affiliate of the Trust in the year 2000, with charity status being achieved in 2001.

A Steering Committee was formed under the Chairmanship of Timothy Darvill, Professor of Archaeology at Bournemouth University. Membership of the Committee, which is voluntary, continues to comprise a number of interested individuals and representatives of a wide range of organisations with interests in the Harbour – including Bournemouth University, Dorset County Council, East Dorset Antiquarian Society, English Heritage, Hampshire and Wight Trust for Maritime Archaeology, The National Trust, Poole Borough Council, Poole Harbour Commissioners and Poole Maritime Trust.

The work of PHHP has extended considerably beyond the initial idea and now encompasses the topics covered by *The Book of Poole Harbour,* the first five parts of which correspond with the studies within the Project:

Part I: The Natural Development of the Harbour
Part II: Man-made Changes to the Harbour
Part III: Settlements in and around the Harbour
Part IV: Industry associated with the Harbour
Part V: Trade, Transport and Recreation.

Whilst much has been achieved, it is apparent that much more still remains to be done. Accordingly it is hoped that the book in its present form will not only encourage public interest in the Harbour, but will lead both to general support and, for those who might wish to do so, to specific involvement in the continuing work of the Project.

Each of the above Parts aims to be as complete as possible, but limitations of space and an attempt to appeal to the general reader as well as to those already knowledgeable have necessitated considerable compression. Each part has accordingly been allocated its own set of references for further reading which it is hoped will encourage those who wish to do so to explore any specific subject in more depth.

Many individuals and organisations continue to be involved with the Project, and many of these have been involved in the production of this book. On behalf of the Project, it is my pleasant duty to acknowledge their considerable and continuing help and support.

BERNARD DYER
President, Poole Maritime Trust
Chairman, Poole Harbour Heritage Project

Brownsea Island from Evening Hill.

The Purbecks from Poole Harbour, Dorset by Bernard Gribble (1872-1962).

PART ONE
The Natural Development
of the Harbour

ONE

Introduction

VINCENT MAY

POOLE HARBOUR is a large lowland estuary about 8650 acres (3500 hectares) in area which drains much of central and southern Dorset, including most of the Isle of Purbeck. Its shoreline, including the islands, is about 100 miles (160 kilometres) in length at Mean High Water. The northern and eastern shore is built upon and includes much of the port activity, in contrast to the mainly open heath and woodland on its southern and western shores. Its four largest islands (Brownsea, Furzey, Green, and Round) are built upon, and include Europe's largest onshore oil and gas field, Brownsea Castle, and several houses.

There are two main channel systems, to the north the Wareham, Ship and North Channels are fed by the Frome, Piddle and Sherford rivers, whilst to the south the Corfe River and several smaller streams join to flow south of Brownsea Island, ultimately all meeting together to flow through the Harbour mouth. The Ship and Swash Channels and, to a lesser extent, the North Channel have been modified by dredging to accommodate larger commercial vessels.

The area of the Harbour compared to other similar harbours has been the subject of considerable controversy. Traditionally, it has been named as the world's second largest natural harbour, Sydney Harbour being named as the largest. However, there are many which are larger, including Scapa Flow in Scotland, Grays Harbor in Washington State USA, and Port Lincoln in Australia.

The Harbour is both commercially very important to the local economy and extensively used for recreational activities of all sorts. The Harbour itself is the responsibility of the Poole Harbour Commissioners whilst the Borough of Poole to the north and Purbeck District Council to the south, including the islands, are the planning authorities.

Poole Harbour has special national and international importance, being designated as a European Special Protection Area (SPA), a European Marine Site, part of the Dorset Area of Outstanding Natural Beauty (AONB), and a Site of Special Scientific Interest (SSSI).

The Harbour in its present form developed about 6000 years ago when post-glacial sea levels, which had been rising rapidly (about 9.6 mm a year), reached their present level. Since then, they fell to about 2.7 metres below present levels during the Iron Age before rising again.

The natural development of the Harbour results from a combination of the geomorphological and ecological processes. These are described in the following two chapters. The human activities within the Harbour and its surroundings are considered in Parts II–V of this book.

TWO

The Formation of the Harbour

VINCENT MAY AND MIKE A'COURT

THE PRESENT-DAY appearance of the Harbour is the result of thousands of years of many different geological processes – glacial, tectonic, changes in sea level, wave and river erosion, and sedimentary deposition – and which obliterate the visible outcome of their predecessors. These processes take place over a wide range of time and space scales. Coastlines stand at the junction between four great earth systems, the atmosphere, the land, seas, and humanity. The present form of the Harbour results from the combined effects of all four, with processes which occur at very short timescales bringing about major changes over the longer timescales.

The story of the Harbour's development begins about 125,000 years ago when the landscape between Purbeck and the Isle of Wight was similar to the Purbeck of today. What we know today as Poole Harbour was a

BELOW Poole Harbour today, showing the principal places mentioned in the text.

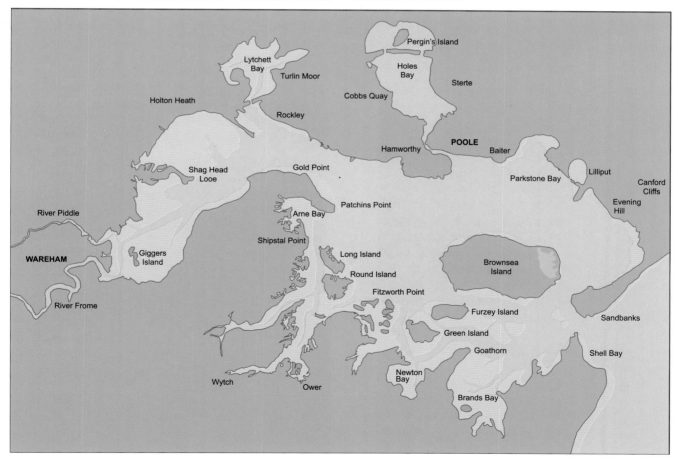

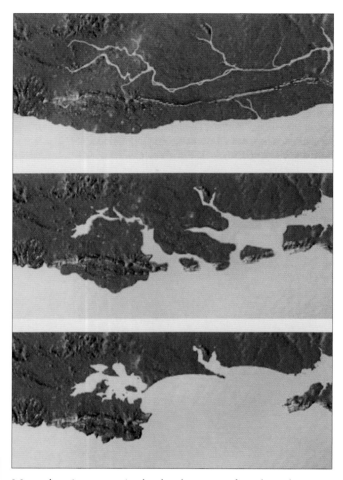

Maps showing stages in the development of Poole and Christchurch Bays and Poole Harbour. For explanation see text.

most likely location of the gaps, just as such features tend to coincide with faults in the chalk ridge in Purbeck.

125, 000 years ago, sea level relative to the land was about 10 metres higher than today. As sea level rose, some of the formerly northward flowing streams may have been captured by more vigorous streams further south and reversed their flow. Tyhurst and Hinton (1997) postulate that the ridge was already breached and that rivers were flowing southwards following a palaeovalley identified by Velegrakis in 1994 (see middle map on left). The Frome-Piddle river was diverted through this gap and would have continued to flow southwards as the climate cooled, sea level fell, and periglacial (tundra) processes prevailed. A similar but slightly later gap broke through the ridge to drain the eastern part of Poole Bay and Christchurch Bay.

As this cold period came to an end, the sea level rose again at rates of as much as 1.5 metres per century (significantly faster than present-day rates). By 9,500 BC, sea level had reached about -40 metres OD and began to remove the southern side of the chalk ridge. Nowell, writing in 1999, suggested that the gaps coincide with faults in the chalk which would have been more readily eroded by the rising sea. Sea level continued to rise until about 8,000 BC it reached about -30 metres and broke through the ridge again. The bays north of the ridge began to open up again as sea level rise and coastal erosion combined to remove much of the land between the ridge and present-day Bournemouth (see bottom

BELOW Green Island. Degraded vegetated cliff in background. Fine yellow sands in right foreground showing phases of deposition and erosion. The central area of the photograph shows a former channel cut into these near-horizontal strata. Present-day erosion is producing rock-falls and undercutting of the upper slope.

valley running west to east, passing north of today's Isle of Wight, before turning south to the embryonic English Channel (see top map above). A river, known as the Solent River, followed this valley, with the rivers Frome and Piddle as its sources, through a landscape which would have been similar to the landscape south of the present Harbour with a series of terraces rising up to a chalk ridge similar in form and height to the Purbeck Ridge. Like the Purbeck Ridge, it was probably broken by gaps such as those at Ulwell and Corfe, with streams flowing northwards through the gaps as they drained the clay vale to the south of the chalk ridge.

The chalk now beneath the sea formed a continuous ridge between Ballard Down and The Needles. Today that chalk forms the seafloor at depths down to about 29 metres at most. About 3 kilometres wide in the west, this sub-marine outcrop narrows eastwards and is marked by a number of north-south trending faultlines. It is generally agreed that the location of the faults is the

map on the left). Poole Bay as we know it gradually came into existence.

The timing of this process, leading to the eventual disappearance of the ridge, is agreed by most authorities to be some 8,000 BC, coincident with the end of the latest, Devensian, Ice Age, and is of major interest in considering the history of human occupation in the area. Before the harder chalk strata could be breached, a large mass of softer rocks particularly to the south of the chalk, had to be eroded away, and this process must have been largely complete by about 8,000 BC.

Until recently it was assumed that this was simply a long-term process of coastal erosion, but in 2007 Gupta and colleagues, reporting on a detailed bathymetric examination of the eastern part of the English Channel, proposed that towards the end of the Devensian Ice Age a dam of rock and ice formed to close the river flowing through the land bridge which linked Britain to mainland Europe, thus forming a lake at the south of the North Sea basin. This lake, fed by the existing major rivers – among them the Thames, the Rhine and the Meuse – together with the run-off from the melting ice cap, would eventually have overtopped and breached the dam, resulting in a catastrophic mega-flood which changed very significantly the geography of the Channel, turning Britain into an island separated from the European mainland. This event may well have

An aerial view of the Arne peninsula, with the Wareham Channel in the background. Patchins Point is in the foreground, and Long and Round Islands to the left.

contributed to the final obliteration of the Purbeck-Wight Ridge as its timing would be more or less coincident with the accepted date of its final breaching.

With stormier conditions and probably higher tidal ranges in the channels, erosion of the sand and clays would have been rapid. The chalk opened into bays, the Purbeck-Wight Ridge was gradually eroded away, and the present coastal shape of Poole Bay developed. Erosion of the sand and clay cliffs supplied beaches which extended across the mouths of the estuaries in alignment with the cliffs. Water flooded into the valleys which carried the Frome-Piddle and the Corfe rivers north and south respectively of a line of islands between Brownsea and Patchins Point. As this was gradually eroded the Harbour became the wide estuary of today, probably about 4000 BC.

Its formation continued, however, as cliffs, beaches and low intertidal terraces formed. The interpretation of these features typically uses the existence of a change of slope from the low-angle terrace to a low bluff where the coast is being actively eroded as a means of describing sea level. These junctions do not represent mean sea level. Their altitude depends upon the combined effects

ABOVE View across the Harbour from the confluence of Wych Lake (right), the Corfe River (centre) and Middlebere Lake (left centre). There are extensive *Spartina* salt marshes.

In the middle centre, Round Island and Long Island are joined by salt marsh. Long Island has a small sand beach extending northwards from an eroding cliff.

Left top, Shipstal Point has a sand and gravel beach fronting low cliffs and extending south on to salt marsh.

Left bottom, a northwards-growing sand and gravel spit is just visible behind the wooded hill. This encloses the salt marshes in Arne Bay which were in the past the source of seedlings for *Spartina* marshes worldwide. The northern side of Arne Bay is Patchins Point where the beach and salt marsh pre-date the invasion by *Spartina*.

of tides, wave heights and wave run-up. For example, they may preserve the position of erosive phases which attain altitudes above mean high water spring tides. Indeed many of those features in the present Harbour cut into the local sands and clays stand at these altitudes. In addition, as the shape of inlets changes so does the tidal range.

Sea level is never static and having flooded the Harbour to its maximum about 4000 BC – marked by a low bluff around much of the present-day Harbour – it stood about 2.7 metres below present levels during both the Iron Age and the late third century AD before rising again and then fluctuating. Today, the estuary has a pattern of a long still-stand at or close to high tide, which means that much of the Harbour is flooded for about 16 hours in every 24. This is likely to have been a persistent pattern once sea levels reached present levels because of the central English Channel tidal behaviour. Tidal range is about 1.8 metres on spring tides and much smaller, about 0.6 metres, on neap tides.

Reclamation of the mudflats around the Harbour from the Iron Age to the present-day has reduced its surface area, but the most significant change in the vegetation and so in the pattern of channels occurred when the Harbour was colonised by *Spartina anglica* (Common Cord-Grass) in the late nineteenth century. Known initially as *S. townsendii* (Townsend's Cord-grass), this hybrid was first identified in Southampton Water and then spread westwards through the Solent. Extensive areas of mudland were colonised and the mud trapped. By the 1920s, *Spartina* covered about 800 hectares, but since then has gradually reduced in area to little more than 300 hectares today.

So the Harbour's present form can be summarized

Spartina anglica salt marsh in the foreground contrasts with the eroding cliffs of Furzey Island and the more degraded slopes of Brownsea Island.

as resulting from the legacy of phases of landform development:

- The Solent River and its tributaries.
- The first break through the Purbeck-Wight Ridge and initiation of the diverted Frome stream.
- Sea level falls and periglacial processes dominate, but the river continues to flow through the gap.
- Sea level rises again rapidly, coastal erosion reduces the ridge, the valleys flood again and the bay is opened up .
- The Purbeck-Wight Ridge finally disappears so that the Harbour is exposed to the present-day wave and tide regime.
- The present sea-level Harbour is established about 4000 BC.
- Iron Age onwards reclamation changes from the shoreline both in the upper Harbour and around Poole.
- Nineteenth century *Spartina* colonises the Harbour changing the intertidal landscape.

The southern shore of Brownsea Island showing the cliff line which developed behind an area of salt marsh in the early twentieth century and is eroded again.

THREE

Flora and Fauna

SARAH WELTON

A VERY SPECIAL PLACE

IT IS THE UNIQUE combination of its size, shape, depth, substrates, small tidal range and other physical features, that makes the wildlife and habitats of Poole Harbour not only special in a local context but nationally and internationally important. The Harbour is protected by many conservation designations, mainly for its internationally important bird populations, the most important of which are the Harbour's recognition as a wetland of international importance and as a Special Protection Area under the European Community Birds Directive. However, although the birds that overwinter,

Fishermen in one of the quiet 'lakes', or creeks, that give the backwaters their character. The Harbour supports an important inshore fish and shellfish industry.

feed, and breed in the Harbour are the most visible of the Harbour's wildlife, they would not be there if it was not for a plentiful food source, safe and sheltered feeding grounds, roosts and nesting sites. So it is not just the birds of Poole that are important, it is also all the plants and animals and the environment that they depend on.

The wildlife of the Harbour is important for people, too. The fish and shellfish support a significant local fishing industry, and wildlife-related tourism – from sea angling to diving and from boat trips to bird-watching – plays no small part in the local economy. Perhaps it is the contrast between the bustling port and expanding holiday area on the north shore of the Harbour and the quiet bays and inlets, a haven for wildlife, along its southern edge, which often surprises the newcomer. This is a contrast which is increasingly difficult to preserve.

THE CHANGING HARBOUR

Without a time-machine, we can only imagine what the wildlife in the Harbour was like before records were kept. However, from our knowledge of the natural changes in the Harbour since its formation, we can make an educated guess. For much of its history, the Harbour would have been surrounded by fringing salt marshes, including the northern shore, much of which has now been reclaimed. Reed swamp would have dominated in the upper reaches where the rivers flow into the Harbour, and most of the plants, which we find today, would have been there in abundance. We know very little about the birds, fish, and other wildlife of the Harbour before the twentieth century, however, other than from their remains in sediments. There is also archaeological evidence – shells and bones are indications of the diet of the early inhabitants – and there are the anecdotal records from fishermen and wildfowlers.

We do have records from the more recent past, and the Harbour itself differs significantly in its patterns of flora from the Harbour of only 150 years ago. This is largely as a result of invasion by the marsh grass *Spartina* and reclamation. This is why research and monitoring are so important in an area such as this – so that future generations can look at the Harbour and understand how it has changed.

The Spartina Story

In many ways the most interesting plant of the Harbour salt marshes is *Spartina* Cord Grass. The arrival, spread and subsequent decline of this grass has been the major force for change in the intertidal zone. *Spartina anglica* is a perennial grass of salt marshes and mudflats. It is, in fact, a hybrid of a native cord grass and a species accidently introduced from North America. It first arrived in the Harbour in the 1890s and by the 1920s had covered large areas of mudflats – an area equivalent to 1,100 football pitches! As this grass traps fine sediments, it was exported to stabilise mudflats around the world. Between 1924 and 1936, more than 175,000 plants from Arne Bay alone were sent to more than 130 sites worldwide. Since the 1930s, *Spartina* in the Harbour has been receding and, by 1980, more than half the original sward had gone. The once-muddy marshes near the Harbour mouth are now firm sands, a change which may be accelerated by rising sea levels.

Although no-one knows for certain why the rapid spread and decline of *Spartina* occurred here, it is thought to be associated with physical and biological changes within the Harbour, such as dredging of the navigation channels and the spread of other salt marsh plants.

Spartina marsh in Holes Bay, with Cobb's Quay in the background.

BETWEEN THE TIDES

When the tide in the Harbour is at its lowest, it reveals a fascinating world of salt marshes, glistening mudflats and shingle and sandy beaches. Although the difference between the highest and lowest tides of the year is less than two metres, the intertidal area comprises about 80 per cent of the total. The Harbour is drained at low water by a relatively stable system of creeks (locally, and somewhat perversely, called 'lakes') and channels, which are pretty much the same as when they were first surveyed 200 years ago. Their movement is constrained by the many promontories and islands, and ultimately by the low-lying, sandy spits of Studland and Sandbanks, which guard the Harbour entrance.

Plants of the Salt Marsh

A salt marsh is a marsh found between the tides, which links the land and sea. The plants we find in the marshes around the margins of the Harbour are very specialised. Few flowering plants can tolerate salty conditions. The distribution of salt marshes in the Harbour is strongly linked to the unusual tides and small tidal range found at Poole and the narrowness of the Harbour entrance, producing a lagoon-like effect. The extent of the salt marsh within the Harbour has been in decline for several years. Salt marsh is generally considered to be a species poor habitat, being dominated by one or two specialised plants. It is also generally split into three distinct zones of differing plants, depending on their tolerance to

The name glasswort came into use in the sixteenth century. The plants were burnt and their ashes used for making soda-based glass.

Sea aster flowers well into the autumn and provides a valuable source of nectar for late-flying butterflies such as the painted lady and red admiral.

inundation by sea water, but owing to the small tidal range, these zones are less apparent than elsewhere. Even here, however, there is all the difference in the world between life in the lower salt marsh zone, where only the few, most salt-tolerant plants can survive and the upper salt marsh, where lots of different plants are found. The lower salt marsh is dominated by *Spartina*; but there are also small stands of the fleshy annual herb, glasswort, changing colour with the seasons from green to yellow to red.

On firmer substrates, communities are dominated by the purple-blue sea aster, in the west, and sea lavender, in the east.

The natural gulleys and creeks enable the marsh to maintain wet, saline conditions and also provide preferred nesting and feeding sites for breeding waders and wildfowl. The creek systems also play an important role in absorbing tidal energy and reducing pressure on sea defences. It is important that the natural drainage system of the marsh is maintained.

In the middle and upper areas of salt marsh, drifts of sea lavender are interspersed with the pale grey foliage of sea purslane. Transitions to fresh water often carry sea rushes, club rushes and distant sedge. On shingle beaches at higher levels the green and scarlet sea beet, maritime, and shrubby sea-blite, add a splash of colour.

Sand, Shingle and Strandline

Scattered throughout the Harbour are small areas of shingle and sand. Where tourist pressure is not too great, a sparse covering of vegetation has developed. There are small areas of vegetated shingle, where scattered plants of sea campion and sheep's sorrel can be found. At a few sites, a strandline community can be found at high water mark. Here, sea sandwort grows abundantly.

Drifts of sea lavender on the eastern side of the Harbour.

Where Freshwater meets the Sea

Known as transitional communities, the plants found on the brackish grassland making up the grazing marshes on the flood plains of the rivers Frome, Piddle and Sherford are dominated by the grass creeping bent. Where the soil is peaty, and freshwater seeps into the back of the salt marsh, the vegetation is very different with dense stands of sea rush, low plants such as creeping bent and fescues beneath.

The Otter Mystery

The Harbour should offer excellent opportunities for otters – plenty of prey and suitable, freshwater habitat, in fact, 'Otter heaven'! The name 'Otter Island' in Lytchett Bay suggests that otters were a feature of the Harbour in the past. Historically, otter records are derived from otter hunt kills. Formal records for otter kills were not kept until the 1930s. Records for the Harbour, collected from 1960 to 1979 lack detail, but they do indicate that otters were widespread in the Harbour up until the 1970s when records became scarcer. Sightings recorded by the Dorset Otter Group since 1997 have been few, suggesting that otters have not colonized the Harbour to the extent they did in the 1960s before the population underwent a dramatic crash. The big question is 'why?' Could it be associated with otters drowning in unregulated eel nets, a shortage of suitable sites for holts, increasing boat traffic, development and roads, pollution, declines in fish stocks . . . or something else? We need to find out more.

The Secret World of Reed beds

If we could penetrate the dense reed beds in the upper reaches of the Harbour, we would find communities of animals totally dependant upon their reed bed habitat. reed warblers and bearded tits use the reed stems as nest supports. Water rails nest in tussocks and feed on invertebrates in the reed bed, and water voles eat young reed shoots as their main diet for much of the year.

A few insects, such as wainscot moths, are so specialised that their whole life cycle occurs in just a few square metres of reed bed. They even overwinter in the hollow reed stems. It is not hard to understand, therefore, that reed beds, which are a dwindling resource in this country owing to agricultural improvements, are a high priority habitat to protect. They were once also

Reed beds provide bearded tits with both food and nesting sites.

an important source of thatch. The reed beds here in the Harbour have been found to be in good condition, supporting a number of notable birds and animals, including the nationally rare bearded tit, marsh harrier and Cetti's warbler. Threats to our reed beds are thought to be damage by sika deer, scrub encroachment, water quality, rising sea levels, and loss by erosion and habitat change.

Merely Mud?

What do you think about mud? Mudflats are unpleasant, smelly areas of barren waste ground when the tide is out, preventing us from getting to the water's edge. However, you might have a different view if you were a wading bird! In fact the glistening mudflats are the Harbour's larders, providing food for the vast numbers of breeding and wintering waterfowl and waders, for which the Harbour is famous. Quite simply, the birds would not be there if the food was not there and the food – mainly worms – would not be there if the mud was not there. So, if worms are not your 'thing', think again! The mud is anything but barren. Surveys of the food resources for birds within the Harbour have shown that the surface of the mud is home to shore crabs, shrimps, and various sea snails but it is the life within the mud that is amazing. Poole Harbour mud is dominated by worms, such as the ragworm and lugworm.

In addition to providing food for birds, the digging

BELOW Lugworms live in u-shaped burrows in the sand or mud. They feed on organic material and excrete the unwanted mud as familiar worm casts.

The bird identification display at Whitecliff Viewpoint, with Parkstone Bay and the Parkstone Yacht Club marina in the background.

of worms for angling bait is a significant activity on the muddy shores of the Harbour. The physical disturbance to the mudflats, caused by cockling and bait-digging, is currently seen as the greatest threat to this habitat. The loss of sediments through changes in the Harbour regime are being addressed by carrying out maintenance dredging of the shipping channels in accordance with a Sediment Management Plan to keep sediments within the Harbour.

BIRDS

When we think of the Harbour, we think of birds. Different groups of birds utilise it at different seasons. The busiest time of all is the winter, when thousands of shore-birds such as dunlin, avocet and redshank flock to feed on the intertidal flats, waterfowl such as wigeon and Brent geese feed on the adjoining fields, diving birds such as grebes and mergansers fish the waters, and water rail and bearded tit utilise the reed beds. The Harbour supports over 20,000 waterfowl at times – a fact which qualifies it for international conservation designations.

Many species have a favourite part of the Harbour. The black-tailed godwit, is mostly found in the muddy bays of Brands Bay, Newton Bay and Holes Bay, whilst its cousin, the bar-tailed godwit, prefers the sandy northern shore along Parkstone Bay. These preferences reflect the distribution of their favoured foods – the different species of benthic invertebrates in mudflats exposed at low tide. The shelduck, which occurs all the year round and nests around the Harbour, also likes the

Man-made islands in the Brownsea Island Lagoon create perfect nesting sites for common and sandwich terns.

The avocet feeds on tiny invertebrates which it sifts from the shallow water of the Brownsea Lagoon with sweeps of its long up-curved bill.

muddier areas. Other year-round residents include black-headed gulls, which nest in vast numbers on islands of salt marsh near Holton Heath, grey herons and, more recently, little egrets, both of which nest on Brownsea Island. The Mediterranean gulls are more common on the Continent, and are winter visitors and rare breeders in the Harbour.

Regular bird counts have shown changes. Of the overwintering visitors to the Harbour. Black-tailed godwit numbers are rising and the numbers of avocets

The mudflats of Poole Harbour provide food for huge numbers of wading birds, such as dunlin.

have not only increased to reach international importance in the last 10 years, but a peak count was recorded in 2001/02 – the largest gathering ever at one site in the UK. There have been declines, too. Peak shelduck numbers have declined and it no longer qualifies for international status. The most significant declines have been with pochard, lapwing, and redshank. When we ask the question why are these changes happening? It could be because of a series of milder winters here and in north-west Europe but if that is the case, why are some species declining while others are increasing?

Of the breeding birds in the Harbour there has been little change in the distribution and status during the last

Shallow seagrass beds provide an important habitat for marine life and a safe nursery for fish. The insert is of a pipefish, a close relative of the seahorse, and which also lives amongst seagrasses.

five years. Black-headed gull numbers have declined but this is happening nationally. The highlight of the last ten years has been the establishment by the little egret on the Dorset Wildlife Trust's reserve on Brownsea Island. Is this a good thing? Perhaps it has contributed to the decline of the grey heron on the Island. Even more recently, spoonbills have become a spectacular sight in the lagoon.

BENEATH THE KEEL

Out of sight, out of mind is often the case with habitats below low water mark. To discover what habitats and species we have beneath our keel in the Harbour presents a new set of challenges. We can walk along the beach or coastal paths and record what we see.

Underwater, however, divers must wear bulky equipment, can only spend a limited period underwater, visibility is often reduced to a metre or less and even making field notes takes on a whole new meaning. Most people assume that the undersea world is a 'desert' devoid of life. If we take time to peer overboard in the shallow water, look at catches of fish and shellfish landed on the fishermen's quay or look at the colourful marine life growing on sea walls, piles and pontoons, we realize it is anything but.

The Shallows

The most important shallow water habitat is the eel grass beds, which occur in the Whitley Lake area, although there is anecdotal evidence of other areas in the past. The soft beds of organic mud support this, one of the few flowering plants to grow in seawater. An important food source for birds, eel grass, is also a habitat of European importance. The eel grass beds provide a safe, warm, shallow nursery for fish, such as bass and mullet and a hiding place for pipefish and seahorses.

Eel grass beds are fragile habitats, susceptible to environmental change. Their growth patterns are known to fluctuate, perhaps as a result of changes in temperature and salinity or from changes in water chemistry, increased turbidity or storm events. There is concern over physical disturbance from anchoring and fishing activities, although more research is needed to understand the effect this is having.

The Channels

The deeper channels might be devoid of life immediately after dredging but underwater surveys, using grabs and dredges and divers, have shown they support different communities of marine plants and animals, depending on depth, seabed, currents and turbidity of the water. Some of the important habitats and seabed species found in the Harbour include forests of peacock worms. This tube-dwelling worm forms unusually extensive forests within the channels of the Harbour. Other invertebrate animals, such as sponges, live amongst the tubes. Where tidal streams are slower and the water more turbid, silt-tolerant animals are found – sea squirts and sponges.

Artificial Reefs

Marine life is quick to colonise any suitable man-made structure, as any boat-owner will know! The walls, piles, jetties, buoys, channel markers and pontoons in the Harbour are no exception. The finger-like sponge (*Suberites massa*), occurs in large numbers upon the dock walls within the channel leading into Holes Bay. This population is probably the largest in UK waters. Other animals commonly found include the breadcrumb sponge, plumose anemone, barnacles and sea squirts. Marine pontoon floats and the unprotected hulls of boats are colonised by the star and light bulb sea squirts, sponges and seaweeds. In Poole Bay, an experimental artificial reef has been laid on the seabed by Southampton University to study colonisation by marine life.

Just Water . . . ?

The water in the Harbour might look like 'just water' but it is, in fact, full of microscopic plants and animals – plankton. Animal plankton (zooplankton) in the Harbour is made up of tiny, shrimp-like animals – copepods – which remain in the plankton throughout their life cycle and the larvae of sea snails, bivalves, worms and crabs. These larvae drift in the currents and the few that do not get eaten become adults and the cycle begins again. The plankton, carried by the seawater, feed many of the invertebrate inhabitants of the Harbour.

ISLAND LIFE

Of the five larger islands in the Harbour, Brownsea Island is the most remarkable. Its 200 hectares embrace a wide range of habitats, including acid grassland, heathland, pine woodland, two lakes, reed bed and alder carr, a brackish lagoon and a varied shoreline. The National Trust has owned the Island since 1962, leasing the northern half to the Dorset Wildlife Trust as a nature reserve.

The whole island is important for wildlife, probably the most famous being the remaining population of red squirrels. Its island location and considerable Scots pine cover have protected this charming native animal from the invading grey squirrel, which has usurped it on its mainland sites. Red squirrels also survive on two of the other Harbour islands – Green Island, and Furzey Island – where they were introduced some thirty years ago. Along with the Isle of Wight these remain the only sites for this endangered animal in southern England. nightjar and woodcock nest in the heath and open woodland, whilst about 80 pairs of herons and little egrets nest high up in the pines in the nature reserve.

The peacock worm builds a leathery tube to raise its crown of feathery tentacles above the muddy seabed.

The wetlands of Brownsea are of exceptional importance for wildlife. The lagoon has an important common and Sandwich ternery and is host to thousands of waders during migration in winter. Over 1000 avocets have overwintered here, and other unusual waders such as ruff, curlew, sandpiper, knot and black- and bar-tailed godwits are regular visitors. Hundreds of shelduck, wigeon and teal feed on the lagoon, and the reed beds support nesting reed warblers, reed buntings, water rail and the declining water vole.

Marine life will colonise any natural or man-made hard surface.

Because of the variety of ponds and lakes on the Island, 17 species of dragonfly breed, including the spectacular downy emerald dragonfly, a local species seen in the spring. Rare fungi, insects, and lichens are still being discovered on this unusual island, where migrating ospreys often roost during the autumn. It is the only Dorset site for an endangered ant, and the only place where a Mediterranean snail lives in Britain.

The intriguing mix of terns, avocets, red squirrels, exotic trees and old buildings make the island a fascinating place to visit. Brownsea is easily accessible with boats running regularly in the spring and summer, paths are firm and dry and there are marked trails. The reserve has several bird hides, providing astounding views of nesting terns in midsummer. That Brownsea Island's unique quality has survived for our enjoyment today is a tribute to the National Trust and the Dorset Wildlife Trust, who both work hard to maintain its unique character.

On the islands of Poole Harbour, native red squirrels have not been usurped by their invading grey cousins.

ALIEN INVADERS

One of the threats to the wildlife in the Harbour is the increasing number of plants and animals from other parts of the world, introduced here either deliberately of accidentally. We have discussed the spread and decline of the cord grass, *Spartina,* but one of the major threats is trampling and grazing by sika deer. Sika deer are native to Japan and East Asia. They were introduced to deer parks and private estates in the 1890s and early 1900s, including Brownsea Island. The Isle of Purbeck now has the largest group of these deer in England and they are spreading around the Harbour. Sheer numbers grazing the salt marshes, disturbing roosting and feeding birds and trampling reed beds must be having an impact. It is a constant battle to keep rhododendron, once introduced as a garden shrub, from dominating the vegetation on Brownsea Island. It is a serious pest. In contrast, two species of cotoneaster, found growing around the Harbour, seem to offer little threat to native plants. In the marine environment, Poole has many foreign invaders. The discarded shells of the slipper limpet are a common sight on the shores around the Harbour. It originated in America, finding its way here over 100 years ago,

probably with imported shellfish. It is a serious pest of natural and farmed oyster beds. The Japanese seaweed, *Sargassum muticum*, was first found at Poole around 1977 and has been a feature of the channel margins in the outer Harbour ever since and a recent discovery was a large, brown, edible seaweed from Asia. The list goes on to include Australian barnacles and a Korean sea squirt, so why Poole? These immigrants are usually transported growing on the hulls of ships, in ballast water or associated with introduced shellfish. Poole has a port, several marinas and extensive shellfish beds.

THE FUTURE

The Harbour has long been recognised for its importance to wildlife. The many designations to protect it and the number of nature reserves that have been established around the Harbour help to emphasise this. The distribution of wildlife in the Harbour has changed in the past and will continue to do so. The challenges

The Isle of Purbeck has the largest population of sika deer in England. They were originally introduced to deer parks in the United Kingdom from Asia.

wildlife faces in the future include increased human pressure for commercial and recreational uses, sea level rises and climate change. Effective management of the Harbour is crucial if wildlife is not to be the loser. Poole Harbour Commissioners act as the lead body for the Poole Harbour Steering Group, which directs the management of the Harbour and implementation of the Poole Harbour Aquatic Management Plan.

This chapter raises a number of unanswered questions and makes us realise that we do not fully understand the complex interactions between the different wildlife habitats within the Harbour and, without further research, are unable to predict how they might change in the future. Whatever changes there might be, let's hope our great-grandchildren will be able to wonder at the diversity of wildlife in this very special place.

Poole Quay from the ferry steps, Hamworthy by Bernard Gribble (1872-1962)

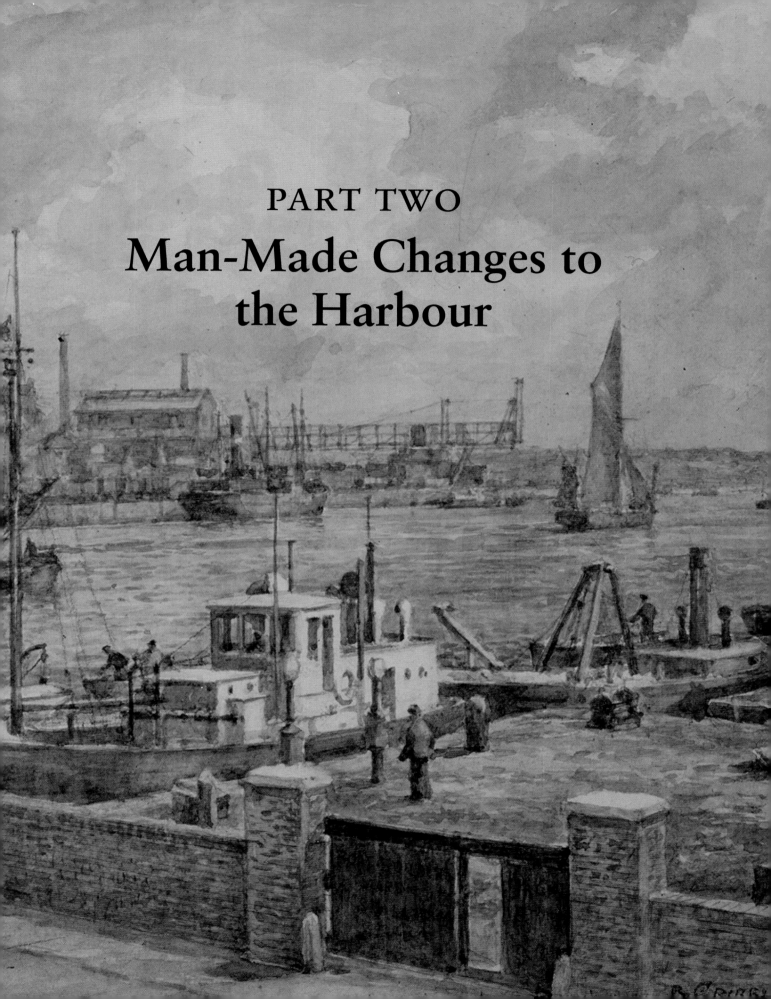

PART TWO

Man-Made Changes to
the Harbour

FOUR

Introduction

GORDON LE PARD

FROM THE EARLIEST settlements around the Harbour following its initial formation, humans have changed it in two interrelated ways: its physical configuration and the quality of the water within it. The results of these man-made changes are considered respectively in the two chapters that follow, 5 and 6.

The major physical changes have been of three types:

- Land reclamation that has changed the actual boundaries of the Harbour, with a corresponding reduction in its surface area.
- Constructions that have facilitated shipping in the Harbour in the form of quays, jetties, slipways, and marinas.
- Dredging, first to maintain access to the port, and, in recent years, to enable the Harbour to accommodate larger vessels.

The extent and location of these changes have varied considerably over time depending on the prevailing economic and social factors and the available technology.

In addition to these actual changes, there have been a number of unrealised schemes that would, had they materialised, have changed the nature of the Harbour to an even greater extent. The six most important of these are summarised in Chapter 5 as of interest historically, but from which lessons might be learned if and when major schemes are proposed in the future.

Water Quality in the Harbour has been affected by five types of human activity: agriculture, industry, sewage treatment, shipping and atmospheric nitrogen deposition. The relative effects of these have varied over time, awareness of their potentially adverse effects on both flora and fauna in the Harbour and humans associated with it, has increased significantly during the twentieth and twenty-first centuries and is currently a major concern of those responsible for the management of the Harbour, as explored in Chapter 6.

FIVE

Boundaries, Quays, Jetties, Slipways & Marinas

GORDON LE PARD

BOUNDARIES

Travelling round the harbour it soon becomes apparent that much of the shoreline is artificial, and not just the developed coast from Sandbanks to Hamworthy, but most of the shoreline of the Wareham Channel. In addition there are other banks, protecting the coastline, to be found at scattered points round much of the rest of the Harbour that may well be evidence of other land development schemes.

The principal boundary changes have been the result of land drainage and reclamation either for agricultural or urban development, coupled with coastal defence to prevent re-flooding of the reclaimed land.

The earliest evidence of land reclamation in the Harbour comes from the town of Poole itself. Archaeological excavation has shown how the development of quays in medieval Poole led to piecemeal land reclamation. There is, as yet, no firm evidence of land reclamation or coastal defence at the Iron Age or Roman settlements at Cleavel Point and Hamworthy, or at the Saxon town of Wareham. Similarly there is no certain evidence of early reclamation of agricultural land. This is perhaps more surprising as elsewhere in the country, notably at Romney Marsh in Kent, or on the Somerset coast, there is considerable evidence of Roman and medieval reclamation. However, there are some intriguing banks lying in the Moors, to the north-east of Ridge, which it has been suggested are the remains of an early sea wall, perhaps Roman.

It was not until the seventeenth century that serious consideration was given to land drainage and reclamation that could have a real impact on the landscape around the Harbour. The East Anglian Fens were being drained and entrepreneurs were looking around for opportunities

One way by which a parish regularly reaffirms its boundaries is by Beating the Bounds, which in Poole's case means going by boat round the Harbour. This shows the 1938 ceremony. The boy is being ceremonially beaten by the Mayor of Poole so as to remind him of the parish boundary points. The somewhat apprehensive girl on the left is about to have a finger pricked so that she also remembers them!

to make money through land drainage.

In 1673-4 extensive proposals were made to drain parts of the Harbour:

'There seems formerly to have been a project, and a very unaccountable one, to embank, inclose, and recover these banks. It was found by inquisition, 13 Car. II. that the waste and oozy grounds in the bay, containing, by admeasurement, 8026 acres, and also *Gofts Bay* alias *Little Sea* bounded almost round with *Parkeston,* forty-one acres – *Holes Bay,* bounded on the E. by Parkston,

A series of regular fields which had once been reclaimed at Middlebere (SY 969 857). At some time in the nineteenth century the sea walls were breached and the land reverted to salt marsh. Most of the banks are only visible from the air.

with a neck of land called *Windmill Point*, and Pool on the E. Hamworthy or South Ham on the S. Upton-wood, Tottenham, and Hickford on W.N. and N.E. 885 acres- *S. Lichet Bay*, bounded by Hamworthy on the E. Holton on the W. and Lichet on the N. 234 acres – *Sheepfall Bay*, bounded by Arne on the S.N. and W. 100 acres – *Middleburgh Bay*, bounded by Arne on the N.W. and Fitzoure on the S.E. which bay divides towards the W. into three creeks; one lying between Arne to the N.W. Middleburgh to the S. and Slepe on the S.W. – another between Middleburgh to the N. and Wych to the S. - another between Wych to the N. and Fritsoure to the S. 350 acres – *Sherwood Bay*, bounded by Fitzoure on the N.W. Owre on the S.W. sixteen acres - *Owere Bay*, lying between Owere on the W. and Newton to the S.E. eighty acres – *St. Andrews*, or *Browsey Bay*, bounded almost all round with Brownsey on the E.S and W. sixty eight acres – *Brand's Bay* lies between Newton to the W. and Studland and S. Haven Point to the E. and S.E. and lands called *Brands* to the S. 305 acres. These premises were granted to *Charles*, Duke of *Richmond* and *Lennox*, for thirty-one years, paying yearly 5 s. that within five years, he imbanked the premises at his own charge, and repaired and maintainded the banks, walls, and fences: a fourth part so imbanked, to be set out for the king. All or great part of the pre-miles were granted 17 Car. H. to

Charles Gifford, esq, for forty-one years, paying yearly 6d. an acre, or a quarter of the yearly value of the lands so imbanked: but this project was found impracticable, and nothing was or could be done in it: yet these waste grounds, if they may be so called, seem to belong to the lordship of Canford . . .'

Though nothing happened at the time, nor indeed for the next fifty years, as the unenclosed mud flats are clearly shown on the 1765 map of Dorset by Isaac Taylor (see page 42), by the end of the eighteenth century a great deal of drainage had taken place. The evidence for drainage in some of the areas mentioned is impressive, but, apart from two areas, the drainage appears to have been piecemeal, small plots, little more than individual fields, being drained rather than a very large area being drained in one big scheme.

The large areas, recognisable by their long straight sea walls, are to be found at The Moors, Swineham Point and at Keysworth, all round the western end of the Wareham Channel. Swineham Point was one of the many schemes around the Harbour to have failed; the sea wall seems to have been breached in the early twentieth century. The land reclamation scheme at Keysworth is particularly interesting. The sea wall that exists today is clearly part of a large scheme; however, aerial photographs show internal banks which may be evidence for an earlier piecemeal scheme.

The piecemeal schemes, enclosing and draining individual fields or groups of fields can be found in many

St Andrew's Bay, Brownsea Island, in about 1860, after having been reclaimed from the sea by Colonel Waugh. Most of the reclaimed land shown is now part of the lagoon.

places around the Harbour. They can be recognised by their irregular boundary, individual farmers building banks that followed existing channels or enclosing slightly higher or firmer patches of mud. As well as the numerous fields that are still in use today, there are about twenty examples of failed schemes, recognisable on aerial photographs, by the remains of banks running across the mud.

SPECIFIC BOUNDARY CHANGE PROJECTS

The Frome Estuary

Whilst some of the larger Harbour schemes considered above did not materialise until the eighteenth century, the meadows alongside the Frome below Wareham were drained during the seventeenth century. Writing in 1774, the historian John Hutchins claimed that:

> 'The tides formerly rose higher and the meadows on the north and south sides of the town were anciently morass, and covered by the water almost every tide, as they are even now on a spring tide, a south east wind and a flood. They have been improved and made firm ground by cutting drains, and raising the banks of the river, within the memory of man.'

During the sixteenth century the Frome estuary had been silting up, a problem that affected several ports along the southern coast of Britain at the time. This led to a massive decline in the port's trade. The draining was as much a means of keeping the port open, by ensuring all the water from the Frome ran down a single, comparatively narrow channel, as with creating additional pasture land. The former idea failed, restricting the channel certainly meant that it would naturally keep it clear of silt, but, by following the banks of the Frome, the channel curved sinuously, meaning that only towed barges were able to reach Wareham.

St. Andrew's Bay

At the eastern end of Brownsea Island lies St. Andrew's Bay, which is probably the best known failed land reclamation scheme in the Harbour as the intertidal mud enclosed by the ruined sea wall now forms an important feeding ground for wildfowl. The Bay was enclosed by Colonel William Waugh between 1853 and 1856, when he carried out various works on the island of which:

> 'No doubt the most valuable improvement of all was the embankment and wall reclaiming St. Andrew's bay from the sea. The magnitude of this undertaking may be imagined when one is told that hundreds of barges of clay were sunk in the deep parts and over a million and a quarter of bricks were used for the wall.'

It is likely that this wall finally failed, owing to

neglect, during the ownership of the island by Mrs Mary Bonham Christie between 1927 and 1939 when she allowed the island to 'return to nature'. However, this is not the whole story, a chart of the Harbour by Captain Sheringham, drawn in 1849, and a plan of the Island drawn in 1853 both show a failed scheme, with broken banks enclosing an area of mud. The chart of Murdoch Mackenzie (1785) also shows the banks, on the same line but with slightly different breaks, which would not be unexpected considering that there is sixty years between the surveys. (For Sheringham's chart, the 1853 plan of the Island and Murdoch Mackenzie's chart see pages 78 and 169.)

Hutchins, quoted above, lists '*St. Andrews, or Browsey Bay*, bounded almost all round with Brownsey on the E.S and W.', as one of the areas which it was considered desirable to drain. It would therefore seem that St. Andrew's Bay was drained in the early to mid eighteenth century, but the sea walls failed and the reclaimed land reverted to salt marsh for eighty or more years. There is no record of this reclamation scheme, but two possible candidates, William 'Auditor' Benson who bought Brownsea sometime before 1722 and who:

'Practically rebuilt the castle, and added to it the great hall, now the music-room; he brought the island into a more advanced state of cultivation than it had been perhaps since the days of its monkish occupation; he lavishly planted it with various kinds of trees.'

Or Humphrey Sturt, who purchased the island in 1762:

'He afterwards, made great additions to the Castle, preserving the great hall built by Auditor Benson, and made great plantations of various kinds of trees; manured and cultivated it with different kinds of agriculture with so much success, that this Island, which hitherto had lain rude and uncultivated, covered with heath and furze, begins to receive the improvements of art, and may in a few years repay the vast labour and cost bestowed upon it.'

Whoever tried to reclaim St Andrew's Bay from the sea for the first time, there can be no doubt that here we have the curious case of land being reclaimed then lost to the sea, not once but twice.

Poole

Much of the land in, and surrounding, the town of Poole has been reclaimed from the sea. This process has been progressing, in a piecemeal fashion, for centuries. Initial land reclamation was concerned with the creation or improvement to wharves; these urban reclamation schemes have been reviewed by Horsey and Watkins.

The Powder House on Baiter in about 1860. Only a fragment still stands, though there are plans to restore it.

Only in the eighteenth century were there attempts to reclaim land for agriculture:

'1722, *Robert Dore* of *Limmington* was presented at a court of admiralty, for inclosing several acres of muddy ground, or flats, belonging to the harbour, at the E. part of Holes Bay, for which he had a grant from Sir J. Webb.'

Through maps and charts it is possible to trace the gradual enclosure and draining of Holes Bay (which was originally the name given to the bay which lay to the east of the town; the bay to the north-west of Poole was then known as Longfleet Bay). This bay was partly enclosed to the south-west by the narrow peninsula of Baiter point. Baiter was the perfect location for structures that were best kept away from centres of population. Hence during the eighteenth and nineteenth centuries it was the home to a gibbet, gunpowder store and isolation hospital. Although there was some smaller reclamation around the edges of the bay during the eighteenth

A detail from the 1886 Ordnance Survey map showing the Infectious Diseases Hospital on Baiter.

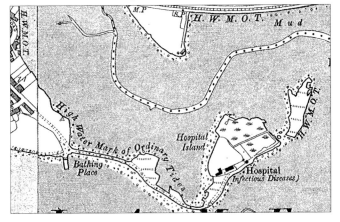

century, reclamation only started in earnest after the building of the railway from Poole to Bournemouth in 1874, which cut off a large section of the bay, to create the present boating lake in Poole Park, and encouraged the draining of more land for building. What was once the site of a gibbet and a hospital for infectious diseases is now a popular residential part of Poole.

The most recent example of land reclamation affecting the boundaries of the Harbour was the infilling of Whitecliff Bay during the first half of the twentieth century, initially as a municipal rubbish dump for the rapidly increasing population of Poole and subsequently to form the present recreation ground.

The reclamation of Baiter Point.

MAJOR QUAYS AND JETTIES

Prior to the latter part of the Iron Age, the normal practice was for all shipping to run on to suitable beaches for loading and unloading. This applied equally to ships large enough for cross-Channel trade as to local Harbour-based boats. This continued to be practised locally well into the nineteenth century, for example at Russel Quay, where special provision continued to be made for boats serving Arne.

However, this changed dramatically in about 250 BC when the first true port facility was established in the Harbour. As far as is known this is the first true port installation in southern Britain and indeed the first on the whole Atlantic coast of Europe.

In the 1950s curious submerged stone structures were discovered in the south-west corner of the Harbour (see pages 66/68). They became known as the Green Island Causeway as they were thought to have been a link from Green Island to Cleavel Point on the mainland. Apart from an initial survey by a party of Boy Scouts in 1959, nothing more was done on the site until the Poole Harbour Heritage Project began work there in 2000.

The Project uncovered two massive stone structures supported with wooden piles and capped with slabs of Purbeck stone. The latter were submerged except at extremely low spring tides which meant that if they were to have been of any practicable use they must have been built at a time when the level of water in the Harbour was significantly lower than it is at present.

Radiocarbon dating of samples from the wooden piles indicated a construction date of about 250 BC, when it is estimated that the level of water in the Harbour was at least one metre below its present level.

One of the structures was found to be 100 metres long and eight metres wide running from Cleavel Point, the other 55 metres long projecting from Green Island,

with a 70 metre gap between the two.

During the second half of the Iron Age, Furzey/Green Islands and the Cleavel Point area supported a significant population and acted as a major (for those days) manufacturing and trading site. Archaeological remains indicate the production and fabrication of iron, the shaping of shale transported from Kimmeridge, the making of pottery products, together with trade with France, and possibly even the Mediterranean.

Such trade would have been greatly facilitated by the use of the 'Causeway' jetties for loading and unloading ships capable of traversing at least the Channel, although a number of other uses for them have been suggested. What is certain, however, is that, with no evidence of a bridging structure between the ends of the two jetties, the 'Causeway' was never a causeway but was certainly the first major port installation in the Harbour against

A drawing by Mike A'Court showing the structure of the landward end of the 'Green Island Causeway', where the massive harbour works with their capping of Purbeck stone slabs crossed the intertidal mud of the Iron Age harbour.

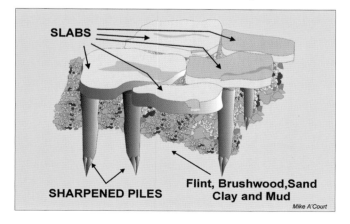

Hamworthy and the Great Quay in 1840, a time when the Hamworthy peninsula was virtually undeveloped.

which ships could load and unload. With rising water levels in the Harbour towards the end of the Iron Age, a new port facility was created at Hamworthy although the Green Island/Cleavel Point port continued to be used well into the second century AD. No trace of jetties or other structures have been found from this period at Hamworthy, and it seems likely that ships were beached for loading and unloading.

Following the Roman invasion in AD 43, Hamworthy became the principal port of the Harbour, serving a major staging post and a network of new roads, as considered in Chapter 9. With no detectable remains, its precise location is unknown, but it was probably on the north side of the peninsula in the little bay that once cut into the north side facing Poole (see the map on page 72).

This site continued to be used throughout the period of Roman rule which ended in AD 410, although for civilian purposes from about AD 65. Whilst a civilian settlement would have continued, this was overtaken as the principal Harbour settlement by the growth of Wareham during the Saxon period, as considered in Chapter 11. With the advantage of serving much of Dorset, by the tenth century Wareham had become one of the principal cross-Channel ports of southern Britain. It is likely that the Saxon quay lies under the modern one, close to the eighth-century minster church of Lady St Mary.

The present site of Poole began to be developed during the early Middle Ages as a rival to Wareham, in a much more convenient position for incoming shipping. Here the story of the quays is one of gradual enlargement and expansion.

During the twentieth century the focus for commercial facilities changed again from Poole itself to the eastern end of the Hamworthy peninsula with significant land reclamation providing the present facilities for commodity-based shipping on the north and east sides of the peninsula and the Ro-Ro facilities for cross-Channel ferries on the south.

Overall, it is interesting to note that with the sequence of main port facilities moving during the past three millennia from Green Island/ Cleavel Point to Hamworthy to Wareham to Poole to Hamworthy, such movement has probably been greater than in any other harbour in the world.

OTHER QUAYS AND JETTIES

In addition to the main commercial centres, a large number of other quays and jetties were developed from Roman times onwards.

Of these the majority were for the export of the mineral wealth of the Harbour and its hinterland. The Romans began exporting Purbeck marble via Cleavel Point when this trade was revived in the Middle Ages and a specialist quay was developed at Ower. The men who quarried the stone had ancient rights to carry the stone down to Ower Quay for which they paid an unusual rent:

'For and in consideration of A pound of Pepper and a foot Ball to be paid by the said company of free marblers on the next day following shrove Tuesday or in four or five Days after except Sabbath day then to be paid the next day following to be paid to the said John Collins his Executors Administrators or Assigns at or in the New Dwelling house of the said John Collins being at Ower abovesaide all which being performed and paid by the free Marblers abovesaid they shall have use occupy and possess the way which was formerly allowed to the said company without any hindrance trouble or molestation of the said John Collins His Heirs or Assigns.'

Pottery, in the form of Black Burnished Ware, was widely exported during the Roman period from several locations around the Harbour to places as far away as Hadrian's Wall and the Rhine frontier in Germany.

By the seventeenth century a new trade had begun, the export of clay. The material was quarried close to the shore and was taken out by a series of small piers around the Harbour, often being known by the name of the local landowner, Russel Quay, Hyde's Pier etc. Russel Quay is the only one of these structures to have been archaeologically investigated. There were a series of small wooden piers, no more than two metres wide, down which the clay could have been carried, as well

The Hamworthy peninsula today is the result of major reclamation. The white building on the far side of the central roundabout, and beyond the railway tracks, which today is the Harbour Office of of the Poole Harbour Commissioners, once the Poole Yacht Club and stood close to the shore (see page 229). The Britanny Ferries *Cotentin* is berthing alongside the *Condor Express* at the Ferry Terminal.

as an artificial hard where ships could have been easily beached. As the nineteenth century progressed, the quays became more elaborate, with light railways running down to Middlebere or Goathorn. Here substantial remains of the timber piers remain, with traces of the light railways that served them (Chapters 18 and 30).

With the development of the clay trade, kilns were built, in Poole they first made drain pipes and sanitary fittings to meet the needs of the building industry during the nineteenth and twentieth centuries. The two pottery sites served directly by jetties were at Lilliput and on Brownsea Island (Chapter 19).

The first of these built in 1867 to serve the South Western Pottery was a massive pier 560 metres long with its outer end reaching to the- then Main Channel to accommodate the loading of relatively large ships. A standard-gauge railway ultimately connected it to the main line station at Parkstone (Chapter 30). It was later converted to a mole, now incorporated into the Salterns Marina (Chapter 32).

The other major jetty served the pottery on Brownsea Island. It was sited at Maryland, with its outer end reaching the Wych Channel on the north side of the Island, with a narrow-gauge rail link to the pottery on the south side (Chapters 18 and 30).

A third significant jetty, but with an entirely different function, was built during the First World War to serve the transfer of cordite from the newly-built Royal Naval Cordite Factory at Holton Heath (Chapters 16 and 30). As with the Brownsea Island jetty, little now remains of Rockley Pier.

For the movement of people and domestic produce, the Harbour provided a highway from at least the Iron Age, as evidenced by the log boat now exhibited in the Poole Museum. From Saxon times, Wareham and, from medieval times, Poole, acted as market towns for the numerous small farms around the shores of the Harbour. Some of these had their own piers but many made use of the passage boats (Chapter 26) with piers at strategic points. They were served by Passage Houses

Poole Harbour from Isaac Taylor's 1765 map. This shows the passage houses on South Haven, Ower, and Gold Point near Arne, where local farmers waited to catch a boat to Poole or Wareham on market days; and several of the early quays, including Hyde and Russel.

where passengers gathered to catch the passage boats, essentially water bus-stops.

The remains of one Passage House survive on Gold Point, which served the Arne Peninsula. This consisted of a small brick building with a more lightly-constructed outbuilding, which bears out the description of one of the Houses from the early nineteenth century as a poor quality inn where very basic food could be had:

'Potatoes, onions and sour beer', and a horse could be stabled.

The passage boats and their piers were superceded by the development of roads and railways during the nineteenth century, their present replacements being tourist boats with piers at places such as Sandbanks and quays at Brownsea Island, Poole, and Wareham. The private jetties serving individual farms have been replaced by jetties serving individual houses around the north and east shores of the Harbour and at Green and Round Islands; by jetties serving the Harbour Yacht Clubs (Chapter 32); and by jetties on Furzey Island and at Goathorn Point serving the BP oil-drilling sites there (Chapter 17).

The Passage House on South Haven Point in about 1890, by which time it was known as the South Haven Inn.

SLIPWAYS

Whilst the initial landing places for ships on beaches were, in effect, slipways, it was only from about the sixteenth century that recognisable slipways began to be built in the Harbour for shipbuilding purposes (Chapter 22). But most of the slipways that now proliferate around the Harbour are even more recent, many not having been built until the twentieth century.

Examples of these are those initially built for Seaplanes at the Royal Motor Yacht Club, Sandbanks, and at Hamworthy for Flying Boats, the latter now used for Royal Marines landing craft; those built in 1927 at North Haven and South Haven Points to accommodate the chain ferry at the entrance to the Harbour; those to accommodate yachts at the principal yacht clubs around the Harbour; those associated with private jetties around the Harbour; and those for public use at Baiter and Hamworthy.

MARINAS

Whilst the idea of a haven to protect boats from extreme weather is not new, a haven for fishing boats in Poole was built in the nineteenth century (Chapter 23), and major marinas associated with yacht clubs and as commercial projects have been a feature of the second half of the twentieth century only (Chapter 32).

UNREALISED PROJECTS

Over the centuries there have been a number of schemes that, had they materialised, would have had a major effect on the structure of the Harbour and its uses.

Proposed New Town and Port

A proposal to build a new town in the south-west corner of the Harbour was made in 1286 during the reign of Edward I. The story of Newton is covered in greater detail in Chapter 9, but it included port facilities to be approached via South Deep that would significantly have affected shipping movements in that part of the Harbour.

Canals

At the peak of the canal-building programme in Britain towards the end of the eighteenth century and the beginning of the nineteenth, there were two proposals that might have significantly affected the Harbour and its water-borne transport:

- A scheme to cut a canal linking Wareham more directly with the Harbour thus overcoming the disadvantages of the sinuous Frome River noted above. It is shown on a map published by Captain Sheringham in 1849, although it had by that date been abandoned.
- An even larger scheme to link the Harbour with the River Avon in Bath was actually started; the remains of the initial work are still visible at its northern end. Had it been completed, the Harbour might have become a major outlet on the south coast for goods from the Midlands.

Both schemes failed due to impending competition from the railway, which reached Hamworthy and Wareham in 1847, as considered in Chapter 30.

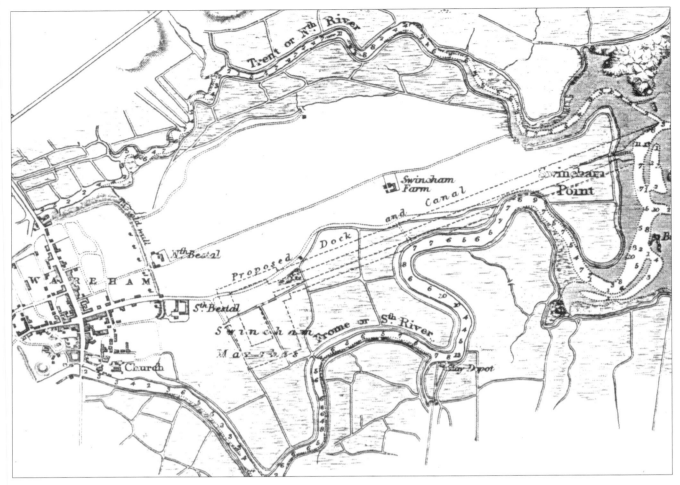

The proposed Wareham ship canal, as shown on
Sheringham's chart of 1849. This immense scheme never
obtained the backing it needed and was swiftly superseded by
the developing rail network.

The proposed Sandbanks Cut drawn onto a copy of the 1891
Poole Harbour chart.

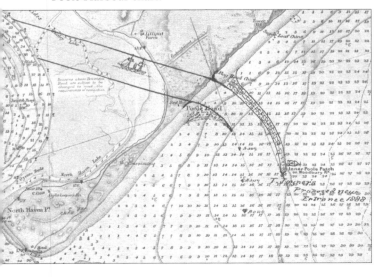

Wareham Docks

In an attempt to revive the maritime fortunes of
Wareham, there were proposals associated with the
above canal scheme to build a major complex of docks
on the south side of the Frome, as also noted on Captain
Sheringham's chart of 1849.

The Sandbanks Cut

In 1888 it was proposed to improve the access to the
Harbour by cutting a new channel through the 'neck' of
the Sandbanks peninsula close to the site of the present
Sandbanks Hotel. Interestingly, it would have followed
one of the possible ancient entrances to the Harbour.
The plan included a massive stone mole running out
into Poole Bay as far as the Inner Poole Patch. Apart
from its original cost and the probable necessity for
continual dredging, it would have made the remainder
of Sandbanks into an island.

ABOVE Salterns Pier, which was intended to become the industrial heart of 1920s Poole. Instead the venture failed and the area was developed for leisure. This is now the Salterns Marina.

RIGHT The coaling wharf, Town Quay, in the 1950s. From the sixteenth century onwards there has been an almost constant need to improve and enhance the provision of quays in the town.

BELOW The dredger *C.H. Horn* at work in the Harbour. The main shipping channel, the Middle Ship Channel, is dredged to 7.5 metres so as to ensure that the port can continue to accomodate commercial shipping and cross-Channel ferries (for a detailed look at the shipping channels see the chart on pages 170/171).

Salterns Docks

It was in the early twentieth century that Lilliput became the focus of schemes that, had they developed, might have turned Poole into a shipbuilding centre to rival the north-east of England. Lilliput was already an industrial centre with potteries, sawmills, and engineering works and was the obvious place for further industrial development that would have involved the dredging of the presently-named Blue Lagoon, as considered in Chapter 19. Substantial funds were raised immediately following the First World War but the scheme failed due, it is thought, to political opposition from traditional shipbuilding centres.

Extension of Town Quay to Baiter

Towards the end of the twentieth century a tentative scheme to extend the Quay to Baiter was considered by the Poole Harbour Commissioners. This could have had a major effect on the present housing and recreational aspects of Baiter and would have involved significant dredging in that part of the Harbour. It was dropped in favour of further development of the Hamworthy site, especially for the newer cross-Channel ferry traffic.

Poole Harbour Place Names

This map of historic and traditional names in and around Poole Harbour was created by Gordon le Pard from the recollection of Harbour users and records made by the Poole Harbour Commissioners.

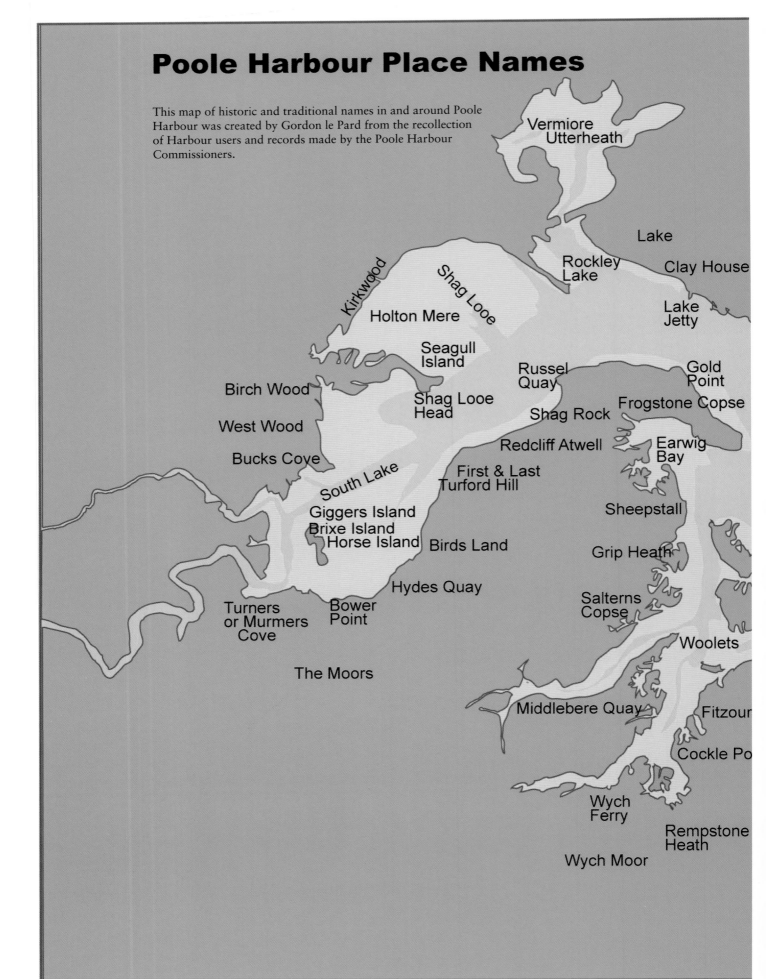

Vermiore
Utterheath

Lake

Rockley Lake

Clay House

Kirkwood

Shag Looe

Holton Mere

Lake Jetty

Seagull Island

Russel Quay

Gold Point

Birch Wood

Shag Looe Head

Frogstone Copse

West Wood

Shag Rock

Bucks Cove

Redcliff Atwell

Earwig Bay

South Lake

First & Last
Turford Hill

Giggers Island
Brixe Island
Horse Island

Sheepstall

Birds Land

Grip Heath

Hydes Quay

Salterns Copse

Turners or Murmers Cove

Bower Point

Woolets

The Moors

Middlebere Quay

Fitzour

Cockle Po

Wych Ferry

Rempstone Heath

Wych Moor

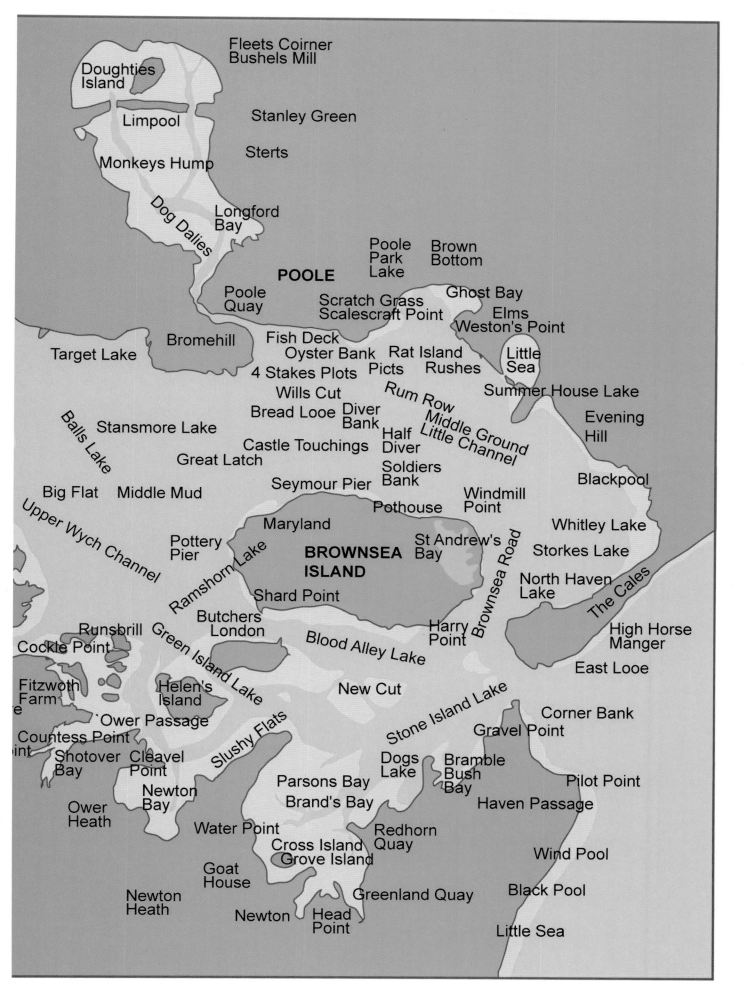

SIX

Water Quality Changes

WILLIAM SHELDRICK AND JOHN WILLOWS

POOLE HARBOUR is a beautiful place with a water line of exceptional ecological importance. Although the water in the Harbour is generally good, its poor flushing characteristics make it vulnerable to pollution. The amount of water displaced by fresh seawater by the ebb and flow of the tide is relatively small due to the low tidal range, the small inlet and the irregular shape and large size of the Harbour. The overall effect is that the water in the Harbour exhibits the characteristics of both estuary and lagoon. The environmental factors that influence water quality are constantly changing and have been exacerbated by increasing human involvement with the Harbour since its formation.

Pollution of the Harbour comes from five main sources:

- Agriculture: Diffuse pollution caused by nitrogen (N) in the form of nitrates and phosphorus (P) in the form of phosphates as nutrients in both mineral fertilizers and animal residues (manure) and other agricultural chemicals in surface runoff water sources in the catchment areas of the rivers and waterways feeding into the Harbour.
- Industry: Pollutants from industry around the Harbour or in the catchment area.
- Sewage Treatment Works (STWs): Pollutants within the effluents discharged from the urbanised area and other catchment areas into the Harbour.
- Port and shipping: Pollution caused by marine or recreational activities within the Harbour.
- Atmospheric Nitrogen Deposition: Nitrogen-based compounds from the atmosphere come from natural, industrial and agricultural sources.

AGRICULTURE

The contamination of lakes and rivers by nutrient runoff is a major problem of the agricultural industry. This results from the very low efficiencies achieved in the use of both mineral fertilizers and animal residues where less than half the N and P nutrient in mineral fertilizers is recovered by the crop and much of the remainder is lost to the soil. For animal residues the nutrient losses are usually higher. In farming areas where there is significant surface water and sediment run off, nutrient losses can be high particularly as soluble nitrates. Usually, agricultural pollution is of a diffuse type but in some cases, such as intense animal farming and fish farms, it can also be regarded as fixed point pollution.

The main catchment areas surrounding the Harbour are mainly of a rolling rural agricultural nature draining into the rivers Frome, Piddle, Corfe, and Sherford – all of which discharge into the Harbour. The total catchment area covers approximately 900 square kilometres and contains no heavy industry.

In 2005 the Environment Agency outlined its Management Strategy for the Frome, Piddle, Corfe and Purbeck abstraction and, in this, the water of the included rivers is described as of high quality, with 97 per cent of it classified as good or very good. However, elevated nitrate levels, mainly from diffuse sources are found in many places. The EC Nitrates Directive requires Nitrate Vulnerable Zones (NVZ's) to be established in catchments where high or rising nitrates have been identified and for action programmes to be implemented in those zones to reduce nitrate pollution (in surface and/ or ground water). Approximately 90 per cent of the catchment area is designated as NVZ.

The large quantities of nutrients in water that flow into the Harbour from both diffuse and single point sources cause algal blooms in the rivers and macro algal blooms (seaweed) in the marine environment. This anthropogenic eutrophication (man-made nutrient richness) can lead to deoxygenation of the water and result in fish and shellfish mortality. The problem of eutrophication is common in areas with high agricultural inputs and is difficult to

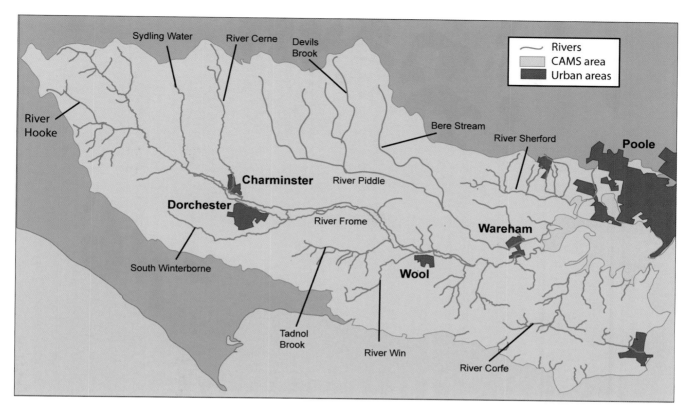

Map showing the Poole Harbour catchment area. The area covers 900 square kilometres, and the water in the principal rivers and streams has been classified as of high quality.

overcome without major reductions in fertilizer use, and/or increases in nutrient efficiency and improvements in farming practices particularly when using manure. To help reduce pollution of agricultural production, the Department for Farming and Rural Affairs (DEFRA) is funding a Catchment Sensitive Farming initiative.

INDUSTRY

Research by Langston and colleagues 2003 reviewed the historic data for metal contamination in the Harbour in the 1970s and 1980s and found contamination was high, particularly in Holes Bay, and was responsible for the poor performance of oyster larvae near Poole Bridge. The metals most likely to be of significance in terms of bio-accumulation and toxicity were cadmium, mercury, silver, copper, zinc and selenium. There was no indication of any metal pollution problems from the major rivers (Frome and Piddle) which enter the Harbour.

Industrial and human pollution in the twentieth century have caused lasting damage to the Harbour, particularly in Holes Bay where circulation and flushing is restricted. Although much has been done to resolve the source of the problems, residual diffuse heavy metal contaminants and bacteriological sources still remain a threat to wild life.

Chemical compliance monitoring of tidal waters is restricted to the outer Harbour where water quality generally conforms to statutory limits. High zinc levels in water (and seaweed) may be due to antifouling and sacrificial anodes, on ships.

Generally, metals in sediments exceed sediment quality guidelines although probable effect levels are restricted largely to Holes Bay, where low energy conditions restrict the dispersal of contaminated particles. Much of the metal loading in Poole sediments may be labile and has the potential to remobilize, for example in dredging operations.

SEWAGE TREATMENT WORKS (STWs)

The rivers entering the Harbour receive treated sewage discharges from 18 STWs in the catchment area, and three STWs discharge into the Harbour directly. It is the responsibility of Wessex Water Services Ltd to run and maintain these works. They have a statutory duty to treat and discharge sewage under consent from the Environment Agency and to ensure that discharges

Holes Bay. Now largely edged by either roads or buildings on three sides, the bay has been the part of the Harbour to have most suffered from pollution.

do not adversely affect the waters of the Harbour in complying with EC directive standards, such as those for bathing and the shellfish industry. The backgrounds for these operations are given below.

In 1974, ten regional water authorities were set up across England and Wales. The new authorities, established under the 1973 Water Act, were to look after the three main disciplines of water management; namely: water supply, sewage disposal, and land drainage. It was in this same year that Wessex Water Authority, with its headquarters in Bristol, took over responsibility for managing the three functions across the counties of Dorset, Somerset, and Wiltshire.

Successful water management and care for the environment relies to a large extent on gathering and monitoring biological data. Recognising this, Wessex Water brought together all its professional biologists and in 1975 set up a biology unit to work across the Wessex region. Called the Regional Biology Unit, the team established a laboratory at the old Admiralty pumping station at Corfe Mullen, across the road from the River Stour. The laboratory undertook investigative work and offered advice on all aspects of marine and freshwater biology, fisheries, sewage treatment, land drainage, water resources, and water supply.

In 1978 Wessex Water published an appraisal document called 'Consultations, and the Further Appraisal of Sewage Disposal Options' as part of the South East Dorset Water Services Study. The document, in response to Dorset County Council's Structure Plan for South East Dorset, outlined a future strategy for water services in south-east Dorset and involved much public consultation. Included in the scope of the document were the conurbations of Bournemouth, Christchurch and Poole,

A sewage works has occupied the present Poole sewage works site since 1922. Originally it only served the Broadstone area as Poole, at that time, disposed all of its sewage through short sea outfalls. The first consented discharge of treated sewage effluent into Holes Bay was in the 1950s. However, untreated discharges probably took place before that date.

Poole was developing into a conurbation. The problems associated with a rising population were added to by the increases in industrial effluents. Public health concerns had seen the first attempts to control discharges introduced in 1936. These were followed in 1937 and 1974 by the tightening of the regulations covering the discharge of trade effluent into foul sewers. However, it was not until 1951 (rivers) and 1960 (coastal waters), that specific anti-pollution legislation was introduced. To comply with the tighter regulations the sewage works was enlarged and modified by introducing two new streams, the western stream to serve a population equivalent of 50,000 was built in 1957-61 and the eastern stream serving 100,000 in 1969-74. This would cater for the interception of Poole's sewage which would no longer go straight out to sea.

The strategy outlined in the 1978 appraisal looked at a nominal 40-year period extending to 2016. As well as the need to improve effluent quality, the 40 year horizon predicted an increase of 110,000 in south-east Dorset's resident population and a summer peak increase of 166,000. To meet the improved standards and population increases, the sewage works serving the area would need to embark on a continuous programme of enlargement and modernisation and this would require a huge financial investment.

Following the appraisal and the many problems it identified, a detailed, two year programme of marine and freshwater surveys was undertaken. The comprehensive scientific study looked at the various discharges from sewage works and industry in order to assess their impact over the next 30 years. The study, which again covered south-east Dorset's water services, was published by Wessex Water in 1980.

The section of the report dealing with the Harbour brought together several studies carried out using ten survey sites. They concluded that Poole sewage works had by far the biggest influence on the water quality. However, two other sewerage works, besides Poole, discharged into the Harbour: the Lytchett Minster works into Lytchett Bay and the Wareham works into

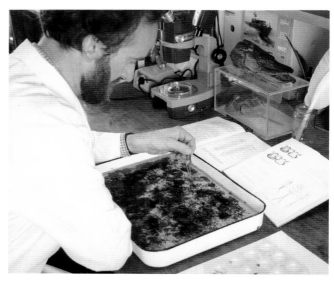

A biologist evaluating the aquatic invertebrate population in a sampling tray for possible sources of pollution at the Wessex Water Regional Biology Unit at Corfe Mullen.

the lower reaches of the River Piddle. All three works were recommended for improvement.

Other problems, of a totally different nature, were also being caused by high levels of nutrients in the effluent discharge from Poole sewage works. Green seaweeds and algae were thriving on the nitrogenous content derived from the effluent. As a consequence, the cooling

The biological, aerated filtration plant at Poole Waste Water Treatment Works. Newly installed in 1996, it took three years to construct at a cost of £35 million and was considered one of the most innovative in Europe.

Until recently *Wessex Explorer* was used for coastal sampling as a means of measuring the accumulation of heavy metals and organic compounds in intertidal organisms such as seaweed.

water intakes to Poole Power Station frequently became blocked, resulting in a reduction in output. Another more noticeable problem was the excessive amount of rotted weed that built up on the mudflats at low water. In the early 1980s, the introduction of an oxygen injection plant resulted in a marked improvement in the quality of the effluent by increasing the available oxygen to reduce the biochemical oxygen demand. In 1985 the injection

A member of Wessex Water's diving team of scientists. The use of underwater cameras and marine sampling of the flora and fauna on the seabed is another way of gathering information about the health of the Harbour.

facility was doubled.

Privatisation of the water industry in 1989 brought changes to the protection of coastal waters. Responsibility passed to the National Rivers Authority (later to be absorbed into the Environment Agency) but the responsibility for maintaining satisfactory effluent quality from sewage works remained with Wessex Water.

In recent years Poole Waste Water Treatment Works (waste water being the present-day words for sewage!) has been transformed. Major works started in 1994 with the addition of a new inlet works. Two years later a major redevelopment saw the introduction of a biological, aerated filtration plant which supplemented the eastern and western activated sludge streams. The plant, which took three years to construct, cost £35 million and is capable of treating 64 million litres of waste water each day or enough capacity for 170,000 people.

The Poole works has seen further major development following on into the new millennium. In 2003, with tighter bathing water standards and the continuing need to improve the water quality for the shellfishery beds, ultra violet disinfection was introduced together with measures to reduce the amount of suspended solids contained in the effluent. To meet tighter compliance regulations being introduced in 2009 for nutrient content, new tertiary sand filters and a dedicated pumping station have been built to further treat sludge liquors. The process will reduce the levels of nitrogen and ammonia and is expected to reduce excessive green weed and algal growth.

The programme of investment since the 1978 appraisal has seen a vast improvement in water quality, and the damaging effects caused by years of discharging poor quality effluents have diminished. However, the need to improve and update treatment processes will continue; the growth and development in East Dorset and elsewhere will see to that, and greater environmental awareness will mean higher water quality standards and tighter regulation. Essentially, therefore, the improvement in waste water treatment seen over the last thirty years is set to continue.

THE PORT AND SHIPPING

Port operations and shipping can pollute the Harbour from surface run off and diffuse pollution such as antifouling paints, sacrificial anodes and oil. Tributyltin (TBT) which was used extensively in antifouling paints until 1987 is found at elevated levels in sediments in the north shore. TBT was found to be having a damaging effect on marine organisms, including some shellfish.

Port facilities provide appropriate facilities for the disposal of sewage, garbage and contaminated bilge water that could have an adverse environmental impact on the Harbour.

ATMOSPHERIC NITROGEN DEPOSITION

Nitrogen deposition as nitrogen oxides is caused mainly from cars and electricity generation. Ammonia emissions are mainly the result of increased animal husbandry. Nitrogen deposition can occur in both wet and dry forms and can be important in agriculture as it provides an addition to N fertiliser. On the other hand it can be harmful to the environment when it drains off into ground and surface water and helps degrade aquatic ecosystems.

There is little specific information on nitrogen deposition in the Harbour and catchment area, but the average total deposition rate for the region is between 17-20 kilos per hectare – which is quite significant.

Overall, human involvement has had a major influence on the quality of water within the Harbour. While in the past it has been seriously affected by the growth of agriculture, industry, and population, this has been accompanied by an increasing awareness of their effects,

The last of what was once a long line of houseboats in Bramble Bush Bay. Their gradual departure has improved the water quality in this quiet corner of the Harbour.

and by measures to correct them, particularly in the recent past.

Monitoring and amelioration take place at many levels. The Environment Agency is responsible for routine monitoring at frequencies defined by various EU Directives and with the involvement of local agencies such as Wessex Water. The data are passed to the Department for Farming and Rural Affairs (DEFRA) who submit these to the EU for review.

Locally, there is an Aquatic Management Plan for the Harbour with the following aim:

'To promote the safe and sustainable use of Poole Harbour, balancing the demands on its natural resources, minimising risk and resolving conflicts of interest'.

The Plan is supported by the Poole Harbour Steering Group, a voluntary partnership that provides a framework for coordination between statutory and other bodies with responsibilities and interests in the Harbour. Its members work together to review, prepare and implement common plans and policies, with a view to promoting the sustainable use of the Harbour, whilst securing the long-term conservation of its internationally important wildlife and natural habitats.

PART THREE

Settlements in and around the Harbour

Town Quay from Hamworthy, Dorset, 1920s by Eustace Nash (1886-1969).

SEVEN

Introduction

LILIAN LADLE

Human settlements have followed closely the natural development of the Harbour from its initial formation at the end of the Ice Age, as discussed in Part I. Settlements have, in turn, had an increasingly significant effect on their surroundings, as considered in Part II. The changing patterns of the resultant settlements are considered in the Part III.

The first known settlements in the general area of the present Harbour during the period 10,000-1,000 BC are described in the following Chapter 8. Prior to about 8,000 BC, much of the present Harbour was wooded, dry land. This and the surrounding area was sporadically occupied by groups of Mesolithic hunter-gatherers who targeted the abundant game, fish and fowl but with little evidence of significant settlement.

During the Bronze Age, however, the woodland was cleared around the edge of the Harbour, and settlements emerged, although many of these had a limited lifespan and were replaced by newer settlements in more convenient locations.

Examples of these are considered in Chapter 9. One of the earliest was at Bestwall, between the rivers Piddle and the Frome towards the east of what is now Wareham, where houses and the first agricultural activities in the area are recorded.

In the middle Iron Age, important trading settlements developed within and south of the Harbour. These included sites on the present Green and Furzey Islands, at Cleavel Point and on the Ower Peninsula. As sea levels rose during the late Iron Age, these sites were gradually abandoned and replaced by Hamworthy on the Harbour's northern edge.

Hamworthy then became the principal port and settlement for the Harbour following the Roman invasion of AD 43; it remained as a civilian settlement following the departure of the Roman army in AD 65. Other small Roman settlements were also developed at this time – for example, at what ultimately became Wareham.

Chapter 9 concludes with an account of a much later intended settlement at 'Newton', in the south-east corner of the Harbour, which did not proceed beyond the planning stage in the reign of Edward I but which otherwise might have had a significant effect on the pattern of settlements around the Harbour.

Chapter 10 is an account of the history of the principal islands in the Harbour, dealing in particular with their known ownership.

In the meantime, during the Saxon period, a small number of settlements developed around the Harbour, and these have generally survived into modern times as farmsteads and villages. The largest became the town of Wareham with its own defences in anticipation of Viking attacks during the period leading up to the Norman Conquest of 1066.

The development of Wareham and its successor, Poole, as the principal town of the Harbour from the medieval period is considered in Chapter 11.

As settlements around the Harbour grew, their defence became increasingly important, as discussed in Chapter 12.

EIGHT

Early Inhabitants

TIMOTHY DARVILL

ONCE UPON AN ICE AGE

THE HARBOUR did not always look as it does now. For much of the last half a million years or so it was simply a low-lying place where several small rivers joined the River Frome, itself a north-bank tributary of the mighty Channel River flowing westwards through what is now the English Channel towards the Atlantic Ocean. Periods of global warming interspersed with phases of intense cold during the middle and later Pleistocene caused sea levels and the surface of the earth's crust to rise and fall, and while this part of north-west Europe was never covered by ice-caps it was certainly a landscape whose environment swung between arctic tundra and sub-tropical savanna several times over. A consequence of these environmental and geomorphological changes was the deposition and subsequent erosion of gravel deposits in the river valleys. Remnants of these can still be recognized, and along the valley of the former Solent River between Hordle and Calshot in the New Forest there is a flight of no less than 14 such terraces tentatively dated to between the Anglian glaciations of 478,000-423,000 BC for terrace 14 up to terrace 1 at about 10,000 BC, marking the start of the Flandrian interglacial in which we now live. Further west, at least ten terraces can be identified along the Frome Valley, including remnant deposits on Brownsea and Furzey Islands within Poole Harbour.

Material for the creation of these terraces was washed into the valley by rivers draining eroded landscapes away to the north and north-west, but amongst the broken rock and clay there are flint tools and weapons swept up from human occupation sites dating as far back as 600,000 BC. Especially rich are the gravels of terrace 6

A reconstruction from the Natural History Museum showing a hunting party in lowland Britain with mammoths and rhinosauruses during the Pleistocene period, which lasted from 1.8 million years ago to about 11,000 years ago.

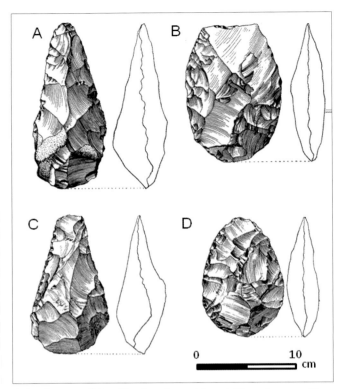

Acheulean tradition flint handaxes (A and C) and ovates (B and D) dating to before 130,000 BC from Ballast Hole (A and C) and Cogdean Pit (B and D) Corfe Mullen [Source: Calkin and Green 1949, figures 2, 3, 7 and 8]

to terrace 11 between Bournemouth and Southampton, with the Dunbridge Hill Gravel Pit being one of the most prolific sources of tools in the Acheulian tradition currently known in Britain. This tool-making tradition, dated to between c.600,000 BC and 100,000 BC and associated with the early hominid species known as *Homo heidelbergensis*, is characterised by beautifully worked handaxes, ovates, and points of various kinds – multi-purpose tools representing the Swiss Army knives of their day.

The Frome Valley gravels are less rich, but the numerous gravel quarries around Corfe Mullen have yielded nearly 200 Acheulean tools dating from before 130,000 BC. A typologically mixed collection has also been recovered from West Howe, and there are more than a dozen stray finds of handaxes from around the Harbour that must also derive from these gravels; one is from Furzey Island. All these pieces suggest extensive occupation of the chalklands of Cranborne Chase and beyond by mobile hunter-gatherer groups whose territories probably extended southwards into what is now France and northern Spain.

The last glacial maximum, known as the Devensian, occurred between 25,000 and 11,000 BC and was a time when people were absent from Britain. Poole was about 100km south of the nearest ice sheet, and with sea levels estimated at 30 metres below modern Ordnance Datum (OD) was more than 50km from the estuary of the Channel River. However, as global warming took hold the ice sheets melted, and from about 10,000 BC competing pressures from isostatic adjustment to turbulence in the earth's crust and eustatic adjustment to increasing amounts of water in the world's oceans meant that relative sea level rose sharply in this part of Europe, first flooding the western valley of the Channel River and then inundating the higher ground further east.

As the bight of the English Channel increased, one casualty was the already dissected chalk ridge linking Purbeck with the Isle of Wight. Once breached there was rapid inundation of the low-lying land to the north and the formation of what would become Poole Bay as the estuary of the River Frome (for an illustration showing this see page 18). Stumps of Scotch Fir found in the submerged forest below Bournemouth beach may relate to this inundation. Freshwater peat sampled at Hamworthy at the north end of the Harbour in August 1956 lay at a depth of -12.8 metres OD and dated to 8783–8294 BC. Downriver near what is now the Harbour entrance similar peat deposits lay at 18.4 metres and -18.1 metres OD and began to form around 7940–7600 BC. Both these glimpses into what lies deep below the present landscape show very clearly that the floor of the Frome Valley and its adjacent low-lying floodplain was wet and boggy in early prehistoric times.

The exact course of the Frome has yet to be determined. It most likely followed what is now the North Channel but with an exit through a now-silted palaeochannel between Sandbanks and Poole Head. A deep borehole drilled at 88 Panorama Road in September 2002 recorded the base of the palaeochannel at -23 metres OD; a 7 metres thick layer of peri-glacial river gravel lay in the bottom of the channel, sealed by a layer of peat at -16 metres to -17 metres OD.

POPULATING THE LANDSCAPE

Anatomically modern humans, *Homo sapien sapiens*, recolonised peninsular Britain from about 10,500 BC and small bands of hunter-gatherers were present in the Bournemouth-Poole area soon afterwards. They were no doubt attracted by the rivers Avon, Stour, Frome and Piddle for fishing, and the surrounding wetlands for birds and small game. Forests dominated by pine and birch cloaked the surrounding higher ground and provided a different range of resources including red deer, pig, and horse. A temporary campsite occupied at about 10,000 BC has been excavated at the eastern end of Hengistbury Head, characterised by flint tools and weapons used in hunting migrating herds of large animals. A slightly later site on the top of Warren Hill, also at Hengistbury Head, was occupied about 8000 BC and was probably a camp used by small-game hunters. Only 18 kilometres to the east was another small settlement of about the same date, but in this case on low-lying land that is now 11 metres underwater at Boulder near Yarmouth, Isle of Wight. Nothing of comparable date has yet been found in Poole Harbour, but the various known peat deposits illustrate the great potential for submerged land surfaces relating to this formative stage in the occupation of southern Britain.

By about 6000 BC, the North Sea and English Channel had joined and Britain was detached from the Continent. In the Frome Valley water levels had risen to the point where the confluence of the main river with various small north-bank tributaries and the larger Sherford, Piddle, and Corfe rivers on the south and east created an extensive wetland. It is likely that Brownsea, Furzey, and Green Islands formed a single low hill with the Frome flowing to the north and perhaps the Corfe River to the south through what is now South Deep; the confluence of the two rivers was probably outside the present Harbour in Poole Bay.

Settlements of the period 6000–4000 BC represented by scatters of worked flints suggesting small temporary settlements have been found on Canford Heath, overlooking the Harbour, in Branksome Dean Chine, west of the Harbour at Swineham, at the East Corfe River site investigated during the construction of the Wytch Farm Oilfield, and on elevated ground overlooking the River Piddle at Bestwall. A pick or tranchet axe now in the British Museum is said to come from 'Lake Poole', and may be from Poole Park or from Lake between Corfe Mullen and Wimborne.

Relative sea level continued rising at an average rate of about 10 mm per century after 5000 BC, but averages are deceptive and preliminary studies suggest periods of rapid inundation punctuated by relative stability and occasional regression through the fourth and third millennia BC as the tidal wetland that can be regarded as ancestral to the present Harbour started to take shape. Erosion of the surrounding landscape within the intertidal zone became marked, and the pre-existing woodlands would have been affected by marine inundation too. Excavations at Worgret beside the Frome in 1988 revealed an old river channel, the base of which lay at -1.3 metres OD with fills containing trunks of alder or birch, one of which was dated to 4140-3940 BC.

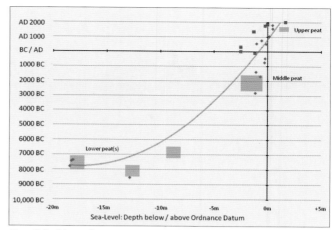

Simplified best-fit regression curve for sea-level change in Poole Harbour 9000 BC to AD 2000. Based on available radiocarbon dates for sea-level index points (blue lozenges) and archaeological observations of old land surfaces and related deposits (red squares). Recorded peat layers are indicated, but it should be emphasised that these are sporadic sightings and some may join laterally when compression and the undulating nature of the valley floor is taken into account.

HUNTER-GARDENERS

From about 4000 BC communities scattered across the British Isles adopted new traditions of food production, monument building, and ways of life that had been established on the adjacent continental mainland for more than a thousand years. In the Stour Valley to the north of the Harbour these gardener-hunters constructed a long barrow at Holdenhurst for the burial of their dead. Just 12 kilometres upstream pits suggestive of a nearby settlement dating to the mid fourth millennium BC have been found at East End and Pamphill north of Corfe Mullen. Along the Frome Valley the nearest monuments and settlements of this period are around Dorchester, nearly 30 kilometres up-river. Overlooking the Harbour from the south is the long barrow on Nine Barrow Down, Corfe Castle, suggesting that perhaps further evidence of occupation should be expected on the Purbeck Hills. Closer to the Harbour, early Neolithic worked flints have been found at the East of Corfe River site.

Within and around the low-lying wetlands of the Frome estuary/Poole Harbour, hunting was probably the main activity down to 2000 BC and beyond as the damp coastal fringe and alder-carr along the river valleys was not especially attractive for early farming. At Bestwall Quarry, excavations covering an area of 55 hectares revealed only a light scatter of worked flints, including leaf-shaped arrowheads and three stone axes. Four pits dating to c. 3800 BC were perhaps ceremonial

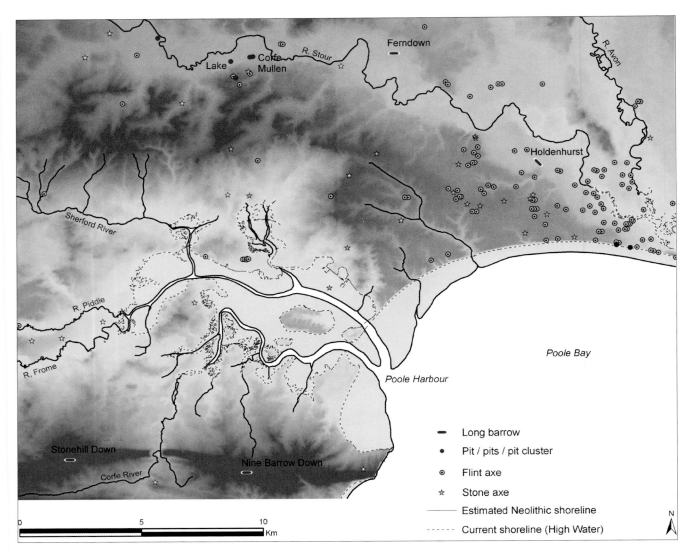

Poole Harbour and its hinterland in the period 4000-3500
BC with an assumed sea-level of c.-4 metres OD in relation to
known bathymetry of the harbour floor and coastal areas (with
thanks to Vanessa Constant).

features cut to celebrate some natural feature in the
woodland, but no certain evidence of occupation was
identified. A similar pit was excavated at Haddon Hill
in Bournemouth in 1936. Elsewhere, leaf-shaped flint
arrow tips have been found at more than a dozen sites
around the Harbour, while Calkin, writing in 1953,
records about the same number of flint and stone axes
from the area, some of which, like those at Bestwell,
were presumably lost or discarded in the woods while
collecting fodder or obtaining timber for building houses
or making artefacts.

The sheltered waters of the Frome estuary and the
low-lying coast at the junction of several rivers would
have made this an obvious area for boats to land,
whether from cross-Channel expeditions or trips along
the coast. Little is known about the boats of the period,
some of which must have been seagoing. A large dug-
out canoe made from the trunk of an entire tree was
found in the bed of the River Frome between Wareham
and Stoborough in 1899 and may possibly be of early
prehistoric date and used to travel the inland waterways
in the area. Sadly it is now lost and therefore cannot be
properly studied. Finds from in and around the Harbour
attest the long distance links that people living in the
area enjoyed. A small dark-green jadeite axe found in
the South West Pottery Clay Pit at Parkstone in 1900
originated in the Barant area of Mont Viso above Turin
in the North Italian Alps. An axe from Highfield Road,
Moordown, is from Sélédin near Plussulien in Brittany,
and one from Bankes Heath gravel pit is dolerite from
the Preselly Hills of south-west Wales. The three stone

Jadeite axe found in the South West Pottery Clay Pit, Parkstone Potteries in 1900, an import from the Barant area of Mont Viso above in the North Italian Alps around 4000 BC (with thanks to Alison Sheridan and Pierre Pétrequin of Project JADE).

Rempstone Stone Circle dates to the Bronze Age, and now lies hidden in woodland below Nine Barrow Down.

axes from Bestwall had all been imported from Cornwall, while a polished stone axe or chisel of ophitic dolerite found at Creekmoor on the north side of the Harbour in the nineteenth century must also have been brought in from western Britain. An axe from Broadstone was brought from Great Langdale in the Lake District. Some of the flint axes from the area may also be imports from distant sources, amongst them a Scandinavian-type axe found in the bank of the Stour near Canford. Also of note is a hoard of five polished flint axes found in 1930 near the corner of Hamworthy Lane and Tucker's Lane at a depth of 0.5 metres, perhaps another ceremonial deposit or a cargo lost in transit.

CLEARING THE LAND

A gradually rising population and greater use of the coastal plain may be glimpsed during the third and early second millennia BC. The ceremonial centre around what is now Dorchester in the Frome valley acted as a regional focus, although more locally the pits at Bestwell were incorporated into a more elaborate circular ceremonial monument. Something rather similar may be glimpsed

at the poorly preserved Rempstone Stone Circle on the south side of the Harbour below Nine Barrow Down with its possible avenue of standing stones to the west. Elsewhere, later Neolithic worked flints have been found at New Mills Heath, the West of Corfe River site and at Bestwall where pits beside the River Piddle contained fine Beaker pottery.

About 2000 BC the area around the Harbour was finally transformed from woodland dotted with clearances to a fairly open agricultural landscape. Grazing was established on the wetland and fields were set out on dry ground. But in many places the quality of the land was such that it could not sustain prolonged cultivation. It was the over-exploitation of this ground during the second millennium BC that quickly caused its degradation and the development of the heathlands that remain as testament to a prehistoric environment disaster through to this day. Moreover, low-lying land was also being inundated as relative sea level continued to rise at a considerable and uneven rate.

Investigations at the East of Corfe River site during construction of the Wytch Farm Oilfield, revealed two phases of activity during the second millennium BC. First, a series of five roughly parallel ditches were established on a north-north-west/south-south-east axis at intervals of about 23-33 metres apart, with a sixth 110 metres away. These are best interpreted as the boundaries of defined plots forming long narrow strips within an extensive field system. Carbonised plant remains include wheat and barley, suggesting the use of these strips as arable plots. Sometime later a stone surface some 20 metres across was built over one of the earlier field boundaries. Spreads of burnt material and a group of small pits were associated with this surface, as well as

A bronze winged palstave found by Philip Butterworth in May 2004 on the Harbour floor near Sandbanks.

about twenty ceramic vessels including biconical and Deverell-Rimbury style pots. A burnt oak stake in one of the pits provided a radiocarbon date of 1459–1254 BC. Interpretation is difficult as it may represent the remains of a settlement or a heavily truncated burial monument. Traces of a similar field system may be present on New Mills Heath, while at Bestwall the excavation described below by Lilian Ladle revealed a settlement of six scattered roundhouses, a fieldsystem, and a handful of cremation burials deposited in Deverel-Rimbury pots relating to this phase of agricultural intensification around the Harbour. Indications of Bronze Age activity in the form of pits and scoops were recorded on Furzey Island, but their purpose is not known.

Burials of the period 2000–1200 BC frequently involved the construction of monumental round barrows, and with more than 50 such barrows within easy reach of the Harbour it is clear that the area was fairly intensively occupied, although not nearly as densely as the lower Stour Valley to the east. Some barrows occur singly, as at Arne Heath on the highest point of the Arne Peninsula, and Slepe Heath overlooking Middlebere. More usually, round barrows occur in cemeteries, as with those grandly positioned to overlook the Harbour for eternity at Godlingstone Heath. A linear cemetery known as Seven Barrows on Northport Heath, Wareham St Martin, actually comprises at least nine bowl barrows and the dispersed cemetery represented by the Worgret Heath Group, Arne, has at least eight bowl barrows, and a bell barrow. The largest mound in this group, known as the King Barrow at Stoborough, was investigated by John Hutchins in January 1767 with quite extraordinary results. He found that the mound was 30 metres across, 4 metres high, and like many barrows in the area was built of stacked turf. In the middle, set on the original

land surface, was the hollowed-out trunk of an oak tree, 3 metres long and 1.25 metres in diameter. Unusually, the body that lay in the oak trunk had been wrapped in animal skins that themselves had been sown together and then secured with a piece of gold wire. With the deceased was a shale cup, perhaps a prestigious personal drinking cup fashioned from locally obtained Kimmeridge Shale. Whether the hollowed trunk was a coffin or a wooden canoe used as a container to emphasize the person's connections with trade and travel is open to debate; sadly everything from the grave went missing long ago. However, it was not the only unusual barrow in the cemetery. A second mound just nearby was excavated in about 1835 and found to contain 25 bronze axes, at least two of which were socketed examples. Further west, but probably part of the same cemetery, was a bowl barrow completely excavated by Geoff Wainwright in 1964 and found to contain two Deverel-Rimbury urns but no remains of any burials.

Trade inland via the rivers, and out of the Harbour into the English Channel and beyond, continued through the second millennium BC as a winged palstave of south-western type found in May 2004 on the Harbour floor near the entrance at Sandbanks attests. Compared with earlier times, however, this was a period of relative quietude in Poole Harbour, as the focus of activity through the later Bronze Age and early Iron Age was well to the east in Christchurch Harbour and along lower valleys of the Stour and Avon.

NINE

The Growth & Decline of Specific Sites

Bestwall
A Landscape on the Harbour Edge

LILIAN LADLE

IN 1992, E.C.C. (Gravels) Ltd., [now Bardon Aggregates], was granted permission to extract gravel from a 55 hectare site on the Bestwall peninsula. The site was bounded by the River Piddle to the north, the River Frome to the south, the historic town of Wareham to the west and Poole Harbour to the east. Archaeological work in advance of gravel extraction has confirmed man's varied activities over thousands of years.

The earliest Mesolithic inhabitants left small numbers of worked flints all over the site. They camped on the northern boundary overlooking the valley of the River Piddle where game and wild fowl would have been abundant. Here, the presence of pits and hundreds of blades, bladelets, flakes, cores and other debitage pointed to an episode of microlith production dating to about 9000 BC. The waste flint was scattered over a working area and the finished tools were taken away and used elsewhere.

Five thousand years later in an oak woodland clearing overlooking the River Frome, four early Neolithic pits were dug, within their fills were pottery fragments and worked flint. These pits were succeeded by a small timber circle and later by segmented ditches enclosing a timber building. Sparse activity all over the site is indicated by finds of pottery, stone axes, flint arrowheads and other tools. Most of the flint was local and fashioned from gravel nodules picked off the ground. Some, however, originated from further afield; chalk flint from Purbeck and chert from Portland. Three granite axes testify

to exchange or even trade with the West Country. The Harbour and rivers would have been significant routeways in journeys to acquire such prestige objects.

There was a significant reduction in tree cover in the early Bronze Age and a shift to an open, agricultural environment with the setting out of the first rectangular field systems. Crops included wheat and barley. Settlement areas could not be defined but pits containing Beaker ceramics, some of them wasters, confirmed pottery production on site.

Radiocarbon dates have confirmed middle Bronze Age activity between 1500 and 950 BC. Within this period, occupation on the peninsula was extensive and included eight roundhouses, developed field systems, cremation burials and large numbers of pits. One house was notable. When it went out of use, two bronze bracelets were left as a 'closing deposit', together with very large amounts of pottery, implying ceremonial feasting on a grand scale. All pottery of this date was manufactured on site; the clay coming from the Purbeck area would have been brought in by boat or cart. Wheat, barley and beans were the main crops and the presence of deep pits and quernstones implied the storage and processing of grain. Shale spindle whorls and ceramic loom weights

Location plan of Bestwall Quarry.

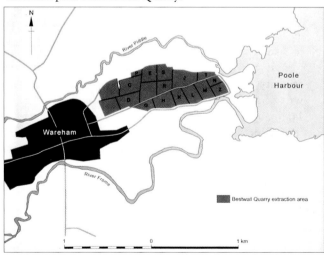

ABOVE An early Bronze Age barbless arrowhead and a Late Neolithic chisel arrowhead, both made from local flint.

BELOW A Neolithic Cornish granite axe – a first hint of coastal exchange and trade?

BELOW A Roman cooking pot which held a cremation dated to the early fourth century AD.

Remains of a Roman pottery kiln with part of the abandoned load in the firing chamber.

were used in the processing of wool.

Settlement continued through the late Bronze Age and into the early Iron Age and a further five houses were in use between 940 and 790 BC. These farmsteads had their basis in agriculture with pollen cores displaying intense arable cultivation of cereals. Pottery making, probably for local use, continued. Metalworking crucibles and moulds were evidence for the production of palstaves and socketed axes.

By the first century BC, two large late Iron Age houses were sited within a ditched enclosure in the southern corner of the site overlooking the River Frome. New field systems were laid out at this time and charred seed and animal bone evidence indicates arable and livestock farming. A wide variety of pottery was made, for domestic use as well as for external markets. Imports included two quernstones from the West Country, amphorae from Spain, and pottery from Brittany and Italy, suggesting long-range contacts and the growing importance of sea-borne trade. The presence of a Durotrigian coin hints at a reasonably high status settlement.

During the Roman period farming probably on a smaller scale continued; crops included wheat, barley, oats, rye and flax. A significant and extremely important pottery industry developed and 32 kilns produced a wide variety of Black Burnished Ware vessels on a huge scale between *c.* AD 220 and *c.* 420. It has been estimated that about one million pots a year were shipped out of the Harbour from Bestwall and from a similar site further up the River Frome at Worget. Clay for kiln construction and for pottery making came from Purbeck. Sand for

pottery filler was locally sourced as was fuel to fire the kilns. This comprised oak and holly from the nearby woodland and chaff from cereal processing. Imported pottery included Samian from Gaul as well as fine ware from pottery production centres in the New Forest, Oxfordshire, and the Nene Valley.

There were at least eight Romano-British burials at Bestwall. Five graves dating from the early third to the late fourth centuries AD were located; all had the remains of hobnailed footwear within the graves and one individual was buried with a coin. The acidic soil precluded the survival of skeletal material, but in two cases body stains were present on the grave bases. Four of the graves were in pairs, and two of these were within ditched enclosures. The large numbers of coffin nails imply that they were reasonably high status burials. Three cremation burials were found, dating from the late second to the late fourth or early fifth centuries. They were all female and buried in Black Burnished Ware cooking pots. In Dorset, cremation was rare at this time.

Perhaps the most surprising find was a hoard of 1558 silver coins dating to AD 275 which was concealed in a Black Burnished Ware pot. A smaller hoard of 34 coins dating to AD 282 was also located. Individuals of

A reconstruction by Jane Brayne of the Roman pottery site by the River Frome at Bestwall.

considerable wealth, perhaps associated with the pottery production site, probably had business interests on the peninsula.

Radiocarbon dating has confirmed ironworking

A selection of coins from the Roman coin hoard deposited some time after AD 275.

and charcoal burning industries beginning in the early years of the post-Roman period and continuing until the mid ninth century. Four small furnaces associated with smelting and one smithing pit were excavated. In addition 1089 randomly occurring 'charcoal pits' were located all over the site. These bowl-shaped features were the remains of small clamps producing charcoal for the Bestwall ironworking industry. The predominantly oak and holly woodland on the periphery of the site, supplied the charcoal burners. Pottery-making on a very small scale and agriculture continued. Grain-rich assemblages were retrieved from charcoal pits and included bread wheats, barley, oats, and rye. By 1086, the Domesday Book records a productive manor with arable, pasture and woodland probably centred on modern-day Swineham Farm.

A Civil War camp on the north-west side of the site was identified through finds of seventeenth century pottery, glass, clay pipes, coins, and metalwork. These, together with lead shot and gunpowder measure caps, have pinpointed the spot where Royalist soldiers gathered before a short, but unsuccessful, battle against superior horse-borne Parliamentarian forces in August 1646.

Farming at Bestwall continued until gravel extraction began in 1992. The result of this has been the formation of two large lakes dedicated to wildlife and which are now the focus of a landscape which has been dramatically altered. The archaeological remains have been completely obliterated, but the results have spectacularly illuminated man's activities over the past 10,000 years.

Green Island and Ower
An Iron Age Settlement

EILEEN WILKES

T HE IRON AGE OF BRITAIN (*c.* 800 BC–AD 43) was a period of intense continental contact. The people of Britain would have been very aware of the advance of Rome through Europe and there is evidence, both archaeological and literary, of a lively trade and communication network along and across the English Channel at this time. On the English coast more than 40 locations would have been suitable 'nodes' on this network. Perhaps the most well-known of these is at Hengistbury Head in Dorset. However, 14 kilometres to the west, Poole Harbour was a busy and well-connected port certainly by the late Iron Age. The focus of the port activities was in the southern Harbour at Ower Peninsula, Green Island, and Furzey Island. This contrasts with today's focus in the north of the Harbour following a relocation of port activities from the end of the Iron Age.

It is suggested that during the late Iron Age the water level in the Harbour was approximately 1.0 metres below today's level. In those conditions, the main islands would exist as larger masses than today and the Harbour, rather than appearing as an open body of water, would instead be more readily defined as a visible network of channels. The main southern channel, today known as 'South Deep', would have led mariners directly to the complex of sites in the south of the Harbour.

Ower Peninsula was the location of a large late Iron Age settlement. The full extent of the site is still not known but geophysical survey has shown that it covers at least 10 hectares. Within this area, the

Map showing the position of the Iron Age jetties on Green Island and Cleavel Point on the Ower peninsula.

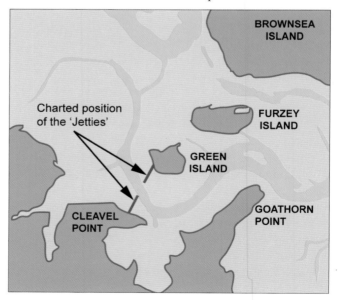

A reconstruction by Victor Ambrus, specially drawn for the 'Time Team' excavation on Green Island in 2000, showing the two jetties on Green Island and Cleavel Point.

settlement is divided into living areas, stock enclosures, and manufacturing sites. People lived in round houses, farmed the surrounding lands and tended their animals, but agricultural activity was not the main occupation of the inhabitants. They were much involved in the production of goods for local use and for export, and in receiving ships laden with goods from other areas of Britain and the Continent. Of particular interest is the continental pottery, finds of which suggest that Ower Peninsula was a site of intense trade from at least 200 BC. These and other imports were used locally in the Harbour settlement and also carried further on in the network, mainly using waterborne transport, to reach sites elsewhere in Dorset and southern England. In exchange, exports from the site included items made of Kimmeridge shale (particularly armlets), pottery (and its contents), metalwork, salt, and one can imagine livestock, agricultural produce and other organic items that leave little trace in the archaeological record. One of the most exciting features of Ower Peninsula and neighbouring Green Island is the pair of jetties already described in Chapter 5.

Green Island was a key element in the port function of the Harbour in the later Iron Age. Evaluation

excavation on the island in 2001-03 showed that it was a focus for manufacturing activity, particularly working Kimmeridge shale into items for the export market. A considerable amount of manufacturing debris was recovered but not a single finished artefact was found, suggesting that all completed items were shipped off the island. Earlier studies concluded that the shale on Green Island, and elsewhere around the southern fringe of the Harbour, was being worked by hand and turned on a lathe during the late Iron Age to produce armlets. Crucially, finds on the island include not just the shale debris but also the flint tools used to work the shale on the lathe. This is an early adoption of lathe technology in Britain that was generally considered to be a Roman introduction. Given the Harbour's continental contacts at this time it was preferentially placed to receive continental innovations and ideas ahead of other areas of the country and before the Romans actually arrived in AD 43.

The pair of jetties respectively from the Ower

Green Island from the air. Just visible on the right is Furzey Island, to which Green Island was once joined.

Peninsula and Green Island are located at the point where the South Deep channel is at its most narrow. This location is ideal as a control point to monitor access into and out of the inner Harbour. The striking visual form of the jetties suggests that, as well as being functional, they also provided a monumental 'gateway' to the prehistoric port, replicating the natural gateway of the two sand bars that form the entrance to the Harbour.

Furzey Island is currently used by BP for oil pumping purposes (Chapter 17). Excavation in advance of BP's development on the island showed that it too had seen extensive Iron Age occupation, but with earlier Bronze Age use as well. A number of Iron Age enclosures were recorded, marked by ditches, the material of which would have formed a perimeter bank. The ditch fills contained late Iron Age local and imported pottery, amphora sherds, hand and lathe worked shale debris, evidence of salt-production, and a small amount of iron-smithing waste, as well as hammerstones and quernstones.

It has been suggested that during the late Iron Age, Furzey and Green Islands were connected to Ower as one extended peninsula until the early Romano-British period when coastal erosion, rising sea level, and changes in the hydrography of the Harbour flooded the land link. Recent fieldwork reinforced the suggestion that Green and Furzey Islands were indeed one landmass ('South Island'), but that before the middle Iron Age it was already separated from the mainland at Ower by the South Deep Channel.

Archaeological evidence suggests that occupation on Furzey Island ended abruptly at c. 20 BC – exactly the date when the main settlement was established at Ower Peninsula. Chiming with modern concerns, perhaps rising sea level created the division of 'South Island' and made access to the area of Furzey less attractive, so leading to a large scale relocation of settlement from Furzey Island to Ower Peninsula.

The relocation from Furzey Island to Ower Peninsula (and the Roman period relocation of settlement and waterside activities to Hamworthy) suggests that the port function of the Harbour was worth maintaining. From its origins on Furzey and Green Islands, that function has continued to the cross-Channel passenger and cargo port of the present day.

This reconstruction by English Heritage of the Iron Age hillfort at Danebury, Hampshire, gives a good sense of similar Iron Age settlements in Dorset, both round Poole Harbour and on hillforts such as Maiden Castle.

Other Iron Age & Roman Settlements

EILEEN WILKES

POOLE HARBOUR in the Iron Age was surrounded by low-lying open heathland through which ran the rivers Corfe, Frome, Piddle (Trent), and Sherford. Although the soils were poor and not capable of supporting much agricultural activity it is possible that the exploitation of marine resources, including salt, the availability of good quality clays, shale and stone, and opportunities for manufacture and trade were sufficiently advantageous for people to inhabit these areas rather than the more fertile agricultural lands of the nearby Dorset chalklands.

A number of Iron Age sites have been identified from the littoral and inner heath which were linked with the Harbour by the riverine and overland routes to its shores. Some of these sites have been the subject of archaeological investigation in recent years, including Bestwall Quarry, Bulbury Hill, 'East of Corfe River', Fitzworth Point, Slepe, and 'West of Corfe River'. From these investigations we can extract an understanding of settlement around the Harbour during the later Iron Age and into the Romano-British period.

The site at Bestwall is conveniently located at Swineham Point where the rivers Frome and Piddle flow into the Harbour. Investigation has revealed evidence ranging from the Bronze Age to post-Roman periods, with a large body of material related to Iron Age and Romano-British pottery production, making use of the local clays.

The reconstruction of a Roman-British farmstead at Upton Park, near Poole.

Approximately six kilometres west of Swineham Point, along the River Piddle, a shaped piece of wood, dated to the Bronze Age, was recovered from under 1 metre of peat. One interpretation for the object is that it was a paddle for a boat. Close to the find spot was a platform of logs that was interpreted as a landing stage. If the interpretations are correct, the preserved wood remains are clear evidence of the use of the riverine route to and from the Harbour in prehistory.

The Corfe River flows from a spring high on the Purbeck ridge from where it passes through the only gap in that ridge, making it particularly suitable to follow as a route between the Harbour and the Purbeck high ground. It flows into the Harbour at Wych Lake. At the confluence of the Corfe River and the Creech tributary, just one kilometre from the shore of the Harbour, are two Iron Age sites known as 'East of Corfe River' and 'West of Corfe River'. The location of the east and west river sites, at a point where two water courses meet to flow into the Harbour, is similar to that at Bestwall. Excavation of the western site revealed evidence of large-scale processes of shale working, iron working, salt production, and pre-Roman conquest pottery production, suggesting it was an industrial rather than a settlement site. The eastern site was the settlement area but also provided evidence of extensive agricultural and industrial activity. As on the other side of the river, those activities included salt production and shale working, and possibly pottery manufacture and iron working. The full extent of the Iron Age settlement at this confluence is not known, but it was considered by the excavators to be of a comparable size to the large settlement at Ower Peninsula, if not larger. It was suggested that both the East of Corfe River and Ower Peninsula settlement sites were 'implanted' with a pre-planned layout of enclosures on a large scale.

Additional settlement, potentially of Iron Age date, is found a little further inland at the site of Slepe. The date for this is not confirmed as it has not been excavated but was recognised on an aerial photograph taken in 1989 as part of BP's geological exploration of the area. Here parchmarks show two superimposed rectilinear enclosures and a series of internal anomalies. The morphology and dimensions of the enclosures were judged to match those of Iron Age enclosures at Ower Peninsula and East of Corfe River. It was concluded that the 'intensity of internal features associated with the enclosures indicates that it is likely to represent a focus of settlement activity'.

A major element in the proposed Iron Age settlement pattern of the Harbour hinterland is Bulbury Hill. As a defended high ground enclosure this was perhaps a further control point, regulating traffic to and from the port via the overland routes. There is no other high ground in the immediate vicinity of the Harbour: it is the first possible point for a high ground enclosure and affords views across the back of the Harbour and the approaches to it. The link with activity in the Harbour is strengthened by finds made there, including an iron anchor and chain. Other Iron Age artefacts recovered from Bulbury were of types which typically had distributions in north-west France and south-west Britain, exactly the areas of contact demonstrated as maritime links for the Harbour. The metalwork and other goods travelled the same routes into the Harbour as the pottery and shale items followed as exports.

Evidence from known settlement sites around the Harbour from the Iron Age and Romano-British periods shows that people were not only engaging in the typical agricultural practices of that time but were also involved in the manufacture of certain products, potentially for export via the maritime network. The number of sites involved with salt production, shale working, and pottery production suggests that the exports were not of a small scale. Local conditions meant that the potential for agricultural produce was not high, but other resources were amply supplied and were easily accessible in the Harbour hinterland. Exploitation of these would have provided an economic base for the Harbour communities and made possible exchanges of goods and produce with other groups, linked by networks both along and across the English Channel.

The Roman Occupation of Hamworthy

KEITH JARVIS & PETER BELLAMY

PRIOR TO AND DURING the Iron Age, the Hamworthy peninsula, in common with much of the Harbour area outside the main settlements such as Green Island, Furzey Island and Cleavel Point, was occupied by a few scattered settlements. Salt production (Chapter 14) and basic agriculture were the principal activities.

The importance of the peninsula increased during the last century of the Iron Age with the probable and gradual transfer of port activities from Green Island and Cleavel Point, apparently as a result of rising water levels (Chapter 5) and the greater convenience for incoming shipping and communication with the hinterland to the north of the Harbour. Overlap between the two sets of facilities, however, continued for some time into the first two centuries AD.

Similar finds at the two locations have indicated active trading with the Continent. Whilst cross-Channel ships would have used the major jetties at Green Island and Cleavel Point, no evidence of similar structures has been found at Hamworthy, and it is possible that incoming ships were beached. The precise location of the Hamworthy port is not known, but it is likely to have been near the present site of the Sunseeker Works and approached via Little Channel.

Occupation of the Hamworthy Peninsula would have increased with the development of the port towards the end of the Iron Age, but it achieved major significance with the arrival of the Romans in AD 43.

The skeleton of a young man of the third or fourth century AD from the 1974 excavation on Hamworthy. At his feet were found hobnails or studs, suggesting that he might have been buried with his boots on.

ROMAN MILITARY OCCUPATION AD 43-65

In AD 43, four Roman Legions invaded southern England. The Second Legion Augusta under the command of the future Emperor Vespasian was responsible for conquering the South West. Whilst meeting little resistance, Vespasian fought 30 battles,

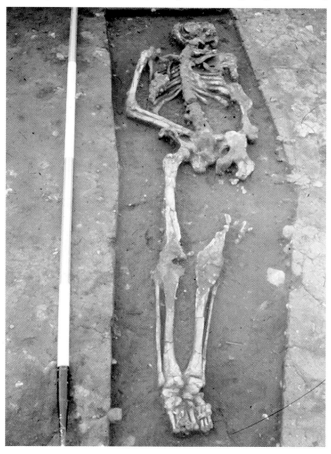

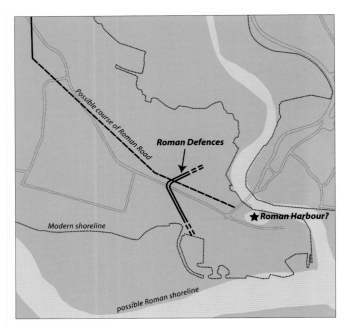

Map of Hamworthy in Roman times. During the Roman period, the sea level was lower and Poole Harbour may have been a series of river channels with low-lying land between. The double defensive ditches of the Roman supply base are only known on two sides – the other two sides remain to be discovered by archaeology. The possible position of the Roman harbour is speculative, based on the location of an embayment marked on historic maps (see page 90).

subdued two warlike tribes, and captured more than 20 well-defended hillforts, which included not only those further to the west and north in Dorset but Hengistbury Head as well as the Isle of Wight.

By about AD 47 a large legionary fortress was constructed at Lake Farm, near Wimborne, to accommodate around 3000 soldiers. Geophysical investigation has revealed a fort plan of 30 acres with a vast complex of timber buildings surrounded by a substantial bank and ditch. Whilst undoubtedly defensive, its principal purpose would have been as a depot for supplying men and materials to other parts of the southwest.

Work by H.P. Smith in the 1930s identified a Roman road passing through Broadstone in a due north-south direction skirting the south-west side of Holes Bay towards the Harbour, the likely site of the Hamworthy port. Many parts of this Roman road still exist and are identified as such by name.

Smith's work at Hamworthy uncovered many Roman artefacts which suggested a military site, but it was only in 2000 that a rather enigmatic double-ditched enclosure with an area of about 20 acres was discovered near the Pilkington's tile factory and immediately north-west of the suspected port site. Work by Terrain Archaeology in 2000-2006 revealed a building, possibly a barracks.

Taking the whole of these discoveries together, the most likely interpretation for the Roman military occupation of Hamworthy during the period AD 43-65 appears to be: a takeover of a port established during the end of the Iron Age, landing men and supplies from the Continent; building an adjacent transit depot; and a road skirting what was then probably an area of low-lying marshland (and is now Holes Bay) before travelling due north to the main legionary fortress at Lake Farm. The intervention of a marsh would explain the deviation from the normal straight line adopted for their roads by the Romans.

During this period of Roman military occupation, the economy of the area changed substantially, with Roman negotiators requiring large quantities of goods such as pottery and salt. Production of both pottery and salt appears to have been done by relatively small groups, perhaps working on a seasonal basis, but we cannot be sure if they remained local cottage industries or developed into major works supplying large military contracts.

LEFT Excavation of Roman saltmaking hearths built over the remains of the Roman military supply base defences found to the south of Shapwick Road, Hamworthy, in 2000. The excavations by Terrain Archaeology were done in advance of drainage works on the site and revealed the double ditched Roman military defences, together with several Roman saltmaking hearths and many small boundary ditches. The hearths were used for boiling brine to produce salt. The burnt clay of the hearths shows up well against the dark soil below.

CONTINUING ROMAN OCCUPATION

AD 65-410

After the army moved out in AD 65, it is possible that Hamworthy became a major civilian port. If so, it would have been one of a small number of places on the south coast of England where a Roman road was connected to a sheltered harbour, and is likely to have catered for a significant part of the export and import trade for the Romano-British economy.

Apart from the Harbour itself, the road to the Lake Farm site gave direct access to the Roman road system to the east, west and north. Archaeological exploration of the Hamworthy site in 2003 found settlement debris and burials inside the military site as well as extensive evidence of salt working.

Romano-British exports would have included salt, perhaps sometimes contained in the Black Burnished Ware pots then being produced in the area. Other exports were probably oysters, shale goods and Purbeck Marble; although the bulk of this was shipped from the south of the Harbour, at Ower and Wareham.

As an interesting postscript to this account of the initial occupation of Hamworthy; although its appearance and the technology used within it have changed significantly during the past 2000 years (for much of the period it was farmland), two of the then principal activities remain in the form of the cross-Channel ferry terminal, immediately to the south of the original Iron Age/Roman port, and the Royal Marine base slightly further to the west of the original Roman military site.

ABOVE Samian decorated bowl, platter and cups. Part of a large service of about AD 45-65 discarded in a well at the Roman fortress at Lake, and – like the amphora below – now on display in Poole Museum.

BELOW A rare example of a complete amphora storage vessel found discarded in a well at the Roman fortress at Lake.

Newton
A Failed Settlement

ALAN BROMBY

In the domesday book of 1086 the Isle of Purbeck was described as an agricultural area with its income derived mainly from sheep farming and salt production. Salt was a major export which was very important to the economy of the area, as described in Chapter 14. It was so important that landowners held land on the edge of the Harbour even if their main land-holdings were on the other side of the Purbeck Hills and some of the salt works were owned by those who had no other land interest in the area. The Domesday Book records salt-workers at Ower who paid twenty shillings a year to the Abbot of Milton

'. . . no plough is recorded but there are thirteen salt workers who pay twenty shillings'.

In 1286 Edward I appointed Richard Bosca and Walter de Marisco to build a new town in a place called *Gotowre super Mare* in Studland parish with the following remit:

'To layout with sufficient streets and lanes, adequate sites for a market and a church and plots for merchants in a new town with a harbour.'

The area on the southern shores of the Harbour has still changed little from the Middle Ages except for oil recovery (Chapter 17), and there is no evidence that it was ever much populated. This is reflected in the lack of churches on the area. During the medieval period church building is an important indicator of the wealth of the population and only one new church was built on the southern edge of the Harbour. This was the church of St Nicholas which was built at Arne during the thirteenth century. It was a single-cell church, a chapel-of-ease of Holy Trinity in Wareham; a chapel-of-ease was established where there were inadequate population or funds to found a new parish church.

The precise location of the intended new town and the reasons for its failure are not precisely known.

John haywarde holdeth one tenement with a cottage and divers closes & p[ar]cells of lande hereafter followeth wi[th] thappurtenances in Newton in the p[ar]ish of Studlande together wi[th] A licence to take berdes or fowle as well in the Lordes commonns as upon the coostes or river of the sea there and paieth therefore yearely .... xiiij [sh]

Treswell's map of 1586 (see opposite page) drawn on behalf of Sir Christopher Hatton, Constable of Corfe Castle and Vice-Admiral and Lord Lieutenant of the Isle of Purbeck and Guardian of the Island of Branksea, shows Newton on the west of the Goathorn peninsula.

With the name Goathorn believed to be a derivation of the original name Gotowre, and with current names of Newton Bay, Newton Cottage, and Newton Copse, its location to the west of the present Goathorn peninsula appears fairly certain. There has however been no direct archaeological evidence for the position of Newton. It was thought that some earthworks, consisting of the footings of three buildings with associated banks and ditches, might be the site of Edward I's proposed new town. On investigation it was found that an oak tree growing in the footings of one of the buildings was approximately 350 years old and this together with the associated pottery dated the house to the seventeenth century.

One reason for its early abandonment may have been the desire of Edward I's sucessors to maintain the whole area as a Royal Forest, which it had been since AD 700. In the Middle Ages a forest was a place of deer, not of trees. The area, which included the heathland and bogs of the southern shores of the Harbour, was strictly controlled, and within it the King reserved for himself the right to hunt certain animals, particularly deer and wild boar. The unenclosed Chase had strict laws to ensure good hunting for the King and his guests.

that no man ought to erecte or build upp any new howses in the heathe or else where wi[th] out licence of the Lorde Constable or the court.

Another reason for the lack of development at Newton, and other sites along the Harbour's southern shore, may be that the landowners were keen to avoid disturbance of their lucrative salt production sites.

East from Newton . . . places of little note, no more than fishers cottages, on ground taken out of the heath'

Had Edward I's project succeeded, the southern edges of the Harbour would have been very different. Newton Bay is now shallow, but it may well have been deeper in the thirteenth century. Its harbour and continuing use as a safe haven for ships would certainly have required dredging to allow ships other than the shallow-draft recreational vessels which use the area today.

TEN

The Islands of the Harbour

IAN ANDREWS

THE FORMATION OF THE HARBOUR as we now know it, following the Ice Age 10,000 years ago, has been described in Chapter 2. Rising water levels meant that the lower land was inundated whilst hills remained as islands of varying sizes and permanency.

The largest islands – Brownsea, Furzey, Green, Round, Long, and Pergin's in Holes Bay (Longfleet Bay) – are described in this Chapter. The footprint of each of these has changed significantly in response to changing water levels, and pairs of these – Furzey and Green Island, Long and Round Island – have at times been joined together.

Many other 'islands' appear at low Spring Tides but are of no permanent interest except possibly in respect of their names – Giggers, Stone, Shard, Utterheath, Vermigore, Horse, and Bucks Cove – and to mariners who encounter them inadvertently at higher tides.

Part of Ralph Treswell's 'A Survey of the Isle of Purbeck', 1586, which as well as the principal islands in the Harbour shows the failed settlement of Newton on the Goathorn peninsula. The 'Mynes' on the east side of the Harbour refer to the raw materials for the alum and copperas industries (see Chapter 15); and the 'Salterne' north of Studland to the saltworkings once common on the south side of the Harbour (see Chapter 14).

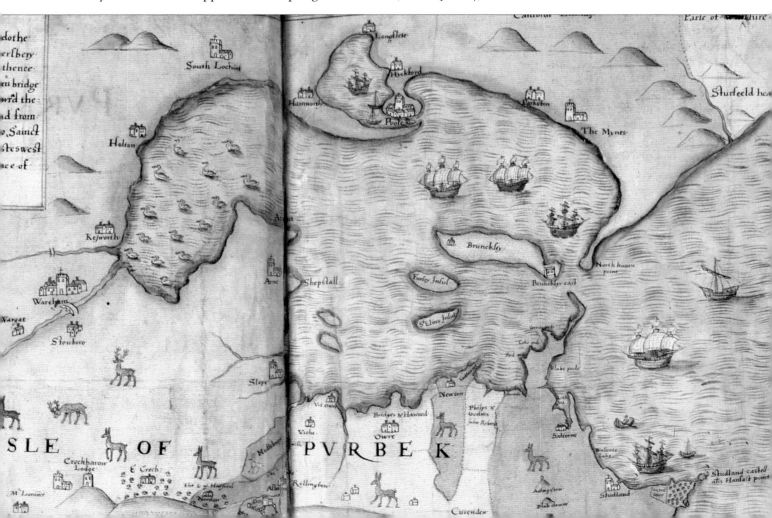

A view of Brownsea Castle in 1774 from Hutchins *History of Dorset*.

BROWNSEA ISLAND

Immediately inside the entrance to the Harbour lies 560 acre Brownsea Island, the largest hilly area that remained above sea level when the Harbour was formed at the end of the Ice Age.

An enchanting island, open to all, in National Trust ownership with part set aside as a nature reserve for Dorset Wildlfe Trust and a campsite for the Boy Scout movement. Its Castle is leased to the John Lewis partnership as a holiday home. And it is a haven for red squirrels, deer, and birdlife.

It is hard to realise that its isolated, peaceful, and natural surroundings lie barely a mile south of densely developed, noisy, and busy city life on the mainland, where grey squirrels prevail.

The Island appears deceptively small in its wider context, but is over a mile-and-a-half long and half-a-mile wide, with a five-and-a-half-mile shoreline.

To date, the earliest evidence of settlement of the Island is through discovery of third century AD animal bones and Romano-British pottery made from the clay underlying part of the Island on a site that now lies below the high water mark, no doubt supplying the needs of the local salt industry.

The next evidence of human occupation of the Island was not until the establishment, late in the tenth century, of a chapel for a hermit dedicated to St Andrew by the Abbey of Cerne, completed in AD 987. There was no need for a congregation as it is highly likely that the chapel was built to establish the Abbey's temporal presence, for example to gain the important money-raising rights of 'wreck' (salvage) in the surrounding waters and mudbanks; the only spiritual need perhaps being to minister for the needs of seafarers arriving and departing these waters and those shipwrecked.

Cerne Abbey and its little chapel were to suffer in 1015 when Viking ships led by Cnut raided the area carrying off all that was valuable. A manuscript records that 'having spoiled the church and monasterie of Cerne [Cnut] took to the haven and sailed thence to Branksey . . . having in it no buildings save a chapel only.' The following year Cnut became King of England and during his reign made reparation for this damage. In 1143 the value of the Island was estimated, not as a round figure, but at a very precise 51s 11d. The right of wreck was a valuable one since it stretched from Kimmeridge to Poole and was confirmed by later monarchs. A reminder of the monastic period remains in the retention of the name of the saltwater bay (now a freshwater lagoon) as St Andrew's Bay (see Chapter 5). No trace has been found of the chapel, but a cemetery containing seven skeletons (radiocarbon-dated as between 1150 to 1350) was found in 1974 some distance west of the present St Mary's Church. The Abbot of Cerne remained in possession until the Dissolution in 1539, after which Brownsea was then vested in the Crown.

From the sixteenth century, Brownsea Island has played a major part in the defence of the Harbour, as described in Chapter 12. The 'castell of Bronkse' was built by Henry VIII in about 1537 and 'the Mayor and brethren' of Poole were supplied from Portsmouth with the necessary munitions. That role continued, in varying

degree, through to the Second World War.

By 1576 it appeared that Queen Elizabeth had given ownership of Brownsea Island to one of her favourites, Sir Christopher Hatton, Governor of Purbeck. Poole Corporation had not been told and requested Sir Christopher to prove it was his. Having done so, they appeared glad to pass all responsibility for the castle, ordnance, and ammunition to him. But relations between the town and the keepers of the castle were far from cordial, especially when the gunner overstepped his powers and sought to interfere with the Poole ferrymen, claiming their tolls, and with Lord Mountjoy (licensed to work clay on the Island for his alum and copperas works), as described in chapter 15.

The Island fell into the hands of several successive owners after Queen Elizabeth's death in 1603. In the Civil War the castle again became a fort, but on the side of Parliament and not the King, and was placed under the control of the Governor of Poole and supplied and strengthened by the House of Commons. Poole must have felt safer once more!

After the Restoration of King Charles II in 1660 the castle was allowed to fall into decay by Sir Robert Clayton, a wealthy Lord Mayor of London and MP for the City of London, a Whig who opposed Royal

An aerial view of Brownsea Island showing the enclosed lagoon.

supremacy. During the Plague King Charles II left London and after dinner on a day visit to Poole was sailed round the island in a boat belonging to a former Mayor, Colonel William Skutt.

Some time before 1722 Brownsea was bought for £300 by the eccentric Mr. William Benson who converted the castle into a private dwelling. Benson was an amateur botanist and man of letters who fancied his skills as an architect. Pleas to the Privy Council and the Attorney General by the Town Council in 1726 that he had deprived Poole of its first line of defence were to no avail and since that time it has remained in private ownership. The castle was rebuilt and enlarged, and special attention was paid to the grounds that were planted with many rare plants and trees. At one stage Benson went mad but later recovered, but not before rumours circulated in Poole that he practised Black Magic there. He sold the Island before his death and it passed for £420 to a bachelor, Mr. John Lock, a master shipwright, from whom it passed on his death and after a dispute with his former housekeeper's claim, to his mother and thence to Mr. Humphrey Sturt of

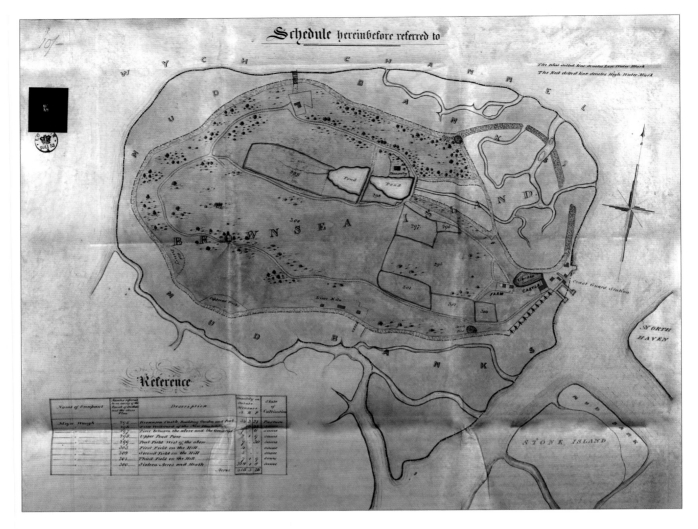

A map of Brownsea Island drawn up following the purchase of the Island by Colonel Waugh in 1853 (who, incidentally, is only ranked as a Major on the Schedule). There is much of interest, including the battery of guns to the south of the Castle, the Copperas Works, Coast Guard Station, and unreclaimed St Andrew's Bay.

Crichel House, who is believed to have spent £50,000 on further improvements to the castle, raising its height to four storeys and adding castellations. He improved cultivation for those living on the island by improving the soil, importing barge loads of manure. On his death Brownsea passed to his only son, Charles, who in the war against revolutionary France raised a Volunteer Artillery from the workers to man the guns. After the Treaty of Amiens in 1802, Charles crossed the Channel and when war resumed against Napoleon was stranded in France and imprisoned. In 1809 he was released and returned to Brownsea, but the hardships he had suffered affected his health and he died in 1815, just days before the Battle of Waterloo. In earlier years he had been a keen yachtsman who once raced against Mr. Weld of Lulworth Castle.

His son Henry Charles inherited but was not impressed by yachting or the Island and sold it for £8,000 in 1817 to Sir Charles Chad, who was an enthusiastic sportsman and yachtsman. At this period there were on the Island two houses for servants, a pub and a house to accommodate the necessary revenue officers as smuggling was then in its heyday. A year after Chad's purchase the Island received its first royal visitor, the Prince of Wales (later King George IV), who was staying in the country at Crichel rather than in London 'to avoid certain amatory scandals.' He is reported as remarking 'I had no idea that there had been such a delightful spot in the Kingdom.' Sir Charles Chad was encouraged to further beautify it, creating a pheasantry (Venetia Park), building a three acre walled-garden and greenhouses and a bungalow on the north side (known as Seymers or Seymours Cottage) commanding a magnificent view of the Harbour, and also a seawater swimming pool.

In 1845 Sir Augustus Foster, a retired diplomat, paid Chad £14,000 for the Island. His tenure was unhappy; he suffered a breakdown of health and committed suicide by cutting his throat. The Island passed to his widow who sold it to Colonel W.P. Waugh, for £13,000, who nursed dreams of making millions out of the clay deposits (see Chapter 19). Colonel Waugh launched out on a programme of expansion. He restored the castle, built a clock tower and a farm complete with cowsheds and outhouses, a laundry, a school and a public house. He also built the present church of St. Mary in 1853/54 at a cost of £10,000, with its transept, nave, and chancel. The oak panelling of the nave and ceiling was taken from the medieval council chamber at Crosby Hall. The Colonel also built the vicarage, which is known as the Villa. He even had tram lines laid down between the potteries and the pier, near which he created the village of Maryland to house the pottery workers. He entertained on a grand scale, with bazaars and the Poole Regatta bringing thousands of local visitors to the Island. He raised £237,000 for his schemes and bought himself out of the Army. The huge loan carried an interest of 10 per cent.

The venture came to an end when it was discovered that the Island clay was of a low grade and little value. A broken man, pressed by his bank and other debtors, a later owner, Charles Van Raalte, told a tale that, were it not true would be comic. Ignorant of his imminent bankruptcy, an eager deputation arrived from Poole to invite Colonel Waugh to stand as their MP. Met by Mrs. Waugh (who was very deaf) she assumed they were creditors who had come to demand their rights. To their overtures she replied by begging them to allow her husband more time in which to repay his debts. So the delegates went back to Poole to spread the news.

The unhappy Colonel fled to Spain. But his impulsive and personally disastrous extravagance had done the island at least one lasting service from which we all benefit today: at vast expense he undertook the reclamation of the St Andrews Bay area, now called the Lagoon (Chapter 5). The Harbour waters are kept at bay by the stout wall he had constructed and from their hide on the fringe of the trees bird-watchers can now train their glasses on the innumerable wild fowl and wading birds. It is now fed from the western lake which in turn is supplied by a freshwater spring.

Colonel Waugh's liquidators put the Island up for sale, but the bidding failed to reach the reserve price of £50,000 and it remained on the market. It is said that the exiled Napoleon III considered its purchase and it was also considered by the Admiralty as a suitable place to establish a Naval College. How different the Island

St Mary's Church, Brownsea Island, built by Colonel Waugh between 1853/1854.

and Harbour would be if the merits of Dartmouth had not prevailed? Finally, in 1870, Brownsea was bought by the Rt. Hon. G.A. Cavendish Bentinck, who enjoyed a twenty-year occupancy before his death. A great collector and art lover he brought many treasures to the castle that were sold on his death, some to the V & A Museum. He lived at the Villa (said to be too large for a Vicar to afford its upkeep) rather than in the castle, as he had given the latter to his son Freddy as a wedding gift. He reopened the potteries with Island inhabitants (then numbering over 250), as its workers.

On Bentinck's death, Major Balfour MP bought the Island. In 1896, while he was in the church attending evensong, a fire broke out in the castle. The Island's shortcomings in the firefighting department all too soon became apparent; it took three hours to load the Poole engine and tow it to the Island, and much of the castle was lost. The cause was not conclusively established but is believed to be connected with the installation of electricity in the building. Balfour immediately set about its restoration at a cost of £20,000 (more than twice what he was to receive when he sold it) and had completed it (with more hydrants) by 1901 when Charles Van Raalte bought it and took up residence with his wife, Florence and children Noel, Margherita, and Barbara.

To the Village Quay, a watercolour of 1905 by Florence Van Raalte. Today, the building on the left is the National Trust shop and café.

Charles was a keen sportsman and a pioneer of the motor car. He was an antiquarian collector and brought many curios to the Island, evidenced in the catalogue of sale after his death, including the finest collection of musical instruments then in the UK (now housed at Kilmarnock Castle). He was a member of the Stock Exchange and a family financial firm, having many connections with London society. It did not take long for him to make his mark, not only on the Island ('a winsome place') but in Poole, in an age of elegance.

Charles's popularity in Poole led to him being elected mayor in 1902 without having been a member of the Council (the only other mayor of Poole not to have been a Councillor beforehand was Lord Wimborne in 1896).

He stood as Conservative and Unionist candidate for Poole and East Dorset in the 1904 General Election but was beaten by the Liberals. At a by-election in 1906 his popularity had increased and many local people were prepared to give their votes more to the man than his cause. His campaigning included touring the constituency in a De Dion Bouilee. When it broke down, his supporters pushed him through the streets of Poole! For many years Poole had been returning Liberals to Westminster, but Charles, while not elected, reduced the Liberal majority from 820 to 21.

He had also written *A History of Brownsea* by 1906 to rescue all the historical references to the Island that might be lost about his 'unique home'. Florence Van Raalte was an accomplished water-colour artist, and contributed her paintings of the island to make it a very attractive book.

The Van Raaltes entertained well. They maintained a staff of about thirty, and ten gardeners kept the lawns of the castle in excellent condition, and the flowerbeds well stocked with profuse and beautiful blooms. A trade with Covent Garden in daffodils transported by train from Poole was initiated.

The Island even had its own band of twenty musicians who wore a special uniform, and played every evening on the castle lawns in summer, or in the great hall in winter, whilst the Van Raaltes dined either alone or with their guests.

Marconi was a frequent guest when he was working at the Haven Hotel and reciprocated this hospitality aboard his giant yacht *Elettra*. Florence even tried to act as a matchmaker for the inventor, who broke his engagement to an American lady to court one of her guests, Beatrice, a member of one of Ireland's oldest aristocratic families. He did not give up when first rejected, and even after newspapers put about rumours of his dalliance with an Italian princess, Marconi impressed her parents as suitable for 'society' and the couple married in 1905.

This was, after all, the Edwardian era and entertaining was the name of the game in those halcyon days. One year the Queen of Romania came with her family to spend a summer on Brownsea.

In 1907 Florence Van Raalte permitted one of her daughter's friends, Robert Baden-Powell, to come to Brownsea and hold a camp there for twenty boys. The camp lasted for ten days, and was attended by six local lads and 14 from Eton and Harrow. The boys were divided into four patrols. Baden-Powell taught them

A view of Major-General Robert Baden-Powell's experimental camp for boys on the Island in 1907, out of which was born the Scouting Movement. Today there are 16 milliion Scouts in 150 countries.

The only known illustration of the Belgian and Dutch trawlers that brought refugees fleeing the advancing Germans to Poole Harbour in 1940 is this sadly poor quality but historic watercolour.

educative games which helped the boys to develop their powers of observation and initiative. They learnt how to cook in the open, and in the evening Baden-Powell told them stories about the Boer War, and taught them songs by the glow of a camp fire. Thus the Boy Scout movement was born on Brownsea Island.

The Van Raalte ownership of the Island was cut short when Charles Van Raalte died of pneumonia early in 1908 whilst on holiday with his wife in Calcutta.

Ownership passed into the hands of his son-in-law, Lord Howard de Walden, who had married Margherita Van Raalte. In 1925, the Island was bought by Sir Arthur Wheeler, a stockbroker. Sir Arthur wanted to turn Brownsea into a money-making concern by opening a tourist hotel on the Island. Fortunately both Poole Borough and Dorset County Councils opposed his schemes. Sir Arthur went bankrupt, becoming the second owner to do so.

The Island was sold by his executors to Mrs Mary Florence Christie in 1927 for £125,000, ushering in a totally different era for she made it a completely secret island ('for nature, not humans') sealed off from the outside world. Her husband died in 1931. Known as Mrs Bonham Christie, her transformation of Brownsea into a forbidden territory was not however immediate. In 1932 she gave permission for five hundred Scouts to land there and celebrate the jubilee of their movement.

Mrs Bonham Christie was determined to keep the Island as a clandestine garden, overgrown and undisturbed, including the mosquitoes. She let everything decay. The village, with its public house and church, were rendered useless. And generally she allowed herself contact with only the barest minimum of human beings. A caretaker and a gamekeeper lived on the Island. The only other visitors were members of Mrs Bonham Christie's family, a couple who used to come across the water to clean the castle, and the postman.

In July 1934 the worst happened – Brownsea caught fire. It started in the Maryland area and was driven by the prevailing south-west wind over half the Island. The church and castle were spared, fortunately. With only few staff, volunteer boatmen, fishermen, seawater (but useless hydrants, because they had not been maintained), extra help had to be summoned from the mainland. It took a long time for boats and barges to be loaded and transported with firefighting equipment, and it was a week before the fire was brought under control and a fortnight before it was finally put out. The cause was believed to be deliberate with the culprit, never caught, possibly an evicted tenant from Maryland, and the motive revenge. Many of the pine trees seen today date from after this devastation to both plant and animal life.

In 1940 Dutch and Belgian refugees escaping the German invasion arrived in their little boats. They had to be screened and were billeted on Brownsea. Miss Mary Llewellin of Upton House brought her family and some Girl Guides to camp and to care for their needs.

For the duration of the Second World War the Island was once again defended against invasion. Soldiers and sailors were billeted there (and ate some of the peacocks; when Mrs Bonham Christie heard this, she wept). Used as a decoy for Poole (see Chapter 12), today wild flowers grow in some of the bomb craters.

After the war the Island was left to itself again until April 28th 1961. On that day, the lone guardian of Brownsea's vital individuality sadly died, aged 98, not in her castle but on the mainland in a nursing home in

Brownsea Castle today is leased by the John Lewis Partnership, all of whose employees can holiday there.

Branksome Park.

The rest is modern history. The Island had been bequeathed to her son, John, to be continued as 'a sanctuary for wildlife', but death duties had to be met. A group of local people including Leslie Miller, John Rutter, Helen Brotherton, Horace Parkyn, Dorset Naturalists' Trust (now Dorset Wildlife Trust), 'Bones' Hoare (from whose building firm's family, Alan Bromby, the first National Trust warden, was later appointed), and other volunteers led the successful campaign to get the National Trust to take on the ownership. They also got the John Lewis partnership interested in leasing the castle, raised the necessary endowment from local people, and catered for the Scouting movement, against a fabricated background threat that it would otherwise become a holiday camp for a certain Mr Butlin! In May 1963 it was officially opened to the public by the National Trust. The Castle was entirely refurbished under the direction of Captain and Mrs George Cooper.

In 1964 Bournemouth Little Theatre Club defied one of the wildlife legacies of the Bonham Christie days by performing *The Tempest,* directed by the legendary Joyce Caton, in a mosquito-infested arena. The audience were given repellant sprays and from this winning production a Brownsea Open Air Theatre company was formed that

performs annually, having got the larvae problem under control.

FURZEY ISLAND

This Island has a long history of human habitation from at least the Iron Age when it was joined to Green island (Chapter 9) until separated by the rising level of water in the Harbour about 2000 years ago. Its archaeology has been well investigated under the sponsorship of BP, who have occupied the Island since 1984.

In that year they acquired its 31 acres to accommodate their first major site in the Harbour (Chapter 17). It now occupies only five acres of the total, the remainder being maintained as a nature reserve.

It was acquired from Algy Cluff, a former proprietor of the *Spectator* magazine whose companies had revived gold mining in Zimbabwe, and in the 1970s had begun to recover oil from the North Sea. Apparently ignorant of the major oil reserves beneath the Harbour (and Poole Bay) he had initially purchased the Island with its relatively simple Purbeck stone house as his seventh home.

The house, now occupied by BP partly as an exhibition centre for their oil-drilling work, was built in 1936 for the then owner of the Island, Dowager Lady Illiffe.

In 1969 a Midlands businessman – Mr Hilton Newton-Mason – had bought the Island from the Illiffe family for £46,000 and continued to own it until it was purchased by Mr Cluff in 1980 in competition with a local wine dealer who had planned to establish it as a 'boozers oasis'. Little did he know that in the first century BC, Furzey's inhabitants had been trading wine with the Continent; or that boisterous passengers returning from Poole Market to Wytch on a ferry in 1759 had capsized the vessel and, of the nineteen on board, only six had survived by struggling through mud to safety on the Island.

GREEN ISLAND,

This, the most southerly island in the Harbour, was once owned by Milton Abbey. It was known as 'St Helens', after a chapel that stood there from the ninth century until the Reformation. Its early history from the Iron Age has been considered in Chapter 9. Together with Furzey Island and Cleavel Point at Ower, it was a thriving settlement producing a wide range of manufactured products, including pottery, iron, and shale objects that were distributed widely to other parts of Britain and the Continent in exchange for non-indigenous products such as oil and wine.

After its separation from Furzey Island, it became an island in its own right with a present area of 25 acres. Outstanding amongst the archaeological remains of the island and the adjacent mainland are two jetties (see Chapters 5 and 9). Whatever their other purposes may have been, they must have played a major part in facilitating the import and export trade of the total settlement.

The importance of Green Island declined with the Roman Occupation of Hamworthy (see Chapter 9) and the Saxon growth of Wareham (see Chapter 11) until late Saxon, Norman and Medieval times, the sole occupants appear to have been concerned with the St Helen's chapel.

After the Reformation the Island reverted to nature until, in the 1920s and 30s, Mrs Ella Barrett leased the Island and, with her gardener, Fred Churchill, grew fruit and vegetables that were taken to market in Poole twice a week.

In the Second World War the Island was an offshoot of HMS *Turtle* in Hamworthy and all signs of the garden were obliterated in the military training exercises.

Recent archaeology has dismissed the possibility of a causeway once joining the island to Cleavel Point but, more excitingly, has confirmed it as Britain's oldest cross-channel port, dating from the Iron Age. Further archaeology has latterly been exposed to the world as part of the Channel 4 'Time Team' programme, that involved digging up the lawn by the house. Articles made from Kimmeridge shale had been found on the Island earlier – perhaps an indication that the occupants 2,000 years ago were trading in 'fashion accessories'.

An aerial view from the south-west, with Green Island in the foreground, then Furzey Island, and Brownsea Island in the background.

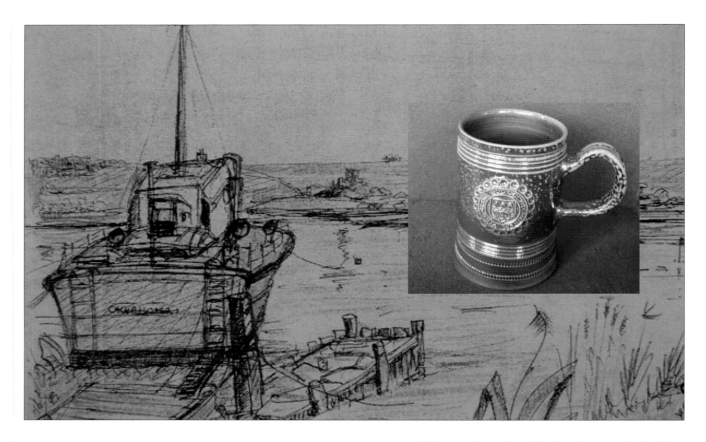

The potter Guy Sydenham's motor torpedo boat *Oklahama* moored at Long Island. Inset is a beer mug, embossed with Poole's coat-of-arms, made by him when working on his pottery on Green Island.

After he left Poole Pottery, the Island's clay was worked and fired in his kiln on the Island by the well-known potter, Guy Sydenham, who lived on a converted motor torpedo boat on its shore between 1967 and 1989. The owner from 1965, Tim Hamilton Fletcher, had been a Kenyan farmer but did not come to live on the Island until 1977. He built the Scandinavian-style house on it with help from the Royal Marines, Poole, who transported materials to the island as a service exercise. When Jo and Tony Davies of Winterborne Zelston bought the 28-acre Island for £500.000 in 1988; other parties interested in purchase were rumoured to include the pop singer Simon Le Bon and Prince Charles. (All of Poole Harbour's islands have, at one time or another, been the subject of wild rumour or playful romancing, which estate agents did little to suppress.) Jo Davies was to become known for a very real achievement – the establishment of the Holidays for the Disabled Scheme, which first operated in 1991. Its continuation has now been confirmed by the Illiffe family, the most recent purchasers (for £2.5 metres in 2005). They have permission to construct a three

storey prefabricated eco-friendly log home to be built in Canada and shipped here with all the parts numbered – the most expensive prefab in the UK?

LONG ISLAND

The seven-acre Island lies about two miles from Poole Before moving to Green Island, the potter Guy Sydenham leased the Island in 1955 from the Ryder family of Rempstone (who since the eighteenth century had owned Green and Round Islands as well until death duties forced their sale in 1935) as a mooring for his torpedo boat. He was working then, as he had done before war service, for Poole Pottery, journeying by a launch with a Seagull engine. Idyllic, the modern car commuter may think. But Guy told a different tale of travelling by this means in all weathers and at all times of year. His hours of work meant that he often had to travel both ways in the dark, using whatever bearings he could and hoping for the best. In the severe winter of 1962-63 the shallows of the Harbour froze. Guy was unable to keep a channel open, so his best hope was to walk over the ice to the shore at Arne and hope to get a lift to Wareham, where a bus route to Poole was accessible. In the early part of the last century both this Island and Green Island

had been exploited commercially for peat, which was sent to London, mixed with molasses, and sold by merchants as animal fodder. Guy's son, Russell, started a pottery of his own on the Island. It is interesting that an earlier pre-First World War lessee, Charlton Xavier Hall of Wareham, was a naturalist and he had reported on the rabbits thriving there and on the Roman pottery sometimes found in their burrows.

The tranquil south side of the Harbour from Arne, showing Long Island (left) and Round Island.

ROUND ISLAND

The Island is just about accessible from Long Island by a walk across a slippery causeway. The ten-acre Island has a 'dream home' designed by Edward Maufe (the architect of Guildford Cathedral) and built in 1934 by the well-known builder, H.J. Hillman of Canford Cliffs, together with four cottages, in only seven months for Mrs Lawrence, the daughter of Lord Illiffe. In 1945 the Island was offered to Poole Council, who declined, and was later in the hands of Stanley Fowler, a machine tool manufacturer from the Midlands. In 1962 a then Poole councillor, Harry J. Palmer, well-known as a builder of quality homes in the Broadstone area, became the owner, paying a reported bargain price of £47,000 after the property had been withdrawn from auction at £72,000! The pier, at 110 feet long, leads to a boathouse and slipway. The Island has its own water supply from a 120-foot well. A guest staying on the Island, the conductor Sir Thomas Beecham, found its peace and tranquillity, broken only by the birdsong, the perfect place to write his biography of the composer Frederick Delius.

PERGIN'S ISLAND

So, finally, to an uninhabited island, shown on OS maps as Pergin's Island, but still referred to by many as 'Doughty's Island', after a former owner of the Upton Estate. Edward Doughty was a Roman Catholic whose benefaction led to the building of the first RC church in Poole, visible from the estate (St Mary's Church in West Quay Road, now demolished). This gorse-covered island, with its sandy shore, 200-year-old mature beech, oak and Scots pine woodland and a central green clearing that may once have been used for grazing sheep, lies at the head of Holes Bay (formerly known as Longfleet Bay). It is now in a Site of Special Scientific Interest (SSSI) and part of the recently declared Upton Country Park owned by Poole Borough Council. Its 15 acres, together with surrounding land, were snatched in 1986 in conditions of great secrecy by Poole's then Town Clerk, acting for Poole Council, from under the noses of developers to protect the whole area from development. This ensured that Creekmoor and Upton will never become merged with the rest of Poole by development.

Poole Canoe Club members occasionally visit the Island, paddling under the low bridge on the railway embankment that bisects Holes Bay. Prior to the coming of the railway there was a boathouse on its shore.

ELEVEN

The Development of Wareham & Poole

Wareham

BEN BUXTON

THE AREA occupied by the historic town of Wareham is an ideal settlement site, with defensive potential. It is situated between two rivers, at their lowest crossing point before they flow into the Harbour, and close to the Harbour and the open sea. It has been occupied since the late Iron Age (the last two centuries BC), if not earlier. Pottery and other artefacts from this period have been found in various parts of the town, with a concentration in the north-west quadrant.

Sherds of Roman pottery dating from the middle of the first century AD, found in the churchyard of Lady St Mary's Church, may indicate that an early Roman fort was built there during the conquest of Dorset. Roman material has been found in various places in the town, indicating that there was a civilian settlement on the site in the third and fourth centuries. Some of the inhabitants no doubt worked at the pottery production sites west of the town at Worgret and to the east at Swineham.

In the centuries after the collapse of Roman rule around AD 400 a community of British Christians, perhaps monks, lived in the area. Five gravestones, made out of masonry from a Romano-British building, were found during the rebuilding of the nave of the eighth-century Saxon church. Each records the name of the deceased, and use Latin script and words. They had been used as building stones either in the original fabric of the church – which became Lady St Mary's – or in later modifications. The stones date from the sixth to the

ninth centuries, so some of them date from the period after the Saxon conquest of Dorset and after the Saxon church was built. They are unique in Dorset, but are of a type found in west Devon, Cornwall, Wales, Scotland, and Gaul.

The Saxons conquered Dorset in the second half of the seventh century, more than two hundred years after the south-east of England. The town of Wareham originated as a lay community which grew up outside the nunnery founded by Aldhelm, Bishop of Sherborne, on the site of what is now the Priory Hotel, in about 700. The church, now known as Lady St Mary's, was built in connection with it. The church was also a minster church, that is, it served a very large area that was later divided up into parishes. Aldhelm is recorded as having embarked for the Continent from Wareham, indicating that it was a cross-Channel port. Wareham – 'the settlement by the weir' – was probably the site of a royal palace by 802 when Beorhtric, King of the West Saxons, was buried in the church.

In 876, Danish Vikings attacked Wareham, in an attempt to conquer Wessex; they had already conquered the other English kingdoms. They marched on Wareham from East Anglia, and also attacked by sea. The earth ramparts, known as the walls, were probably built at

One of the five seventh century memorial gravestones, cut from a fragment of Roman shaft, found during the rebuilding of St Lady Mary's Church.

The west section of Wareham's Saxon ramparts, built by King Alfred towards the end of the ninth century, and now recognized as the best-preserved Saxon defences in Britain.

around this time, or perhaps before, by Alfred, King of Wessex. It is recorded that the Danes spent the winter in Wareham, and that Alfred negotiated a deal whereby they left; he defeated the Danes in 878. The ramparts were topped by a wooden palisade and enclosed the town on three sides, the River Frome forming the defence along the fourth (south) side. On the east and west sides of the town the ramparts had a ditch in front, from which the material of the ramparts was dug, while on the north the rampart was built at the top of a natural steep slope above the valley of the Piddle. The rectilinear pattern of streets was probably laid out at this time, although the main north-south and east-west routes would have been established by then. It is likely that only the central area was built up, but even here very little evidence of Saxon occupation has been found in excavations. Wareham was one of a series of fortified towns (burhs) in Wessex, and one of four in Dorset, the others being Bridport, Christchurch, and Shaftesbury. Town life flourished in these havens of safety from Viking aggression.

Viking raids on southern England were renewed in the late tenth century and Wareham was attacked in 998 and 1015, the latter by Cnut who used the Harbour as a base for raids throughout Wessex. It was probably during this period that a stone wall was built along the top of the ramparts. Wareham became the most important town in Dorset in the late Saxon period, and had two mints. The body of King Edward (the Martyr) was buried in Lady St Mary's in 978. By the time of the Norman Conquest the nunnery and its church had been given to the Norman abbey of St Wandrille. St Martin's church was built in the early eleventh century, and another church was built on the site of the church later known as Holy Trinity.

Following the Norman Conquest of 1066, a motte-and-bailey castle was built in the south-west corner of the town, in a commanding position overlooking the River Frome. Timber was used as a building material at

A nineteenth century watercolour of Lady St Mary's Church, and one of the few visual records of its Anglo-Saxon origins.

Wareham Quay today, with Lady St Mary's Church in the background.

first, but in time this was replaced by stone. The castle became a royal residence and prison, and Wareham was caught up in the conflict between Stephen and Matilda (1135-53), during which it was set on fire. The town was granted a charter by King John in 1211 (although this was short-lived; the present charter dates to 1703).

By the fourteenth century two further churches had been built in addition to the existing three Saxon churches, and four chapels. None of these later medieval foundations survived into modern times. Lady St Mary's Church and its possessions were given to the Norman Abbey of Lire in 1150 and it became a priory; in 1414, it was granted to the Priory of Sheen, Surrey.

The castle was abandoned in favour of Corfe Castle in the fourteenth century, and the massive walls of the keep – over four metres thick at their base – were quarried away. The curved line of the bailey of the castle is preserved in Pound Lane, Trinity Lane, and West Street. Wareham thus lost its royal status, and its status as a port was also undermined by the rise of Poole in the thirteenth century. Wareham's location on a tidal river was a disadvantage at a time when

trade was increasing and bigger ships needing deeper water were being built. Another blow came with the Dissolution of the Monasteries in 1536 and the closing down of the priory.

John Leland, visiting around 1540, described Wareham as 'fallen down and made into gardens for garlic.' However, the town was significant enough during the Civil War (1642-6) to be fought over by both sides, and the defences were again refurbished by the Royalist defenders. After the war, Parliament ordered the walls to be slighted, but this was never carried out. The defences were pressed into service yet again in the Second World War, when the rampart between West Street and Cow Lane, known as Bloody Bank, was steepened as an anti-tank measure.

A consequence of Wareham's decline was that its Saxon defences, although modified over the centuries, have not been destroyed by later urban development, with the result that they are the best preserved of any burh in England. They are thus of national and international significance. St Martin's Church has also survived with relatively little modification, and is the best preserved Saxon church in Dorset.

Wareham remained a minor port into the nineteenth century. Clay was exported, while grain for the breweries, and coal, were imported. The arrival of the railway in 1847 reduced trade still further.

The centre of Wareham suffered a devastating fire in 1762, and many of the buildings in the town centre today date from the rebuilding soon after. At the time, most of the back streets of the town were still lanes between gardens. These areas were developed over the next 150 years. The arrival of the railway had little impact on Wareham, apart from providing a focus for development north of the town at Northport. There was no significant development outside the Saxon walls until about 1920, when Northport began to grow, and most of the subsequent growth has been there, at Northmoor Park.

An eighteenth century engraving of St Martin's. The picturesque ruin in the engraving has since been restored, and is the best preserved Saxon church in Dorset.

Poole

IAN ANDREWS

A S THOMAS SYDENHAM wrote perceptively in his 1839 *History of Poole*, 'Few literary tasks are enveloped in greater difficulties than those with which the topographer meets in the attempt to trace the history of a town up to its origin.' The earliest written mentions of Poole occurred in a document from 1170 relating to its shipping movements and one in 1196 describing the newly-built St James's Chapel in 'La Pole', a chapel-of-ease to the oldest building in present-day Poole, Canford Church, which came under Bradenstoke Priory. In 1229 the Feet of Fines refers to 'Kaneford and Poole' together. The first chronicler to refer to Poole was John Leland in his *Itinerary*. Writing between 1535 and 1543 (ie at about the time Poole seamen were making the first voyages across the Atlantic to Newfoundland), he noted:

> Pole is no Town of auncient occupying in Marchantdise: but rather of old Tyme a poore Fishar Village and an Hamelet or Member to the Paroche Chirch.

And this has become the mantra for successive travel writers, who like early map-makers did little by way of their own research or surveys, merely embellishing and augmenting the work of their predecessors and repeating an often inaccurate oral tradition.

In one respect Leland misled successors in respect to the relationship between Poole and Wareham. He wrote:

> I can gather no otherwise, but whereas of old Shippes cam sumwhat nere Wereham up the Haven, and there had vente of their Wares, and synnes Shippes lost their Rode ther for lak of Depth of Water Shippes kept and resorted nerer to Pole Toun, and so it by a little increased.

This was embellished by later writers to refer to the 'sea having left Wareham' or 'silting', but this is not borne out by modern research which shows the sea has been rising over the centuries, flooding many sites on the littoral (eg at Brownsea Island) that were once above High Water. In truth the size and capacity of vessels had increased, requiring a greater draught and simpler approach than Wareham could offer.

The area Leland speaks of is specific:

> It standith almost as an Ile in the Haven and hangith by the NE to the mayne land by the space almost of a flite shot. And in this plaace is a Dike, and to it often commith thorough out the Haven Water, and here is an embatelid Gate of Stone to enter into the Town . . . King Richard the 3 began a pece of a Town Waulle at one end of the Kay; and promised large things to the Town of Pole.

In other words Poole in the narrow sense was a defended Island, as the 1634 map indicates. 'A Key for the Shippes standith SE', Leland adds.

But if one takes a generic view of Poole and its contact with the outside world, it was as part of Canford, then

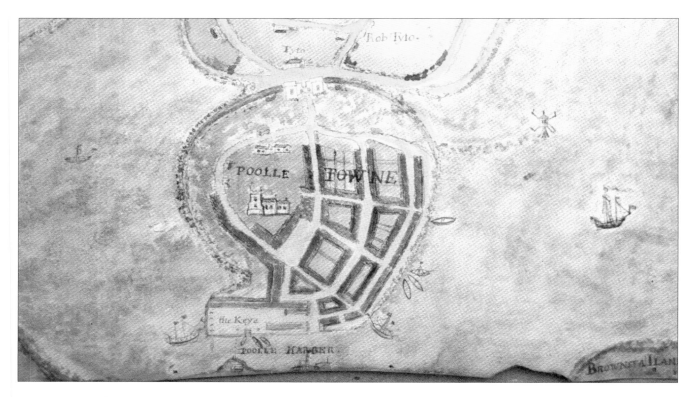

ABOVE A detail from an early seventeenth century map of the Manor of Canford, of which Poole was part. Note the Town Gate and windmill on Baiter.

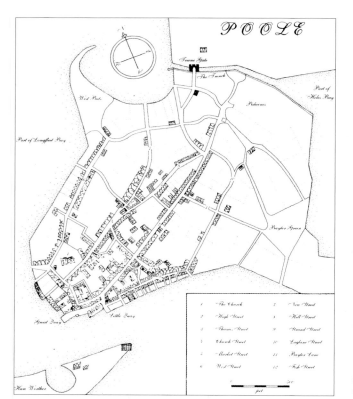

held by Ulwen, that was included in the Domesday Survey of 1086 (if not by name). Leland continues that the 'Haven' or Harbour encompassing 'welle toward 20 miles' was clearly of importance, if only for fishermen, and the distance from the Haven Mouth 'to a Fishar Town called Sandwiche (Swanage)' is given as 3 miles. By land and ferry its connection with 'Lichet' is referred to, although Hamworthy as such is not named. It is from these areas that those coming to the weekly Thursday market in Poole, that had been chartered since 1239, would have come.

The Lord of the Manor, Sir William Longspée, sold a charter of liberties to the burgesses of Poole in 1248 to raise funds for his participation in the Seventh Crusade. Consequently, Poole gained a small measure of freedom from feudal rule and acquired the right to appoint a port reeve (mayor) and to hold a court within the town. The Canford 'Lawns' formed a royal hunting ground and John O' Gaunt's kitchen dates from this time.

'Ther be Men alive that saw almost al the Town of Pole kyverid with Segge and Rishis,' was one medieval description of the town, but nonetheless a census of 1574 lists it as including 1,373 residents – a quarter of the number residing in the town 200 years later.

LEFT Poole in 1634. Both the Little Quay and Great Quay are shown prior to their later realignment. Note the bulwark on the tip of Hamworthy and the small bay on its north side.

THE TOWN

Turning to physical evidence, it is true that little of prehistoric antiquity has been discovered within the narrow confines of the town, even by rescue archaeology in the twentieth century, slum clearance and redevelopment. But many sites remain unexplored in what was clearly a densely occupied area, with substantial and important medieval buildings pre-dating Leland by several hundred years at least, including the fourteenth century Town Cellars (one of the longest in the country till severed by Thames Street in the nineteenth century). Poole was created a port of the Staple in 1433.

Archaeological digs have revealed hitherto unknown features, not all conclusive, indicating that Roman activity had been centred not on Poole but on Hamworthy as a port, transit point and pottery site (as well as

LEFT Two views of the medieval Town Cellars, which were originally built for the storage of wool. Today the building is the superb Poole History Centre.

BELOW A reconstruction by Graham Smith showing the Town Cellars as they might have looked prior to being severed in the nineteenth century to create Thames Street. Once again, the quay is shown prior to being realigned.

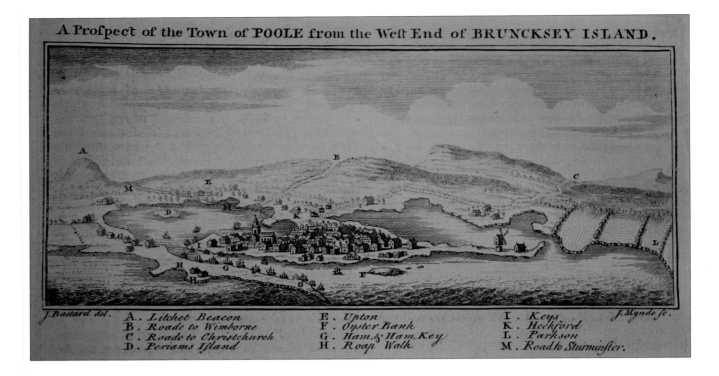

A Profpect of the Town of POOLE from the Weft End of BRUNCKSEY ISLAND.

J. Baftard del.

A . Litchet Beacon
B . Roade to Wimborne
C . Roade to Chriftchurch
D . Periams Ifland

E . Upton
F . Oyfter Bank
G . Ham & Ham, Key
H . Roap Walk

I . Keys
K . Heckford
L . Parkfon
M . Road to Sturminfter.

J. Mynde fc.

An eighteenth century 'Prospect' of Poole showing the Old Town and first St James's Church. Once again the windmill on Baiter is included.

possessing valuable hand mills) rather than a settlement (see Chapter 9). Yet recent work in the Old Town yields evidence of salt-working, boatbuilding and oyster fishing in the medieval period. There is also briquetage from the Iron Age and Romano-British periods, as well as rare Saxon vessels from what is popularly known as the Dark Age – when Poole was also known as Fromemouth – after the Romans departed in the fifth century.

From the early sixteenth century, there is evidence of much reclamation along the original shoreline, with dumps containing foreign imported material (mainly pottery) of Dutch and Norman origin, indicating it was an area of considerable shipping activity across the Channel. The town's first seal is one of a rare few bearing the image of a boat with castellated stern and forecastle (see page 147) and was probably the first to show a vessel with a then 'state of the art' rudder. We also learn from thirteenth century documents that the town was responding in 1229 and 1230 to requests from the King for four ships, stores, and 94 men and for all ships large enough to carry 16 horses required for the wars with France. The reclamations were often of stakes (piles), to which larger ships could be tied, instead of the earlier

practice of beaching to unload them. Merchants from nearby Wareham, which was burned in 1139 during a Civil War, may have helped found Poole.

In 1364 the Winchelsea Certificate confirmed Poole's harbour jurisdiction as extending from North Haven right up to 'Redclive Atte Welle' on the outskirts of Wareham and not far from the junction of the River Frome with the Harbour. A boundary stone marking this limit of former jurisdiction is maintained at this point to the present day by the Society of Poole Men when they re-enact an Admiralty Court at the Beating the Sea Bounds ceremony (see page 35).

By 1433 a Charter was granted by King Henry VI 'considering that the town and port of Poole are notably inhabited and that a great multitude of people are there and that the port is sufficient and secure', giving it the status of a customs port, in place of Melcombe (now part of modern Weymouth), the previous but heavily declined staple port in Dorset.

By 1569 Poole had achieved the dignity and status of a county (separate from Dorset) and as a town under a charter from Queen Elizabeth I, as Southampton had done. It could now be described as 'one of the most considerable ports of the West of England'. By 1600 Poole had established itself, and went on from strength to strength, with much investment in new buildings – no longer a 'poor fisher village'!

TWELVE

The Defence of the Harbour

BRIAN ELLIS

PRIOR TO THE ROMAN INVASION IN AD 43, people living around the Harbour area had not found it necessary to protect itself against neighbouring tribes, as had been the case in other parts of Dorset with the building of hillforts in places such as Chalbury, Badbury Rings, and Maiden Castle. The nearest approach to a high ground defended enclosure was at Bulbury Hill, the principal purpose of which may have been to control the traffic associated with the Harbour rather than specifically for defence.

Even the Roman invasion would have been relatively peaceful in that there was no indigenous force established at a defensive focal point in or around the Harbour to oppose what would undoubtedly have been a superior invading force.

The establishment of the Roman force at Hamworthy following the invasion is covered in Chapter 9, which makes it clear that its principal purpose was as a staging post for troops and their supplies and as a power base rather than specifically for defence against the indigenous population or anyone else. There is some evidence that a minor garrison was established at Wareham at the same time, again as a power base rather than specifically for defence.

Following the end of Roman rule in AD 410, Hamworthy declined as the principal Harbour port and was superceded by Wareham, particularly after the takeover of the latter by the Saxons in the late seventh century. With its river systems it was more easily defended than elsewhere.

Wareham grew under Saxon rule and became increasingly fortified with its bank and ditch walls. In spite of this, the Danes invaded Wareham three times, the first being in 876. On the second occasion, in 998, they used the town as a base for attacks further up the coast. In their third attack on the town in 1015 the Danes, led by Cnut, arrived by sea from Devon.

In the years following the Norman Conquest in 1066, a wooden motte and bailey castle was built in the south west part of the town which was replaced with a stone keep. However, it was soon superceded by the much larger Corfe Castle with its better view of the upper Harbour, and Wareham Castle fell into disrepair. There is some evidence of a castle at Corfe prior to 1066, but the construction of the present castle began around 1086.

With Poole growing in importance during the medieval period as the principal port of the Harbour, it became increasingly important to consider the defence of the whole Harbour, rather than just its western end in Wareham or the newly-built Corfe Castle

However, in spite of this, until the Second World War the Harbour was never heavily defended. It was penetrated several times in the Middle Ages – most notably in 1377 when part of Poole was burnt by the French, and again in 1405 when the took was attacked by a combined Spanish and French army. There were several reasons for this: firstly, the Harbour was used almost wholly for civilian purposes; secondly, it was reliant upon natural defences such as its shallowness, the mudflats and the narrowness of its entrance; thirdly, as declared by Poole's governor during the Civil War, the Navy could always be relied upon to defend Britain's shores:

'towards the sea Poole is not yet fortified, we there trustynge to our ships.'

From the early centuries of the new second millennium AD the main threats to the Harbour were hostile powers across the English Channel and, during the sixteenth, seventeenth and eighteenth centuries from pirates, both local and from the Barbary Coast in North Africa. The town and quays of Poole itself seem to have been defended from 1433 merely by a ditch and the Town Gate.

With the development of cannon, small gun batteries appeared in the sixteenth century, such as the bulwark on the tip of the Hamworthy peninsula (shown on the town map on page 90). However, it was also in this

A detail showing Poole Harbour from the 'Plat' sent to
Thomas Cromwell by Lord Russell following his Survey
of Dorset 1539. It is the earliest known illustration of the
Harbour, and as well as the beacons, and Poole's Town Gate,
it includes fortifications at Poole, Hamworthy and Brownsea
Island.

century that development began on the obvious position,
commanding the narrow Harbour entrance – Brownsea
Island. With the introduction of artillery the Island's
position was ideal for controlling the maritime traffic of
the Harbour.

The first documentary evidence of fortification on the
Island is expenditure of 93s 9d in 1532 on the Castle
when the Island still belonged to the Benedictine Cerne
Abbey. After Henry VIII's break with Rome, the threat

of invasion by France and Spain became much more of a
possibility. In April 1539 the Dorset coast was surveyed
by Lord Russell and a *'plat'* was sent to Thomas
Cromwell. It envisaged that fortifications should be built
at 'Bowarnemothe', Poole, Brownsea Island, Redcliffe
Point, Weymouth, Sandsfoot, Portland and Lyme Regis.
Not all the recommendations were acted upon. The
King financed artillery castles at Portland and Sandsfoot
and provided some financial help for Poole Corporation
to improve the castle on Brownsea. This work seems to
have been completed by 1547. It must be emphasized
however, that the Castle was not part of the national
defence scheme – the 1539-1543 *'device'* programme that
created the massive fortifications such as Deal, Portland,
and Southsea Castles. The defensive work on Brownsea

was very simple, consisting of a tower and a platform mounting at least three cannons of different sizes. Almost as soon as it was completed, the Castle's story seems to be one of continuous reported shortcomings, and subsequent improvements. It had achieved its final form by the time of Elizabeth I when there was a strong possibility of a Spanish invasion. The Castle garrison was intended to be provided by the 'able-bodied' men of Poole; however, it seems the Borough provided funds for a permanent garrison of six. In 1576 the Castle passed into the control of Sir Christopher Hatton, the owner of Corfe Castle, and between 1584 and 1588 £200 was spent on repairing the Castle. In 1588 the Norris Survey reporting on Dorset's coastal defences said of

> 'Corfe Castle, Brownsea Castle, the towns of Wareham and Poole, but the fortifications of the latter are indifferent and of no use except Brownsea were provided with arms and artillery'

Apart from Brownsea Castle, another fort appeared at Handfast Point in this period, and Corfe Castle still had a part to play as shown by Treswell's 1586 plan showing a battery of six cannons in the outer bailey. It is uncertain whether Wareham's ancient earthworks were expected to have a role in the area's defence (as they did in 1940). There is also some evidence that a battery may have existed at North Haven at the entrance to the Harbour from Tudor times.

Brownsea Castle continued as the main Harbour defence into the seventeenth century. During the Civil War, Poole was a leading Parliamentarian stronghold. Along with Lyme Regis, Poole was alone in Dorset in not submitting to Royalist forces and after snubbing Charles I in August 1642 strengthened its defences.

As well as Brownsea Castle, the Harbour entrance was protected by a 180-ton guardship the *Ark*. New artillery was delivered to Brownsea from the Isle of Wight – could this be the surviving seventeenth century cannons on Brownsea today? Poole and its Harbour, apart from an unsuccessful Royalist plot in 1643, unlike other Dorset towns, did not see any conflict but acted as a base for military and naval expeditions for Parliament – the best known being the actions against Corfe Castle in 1643 and 1645-6. During the Commonwealth, Poole seems to have continued its military role, both as a minor naval base during the war with Holland and as a Republican stronghold in comparison to mainly Royalist Dorset. In 1660 the monarchy was restored and Poole's fortifications seem to have been largely dismantled, although it is unclear how far this applied to Brownsea Castle. Certainly Brownsea was still considered a key part of Poole's defence when, in June 1690, a large

This detail from a map of 1597 shows the simple square single-storey stone building on Brownsea Island surrounded by a moat and with a hexagonal gun platform on the seaward side enclosed by a low wall. Three guns are shown but the platform is empty of guns and the wall appears to be partly broken down. The Castle was probably relatively unchanged until William Benson began its conversion to a residence in the early eighteenth century.

French fleet appeared in Poole Bay. The town's defences were reactivated and a watch was established at the Castle. However, as in 1588, no hostile landing was attempted in the area.

Although not a naval base, Poole like many other ports was a centre for privateers or legalised pirates> It was also a target for foreign privateers, as in 1698 when two French privateers entered the Harbour. This suggests that by this date the Castle was no longer capable of defending the Harbour entrance. This seems to have been finally accepted in 1726 when Poole Borough appeared to abandon its case against William Benson, the owner of the Island since 1722, when he began converting the Castle into a dwelling house. In a similar fashion Poole's land defences seem to have been given up after a final flurry during the Jacobite uprising of 1745-6.

Until probably the end of the Napoleonic War in 1815 the Harbour's defences seem to have relied on batteries at the Harbour entrance and Poole Head (now Chaddesley Glen). The guns were provided by the Ordnance Office, the town building the batteries and providing ammunition and the men to man them. They are shown on Isaac Taylor's map of Dorset in 1765 (see page 42) and appear in an Ordnance Report of 1779 which mentions four batteries with a total of eighteen

One of a set of light-hearted drawings by a Leading Seaman Lucas showing parties of men going to the wreckage of an aircraft during the Second World War.

guns. An illustration in Hutchins dated 1774 shows a battery of twelve 9-pounder guns on Brownsea adjacent to the Castle, by now a residential property. However, a report of 1803 to the Mayor of the Town and County of Poole describes the defences of Poole seaboard in less than reassuring terms;

> 'the battery at South Haven Point consists of three nine-pounders dismounted in better condition than the other guns . . . A battery on Brownsea Island consisting of seven twelve-pounders and one nine-pounder dismounted all serviceable gun with some shot and implements . . .

BELOW The 7th Battalion, the Green Howards, training in the dunes at Sandbanks in July 1940 (IWM H 2669).

The Committee since their return are informed that two hundred and eighty two six- and nine-pound shot were taken from Studland Battery for ballast by Caleb Sturney whose boat was upset, part were recovered and on board the *Marianne* belonging to Mr Sturt'

Charles Sturt, the owner of the Island from 1789 -1812, commanded and presumably set up the Brownsea Island Artillery Volunteers in 1798. They probably manned some of these defences and were almost certainly recruited from the Sturt Estate at Crichel. As well as the Artillery defences of the Harbour there was also the warning system provided by the Admiralty Signal Stations first set up in 1798 to replace the ancient beacons. Those falling within the Harbour area were on Ballard Down and Hengistbury Head. In spite of the place-name there never was a Martello Tower in Poole.

After Waterloo it appears that coastal defence of the Harbour was again downgraded. During Victoria's reign, the introduction of steam and iron-clad warships with greatly increased firepower led to vast expenditure on naval harbours such as Portsmouth, some commercial ports such as Bristol, and the development of a new naval base at Portland. As far as Poole is concerned there was a Royal Naval Reserve battery in Hamside with up to five guns in existence from 1890-1903. There is a plan of Brownsea Island of 1853 (see page 78) showing a 10 gun battery adjoining the Castle but it is unlikely that this ever existed. It has been suggested that Poole Harbour's position brought it within the area controlled by the enhanced fortifications at the Needles; therefore no elaborate defences were needed.

In spite of being a naval base for minesweepers in the First World War, apart from a guardship, a boom across the entrance, and the organisation of coast watches, coastal defence seems to have been minimal.

Matters were very different from 1940. The story of Poole itself during Second World War has been fully described elsewhere, so this account will concentrate on the defence of the Harbour area. In 1940 Germany had won control of the continental coastline from Norway to the Spanish frontier making the North Sea and English Channel a moat and Poole in a frontier zone. The summer of 1940 saw the greatest defensive works ever built in Britain with over 18,000 pillboxes alone. Poole, being only 60 nautical miles from the German controlled base at Cherbourg, seemed a potential target for invasion. Brownsea Island again became the focus of Harbour defence, being the site of an Emergency Coast Battery armed with two old naval guns, the records state 4.7 inch calibre but eyewitnesses state they were 6 inch Mark XII guns on Mark IX mountings. The battery was set up by

TOP LEFT Winston Churchill, who enjoyed bricklaying, laying a brick at a pillbox being built on Sandbanks. The brick was inscribed '19 WC 40'. The pillbox was eventually demolished and the brick retrieved by the then Borough engineer (IWM H2270).

TOP RIGHT The beaches were an integral part of the Harbour's defences. The Sea Flame Barrage of burning oil being fired at Studland in 1941 (IWM H7020).

ABOVE One of the two large guns positioned on Brownsea Island above the Castle as part of the coastal defences erected after Dunkirk, and manned until 1944 (IWM H2456).

ABOVE The Poole Harbour Defence Launch, which in due course took over the task of patrolling the Harbour from the various civilian yachts and boats requisitioned by the Navy at the start of the Second World War.

LEFT Although not in the Harbour, the beaches were an integral part of the Harbour's defences and the standard beach scaffolding is shown in this picture from 1946.

BELOW LEFT For a while after the war old landing craft were used to form a temporary breakwater near the Quay.

the Royal Navy, but then manned by the Royal Artillery. The battery had two emplacements to the south-west of the Castle, with its accompanying searchlight towers. There were pillboxes, other obstructions along the Poole Bay and Harbour coastline, and a control point on the highest point of Sandbanks. Later, in 1941, the Army felt Poole would be more in danger from a land attack so Poole itself became a *defensive nodal point* (anti-tank island or redoubt). Other defences included blockships, a boom across the harbourmouth, patrol ships, and a minefield controlled from Brownsea.

A defence dimension which had not been a major issue in the First World War was aerial attack. Initially the nearest fighter station was at Warmwell (near Dorchester), and anti-aircraft batteries were set-up around the Harbour, but the most successful form of defence in practice was the decoy. The idea was simple: to deceive enemy pilots into drop their bombs on open ground. The three Royal Navy-operated decoys in the Poole area were at Arne (HH1) and Gore Heath (HH2) to protect Holton Heath Royal Naval Cordite Factory, and Brownsea Island (PE1) to protect Poole, as described

on the following two pages.

Although not specifically concerned with its defence, the largest military force in its history passed through the Harbour in 1944 in preparation for the Normandy landings; Operation Overlord, the invasion of Western Europe by the Allied Forces on 6th June 1944.

With the successful invasion of Europe in sight, the defences of the Harbour began to be downgraded and, although coastal defence continued nationally until 1956, locally it ended in 1945. However, reminders of the Second World War defences remain in the form of pillboxes, 'dragon's teeth' obstructions, gun emplacements, a

Poole became Dorset's third Royal Naval Base after the fall of France in 1940. Shown here are Royal Navy gun craft of the Support Squadron from HMS *Turtle* based at Hamworthy and US coastguard cutters of Rescue Flotilla I which saved 1437 men and one woman on the Normandy beaches during the June 1944 D-day landings.

searchlight tower and bunker on Brownsea Island, and the decoy sites with bomb craters. And, as reminders of progressively distant past defences there are the remains of the original Tudor fort below the terrace of Brownsea Castle, and the Saxon walls around Wareham.

Brownsea Island Starfish Decoy

ALAN AND DONALD BROMBY

EARLY IN THE SECOND WORLD WAR bombing decoy sites, that deliberately created simulations of burning towns, were constructed in Britain. The code name for this type of site, was 'Starfish', itself from the original code, SF, for Special Fire.

Starfish sites were used to decoy German night bombers from bombing real towns or factories by operating a series of controlled fires during an air raid to replicate an urban area targeted by bombs. In the UK there were approximately 400 decoy towns and factories and these were bombed about 100 times attracting many bombs intended for towns and cities and saving several thousand lives and much material damage.

Several sites selected by the Admiralty in a series to protect certain dockyards and manufacturing sites included Brownsea Island in Poole Harbour and Holton Heath. Work on these sites started in 1941. Brownsea Island was in the private ownership of Mrs Bonham Christie and had been closed to the public for many years. The decoys were established at the western end of the Island about three quarters of a mile from the inhabited area and the Castle. The pyrotechnics effects department

The remains of the Starfish Decoy control bunker today (SZ 015877).

of Elstree Film Studios was commissioned to design a system of fires and explosives to achieve the deception. The decoys comprised an arrangement of adaptive and innovative technology; this included rows of large wire baskets each one packed with wood shavings soaked in paraffin and creosote. A number of bath tubs filled with wood and coal were alternatively flushed from two lavatory cisterns, one containing paraffin and the other water, to simulate the visual appearance of exploding bombs. The devices were set up in the area surrounding the hill above the old Pottery Pier,

Two large air raids on targets in Poole Harbour in which Admiralty decoys were involved are documented in Admiralty minute ADM1/17816. dated. 24 July, 1942 as follows:

Poole – 24/25 May 1942
The first flares were dropped through clouds over Poole just before midnight and the first bomb fell a few minutes later. It fell on the decoy site itself actually setting off a number of cordite flashes. An order was immediately given to start the S.F. fires and for the next hour and a quarter 60 enemy aircraft bombarded the site. No damage was done to the target and the small number of casualties which occurred that night were caused by a few bombs which fell at random on the countryside. Had this weight of attack reached the congested town of Poole, with its boat building yards, the results would have been very serious.

Holton Heath – 3/4 June 1942
Ten nights after the foregoing incident, much the same weight of attack would seem to have been intended for the R.N. Cordite factory. In this case the weather was clear and less favourable for decoy action, but the success was even more marked.

There was every indication that the attack would find the target but it was definitely drawn off by the well-timed lighting of the Q.F. fires. More than 112 high explosives and five thousand incendiaries fell around the decoy and the heath fires which were started by the enemies own action, but no bombs hit the cordite factory and there were no casualty or damage elsewhere.

This saving of the principal R.N. Cordite factory from being put at least temporarily out of action must be placed very high on the credit side of the Admiralty decoy system.

Many years have passed since the Starfish sites operated. Due to the ephemeral nature of the decoys, and the fact that they covered very large areas of land, there is little identifiable physical evidence to remind us that they even existed. A few of the substantial structures such as the control centre and associated generator housing have survived, but nationally there is little

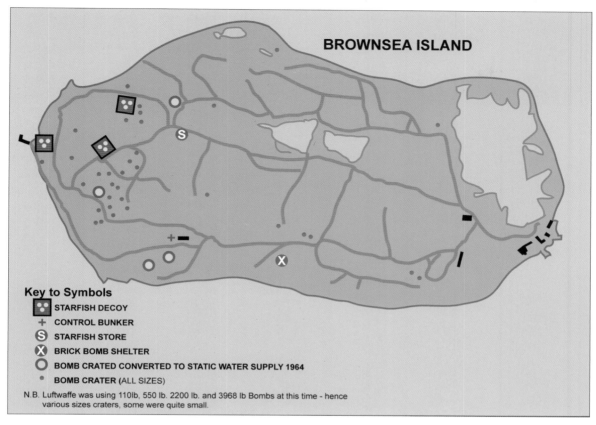

BROWNSEA ISLAND

Key to Symbols

- STARFISH DECOY
- ✛ CONTROL BUNKER
- Ⓢ STARFISH STORE
- Ⓧ BRICK BOMB SHELTER
- Ⓞ BOMB CRATED CONVERTED TO STATIC WATER SUPPLY 1964
- • BOMB CRATER (ALL SIZES)

N.B. Luftwaffe was using 110lb, 550 lb. 2200 lb. and 3968 lb Bombs at this time - hence various sizes craters, some were quite small.

evidence of the bomb craters – though it is they that most clearly demonstrate the success of the decoys in drawing the explosives carried by the enemy bombers away from the true target. Most craters were filled in soon after the raid or eradicated by post-war developments.

In the case of the Brownsea site we are fortunate that many of the craters remain, as do other items such as the buried control bunker and various other brick-built surface shelters. We are also fortunate that several people closely connected with Brownsea Island and its history over many years have developed and maintained a record of the Brownsea Starfish site, helping to remind us of what happened there on the night of 24/25 May 1942.

The progress of about sixty enemy aircraft that had approached England from the Pas de Calais and made landfall at St Catherine's Point was already known at the RAF's radar counter measures headquarters in Hertfordshire. Poole was believed to be on the enemies' list of targets. After an initial attack had been carried out by enemy path finders, the naval personnel in their bunker on Brownsea Island were telephoned by the Controller of Strategic Night Decoys and ordered to ignite the decoy devices

For the next hour or so, the sixty attacking aircraft dropped their bombs on the decoy target and it was estimated afterwards that out of 166 tons of bombs used that night, all but 9 tons fell harmlessly within this area. Unfortunately, several people were killed and there was some damage to houses, mainly in Hamworthy. These were probably caused by a few bombs from the pathfinder aircraft dropped just before the decoys were ignited. There is little doubt that if the decoys had not been activated that evening and the full bomb load fallen on the congested town of Poole many hundred of lives could have been lost.

PRESERVATION

There are several other towns in Britain like Poole that owe much to Starfish decoys but research shows that the remains in Brownsea Island and their records are probably unique, particularly with regard to the evidence of bombs during the raid. There are craters still visible on Brownsea which were recorded on a reconnaissance sortie by the Luftwaffe on 28 October 1942. It is important that the craters and structures on Brownsea should be protected and preserved and the documentary evidence of the Starfish site displayed to visitors to the Island as an important part of Poole Harbour's history and heritage.

Poole Pottery, Dorset, c.1925, Eustace Nash (1886-1969).

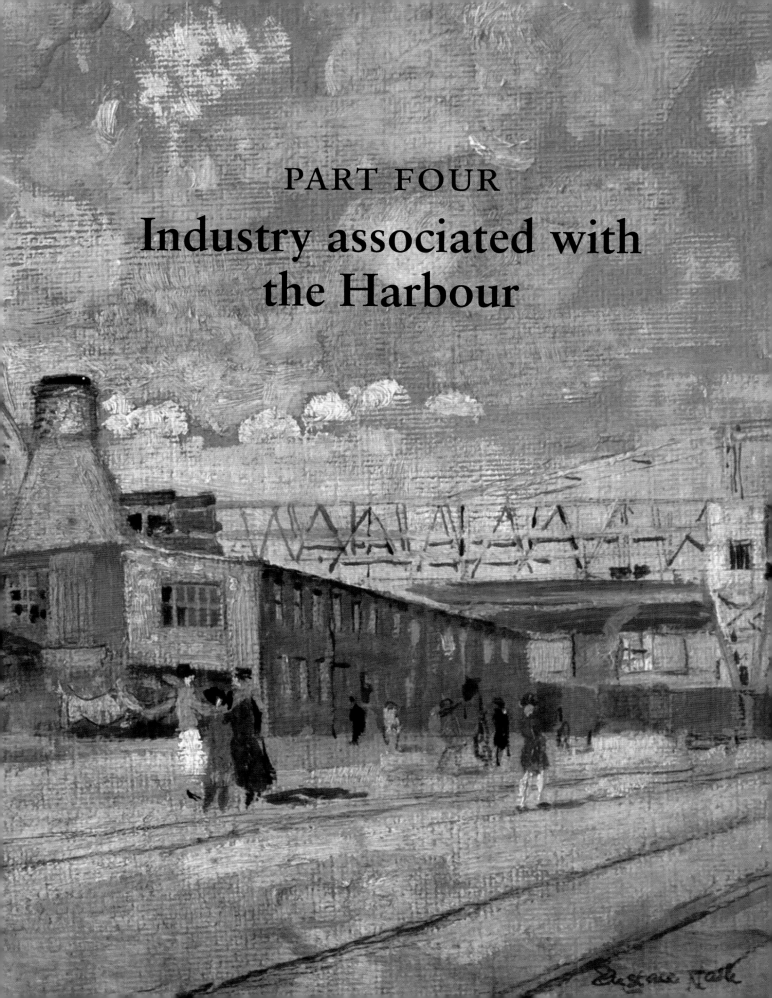

PART FOUR
Industry associated with the Harbour

THIRTEEN

Introduction

WILLIAM SHELDRICK

Early Days to the Eleventh Century

POOLE HARBOUR has been associated with many different industries since the prehistoric period. By the first century AD, some of these were of national importance. Their basis was the recovery of resources from land and sea. The first major industry in the area was the production of pottery based on the high quality clays that outcrop around the Harbour. A distinctive Black Burnished Ware first appeared locally about 300 BC, and by the early first century it was being distributed as far afield as the Channel Islands and northern France.

The Iron Age log boat found preserved in the Harbour off Brownsea Island shows that boatbuilding was taking place in the Harbour more than 2000 years ago. Archaeological evidence also indicates that in the Iron Age salt was being produced in many places around the Harbour and that, by the early Romano-British period, the industry was well established. There was a continuous growth in the fishing industry during and following the Roman occupation.

Twelfth to Sixteenth Centuries

There seems to have been little change in the pattern of industry around the Harbour up to the Middle Ages, with Wareham being the main port. Poole was founded in the late twelfth century as a small fishing village, but soon became a flourishing port. Fishing increased steadily and the products were salted and shipped in barrels to London and some European countries.

Following the discovery of the great shoals of cod off Newfoundland, fishing vessels from Poole set out across the Atlantic, and by the end of the sixteenth century the town's overseas cod fishery was well-established. It also encouraged the growth of many other industries, such as shipbuilding, rope and sailmaking, baking, and brewing. The local production of alum and copperas (ferrous sulphate) marked the beginnings of the chemical industry in England.

Seventeenth and Eighteenth Centuries

Copperas production on Brownsea Island finally ceased in about 1705, leaving industry in the Harbour to be dominated by the Newfoundland trade. To support it an important shipbuilding industry developed at Hamworthy. The centre of salt production moved to Lilliput, to an area still known as the Salterns, but the eventual mining of salt in Cheshire from the end of the eighteenth century made most other sources of salt production uneconomic. Brewing continued to flourish, with major breweries established in Poole by the middle of the eighteenth century.

The excellent quality clay from around the Harbour had been used for pottery production for many centuries, but it found a further use in the seventeenth century in the manufacture of tobacco pipes. Shipments of pipe clays from Poole became one of its most important cargoes.. Poole ball clays were ideal for producing high quality pottery, and an expansion of potteries in the Midlands increased the demand for Poole clay.

The end of the Napoleonic war in 1815 resulted in a rapid decline of the Newfoundland trade with Poole, and from about 1820 to 1850 the area also suffered a serious recession in fishing.

The clay industry continued to prosper. Quays and jetties were built on the south side of the Harbour at Ower, Middlebere, Goathorn, and Redstone Point. Whilst some of their remains are still visible, they progressively became redundant and almost all clay now leaves the immediate area by road or rail, instead of across the Harbour. The availability of both high-grade and lower-grade clays together with an increasing population and a rise in housebuilding encouraged the local pottery industry. The production of fine and decorative china and tiles was concentrated in Hamworthy and Poole, whilst domestic and municipal drainage products of all types were manufactured at various sites around the north side of the Harbour and on Brownsea Island.

During the second half of the nineteenth century and the early twentieth century a number of engineering companies were established locally. Whilst less dependent on the resources of the Harbour, their products – steam engines, pumps, compressors, and oil engines – were aimed largely at maritime outlets. Outstanding amongst these has been the company now known as Hamworthy PLC, which continues to be a major employer in the area. Outboard motors for small craft were produced by British Seagull on the Quay and subsequently at Fleets Bridge between 1938 and 1996. During the Second World War the company produced a large number of motors for light assault craft, and also built pontoon bridges.

A nineteenth century chemical industry associated with the Harbour was the production of town gas at the Quayside works from 1863. With considerable subsequent extension at the new Pitwines site, this flourished until the 1950s when it was superceded by the national gas grid.

A major chemical-based factory – The Royal Naval Cordite Factory – was built in 1915 at Holton Heath to provide the Navy with explosives during the First World War; it continued through to the end of the Second World War.

The last major chemical works in Poole was British Drug Houses (BDH), which made fine chemicals in West Quay Road from 1946 until 1973, when Glaxo sold it to Merck of Darmstadt, who finally closed the plant in 1993. A few small chemical companies continue to operate on some of the industrial estates around Poole, but despite its pioneering role in this field in the sixteenth century the area is no longer the centre of major chemical production.

Poole continued its tradition of shipbuilding throughout the period in response to changing demand. At the end of the First World War the Dorset Shipbuilding Company with strong local support planned to construct a major shipyard and industrial complex at Lilliput that would have employed 10,000 workers. This did not proceed; had it done so, it would have had a major effect not only on the immediate vicinity of what is now the Blue Lagoon but on the economy and environment of the whole Harbour area. Between the Wars the shipyards at Hamworthy and Poole were concerned primarily with ship repairing and the construction of small craft. The latter became of particular importance during the Second World War, and many of the landing craft that sailed to Normandy in 1944 were constructed locally. Post-war shipbuilding has been concerned with leisure craft, first at Southern Ocean Shipyards and, since 1978, by Sunseeker International Ltd, which now employs well over 2000 people in the construction of luxury motor yachts – primarily for the export market.

Of particular significance to the whole Harbour has been the exploration and extraction of oil and gas from reservoirs beneath the Harbour and Poole Bay. This began in the 1970s with drilling rigs on Furzey Island and subsequently on Goathorn Point. With a gathering point at Wytch Farm on the south side of the Harbour, it has become Europe's largest on-shore oil field and the sixth largest oil field in the UK. It is operated by BP Exploration Operating Company Ltd who have maximised the recovery of oil and gas as economically as possible with the least disturbance to the environment. With significant remaining reserves and improved drilling techniques, production seems likely to continue for many years to come.

FOURTEEN

Salt Production

SARAH-JANE HATHAWAY

SALT HAS PLAYED a huge variety of roles throughout time and across different cultures, leading to a variety of symbolic cultural meanings as well as having many important practical roles. Cultural symbolism has included the incorporation of salt within superstitions, folklore, symbolic practices, and taboos, which is unsurprising when considering the long history of use and the many physical properties salt incorporates. These include food preservation, antiseptic, strengthening clay (before firing), taste, and biological fulfilment amongst many others. We only need to look to the many sayings that still exist within the English language to observe one way in which salt has been attributed a cultural marker. Sayings such as 'Salt of the Earth', 'Take with a pinch of salt' and 'Worth their salt' are all still in use today and are vestiges of the symbolic nature of salt's ability to convey a multitude of meanings.

In Britain, there is evidence that salt has been produced from the sea since at least the Bronze Age, but it is during the Iron Age that we have evidence for an increase in coastal production sites, with the demand for salt clearly growing. It is during this period that we see the first evidence for salt production in the Harbour area.

Seawater contains on average 3.5-3.7 per cent of salt. However, salinity levels can vary in different areas depending on the topography of the coast and the presence of freshwater rivers. Areas of enclosed water such as estuaries and inland brine springs are generally thought to be the most fruitful areas to produce salt as the salinity level can be much higher. In both these areas, the figure can increase to as much as 8 per cent. Therefore it is not surprising that there is a long history of salt production in the Poole Harbour area. The Harbour contains many discrete areas where saltwater could be either gathered directly from the sea, perhaps using ceramic containers, or directly channelled into sites set back a little further than the coastline.

The main way we can recognise that salt has been produced on, or nearby to, a coastal site is by finding a particular form of clay 'equipment' called 'briquetage'. This term originated in France during the twentieth century, and was first used to describe the large amount of ceramic debris found on Iron Age salt production sites which utilised inland brine springs.

Reconstructed sub-rectangular briquetage container used to heat brine from Poole Harbour, created by Keith Jarvis in 2003.

COASTAL SALT PRODUCTION IN THE HARBOUR AREA

For the Harbour area, rectangular or circular thick and coarse containers were made from local clay and sand, as well as 'pedestal' supports which held the containers and were generally just made from simple twisted rolls of clay. The Harbour's abundant supply of clay meant that large amounts of this material could be made each year, alongside pottery. Clay was also used to create the features needed to produce salt, including hearths and special clay-lined tanks used to help seawater settle, and the seawater to partially concentrate (into brine) in natural sunlight. It is a skilled process as it required a great degree of preparation and knowledge of the heat that was needed to produce salt. Once the brine had been produced, it could then be transferred to a thick clay briquetage container, which was held with pedestals over a hearth used for heating the brine. The amount of heat and time taken to produce the salt depended on the type of salt required, for example fine or coarse salt. Once a wet salt mixture had been produced and most of the water evaporated, the salt could then be heated and dried using a gentler heat.

Vast amounts of briquetage have been found in the Harbour area. To date the area has produced at least 179,361 kilos of briquetage, and this is just a sample of the briquetage actually buried within this area, as due to its heavy and coarse nature, it is often left in the ground! This is a good indication of how important this process was to the economics of the Harbour during this time. Salt appears to have been produced in the Harbour area and the Isle of Purbeck from the early to mid Iron Age, through to the third and fourth centuries AD. Three areas have proved to be a particular focus for production: Kimmeridge Bay, Ower, and Hamworthy.

Archaeological excavations at Kimmeridge Bay revealed extensive areas of debris associated with salt production, such as burnt fuel, ash and briquetage, as well as occupation debris such as pottery and animal bone. The debris here was reported to have measured 10 feet deep in some areas! Burnt shale indicated its use as a fuel; shale being an abundant resource in the area. The advantage of using shale is that it is slow burning (which is good for salt production as a low steady heat is

Late Iron Age to early Romano-British clay briquetage supports from Hamworthy.

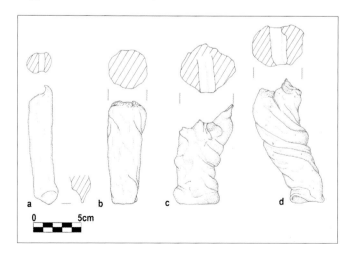

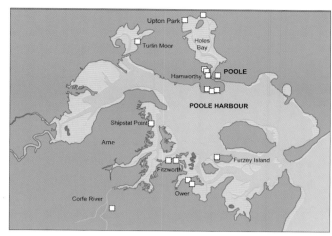

Iron Age and Romano-British sites associated with salt-making round Poole Harbour.

best for making salt crystals): however, the disadvantage would have been that burning shale produces a heavy smoke and sulphurous smell.

Excavations at Ower revealed an extensive settlement which intermittently continued in use from the late Iron Age through to the late Roman period. Briquetage was present through most of the settlement phases, indicating that salt production (as well as pottery production) was an important 'economic component' of this settlement. Briquetage had even been used to create a hard-standing around the settlement, which is testament to the robust nature of this material. The general increase in salt production during the late Iron Age at Ower could be due to the occupants salting pork on the site, which is evidenced by a relatively large pig bone assemblage with evidence for joint processing. There may also have been a site nearby to Ower alongside the Corfe River that needed the freshwater to process salt, perhaps to cleanse it of impurities. This would explain the discovery of briquetage in this particular area.

Finally, a series of excavations in the Hamworthy area offer a particularly interesting insight into salt production towards the end of the Iron Age and at the beginning of the Roman period. Early excavations by H. P. Smith in the mid-twentieth century revealed a series of pottery kilns, some of which were used to make a distinctive style of black pottery called Black Burnished Ware. Some of the pottery kiln furniture found during this excavation is likely to actually have been briquetage used for salt production. The two are very similar and difficult to separate at sites where both processes took place. Mention was also made of two channels inland running from Holes Bay towards the site, which ended in small shallow circular depressions. It is likely that these features were 'feeder channels', supplying saltwater to the site for salt production. Later excavations revealed more about salt production in this particular area, including a series of ditches and gullies, clay pits, and a rectangular hearth. This hearth was a simple hole cut into the ground and lined with clay; briquetage supports would have been placed on the sides, containers would have been placed on the top and brine heated to make salt crystals. In contrast to the south side of the Isle of Purbeck, wood was used as a fuel in this particular area, as shown by wood charcoal found within the hearth at Hamworthy.

Poole Harbour was a hive of production activity during the Later Iron Age and Romano-British periods, with shale working, pottery production, iron working and salt production, all combining to create an industrial complex within the Harbour. It seems very likely that people would have knowledge and skills that were used for multiple production processes. Pottery and salt production, naturally form a relationship in that they both require a large amount of raw clay, not only to make pottery and briquetage, but also to provide the structural material to make the hearths and kiln features. Both also required a steady supply of fuel (mainly in the form of wood). The knowledge of pottery production techniques would also be useful in the production of briquetage.

Salt continued to be made within the Harbour area during the early medieval period, evidenced by the number of entries in the eleventh century Domesday Survey. Records of the 'salinari', which refers to the salt-workers themselves, were made for two areas within the Harbour; 13 for Ower and 32 for Studland. It is particularly interesting that Ower continued to be a focus for salt production within this period as it had been previously. It has been speculated that the 'Studland Circles', a series of bowl-shaped impressions covering the Studland Peninsula, are associated with salt working. No evidence has yet been found to support this, and it is possible that the circles may have been associated with the copperas industry instead. It is hoped that further investigations by the Poole Harbour Heritage Project will help to elucidate the function of these mysterious earthworks.

Little is actually known about the different techniques used to produce salt in the early medieval period, however many sites, especially those in the Adur Valley of East Sussex, used a technique called 'leaching'. This technique involves washing silts and sand that are impregnated with salt, removed from coastal areas.

Later post-medieval salt production within the Harbour area employed a systematic and more technologically elaborate method of production. It involved the use of large metal pans (instead of ceramic) in 'salt boiling houses' where seawater was fed in through artificial salt pans on the coast, which are often visible on maps as a square grid system in the sea. This grid system was still clearly visible on an 1811 Ordnance Survey map at Lilliput, an area still referred to as 'Salterns'(see page 211), (although this name usually refers to the presence of salt marsh, which is an indication that there was a good salinity level).

In the eighteenth century, extensive rock salt deposits were found in Cheshire while exploring for coal seams. The vast amount of salt eventually extracted from these deposits gradually resulted in many coastal salt works ceasing to produce, unable to compete.

FIFTEEN

Alum and Copperas

GILL BROADBENT AND ALAN HAWKINS

SAILING OVER TO BROWNSEA ISLAND on a summer's day it is hard to imagine that the island, now peaceful and tranquil, was once one of the centres of alum and copperas production. Or, when shopping in Lilliput on an equally pleasant summer's day, that this was another centre for the production of copperas based on raw materials dug from 'the mynes' on Evening Hill. The manufacture of these basic chemicals that grew up around the Harbour in the sixteenth century enables Poole to claim that it was the birthplace of the chemical industry in England.

Alum was mainly used as a fixative in the dyeing of cloth and for tanning and softening leather. Copperas was also used as a fixative, as a black dye, and in the manufacture of ink. Though little known today, both alum and copperas were much in demand all over Europe at this time, especially in the textile industry. The flamboyant and colourful fashions of the day creating a big demand for these chemicals, which in turn accounted for the high prices they commanded.

Although the specific processing techniques used around the Harbour are still not fully understood, by the sixteenth century the general methods for making alum and copperas had been known for many years, originating in Egypt around 2000 BC. However, much of the terminology of the alum and copperas industries was developed before the chemistry of the materials involved was properly understood and over time misinterpretations of the industry and misnaming of the chemicals concerned has occurred.

Alum is the more versatile of the two, the essential ingredients necessary for its production being aluminium silicate and pyrites, both of which can be found in the clays around the Harbour. When heated together they combine to form soluble aluminium sulphate. Following lixiviation two types of alum can be produced: ammonium alum by the addition of ammonia in the form of urine, and potash alum by the addition of burnt kelp or wood.

The south shore of Brownsea Island, and the possible site of the seventeenth century Copperas Works (see map on page 78).

ABOVE Melanterite crystallising out from the sediments on Brownsea Island in 2007.

ABOVE LEFT Brick structure eroding from the cliff at the south shore on Brownsea Island prior to excavation.

LEFT A view of the excavation of the brick floor undertaken by Poole Harbour Heritage Project on Brownsea Island in 2008.

There are two methods for making copperas, which in the pure form is ferrous sulphate, and, in the natural form is melanterite. In the first, raw material in the form of clay, is boiled, the resulting liquid evaporated, cooled and crystallised. In the second and more common method, nodules of pyrites are weathered with air and water to produce dilute ferrous sulphate. This is then concentrated and crystallised to form copperas in a process cycle that can take several years. It is this latter method that was recorded by Celia Fiennes in her diary following her visit to Brownsea Island in 1686.

In 2008, a two-year archaeological investigation into the Harbour's alum and copperas industries began with an excavation on Brownsea Island. The excavation was an attempt to establish whether or not features eroding from the cliffs on the south shore are connected to the late seventeenth century works described by Celia Fiennes. This fieldwork, funded by English Heritage, is part of a wider investigation into the Dorset alum and copperas industries which is being conducted by the Poole Harbour Heritage Project.

In the sixteenth century the main source of alum was from the Papal States in Italy. However, increasing Papal control over both its price and importation into England and the general unrest on the Continent, led to endeavours, actively encouraged and controlled by the Crown, to produce domestic supplies. The Crown's involvement in this enterprise and the expectations that large fortunes could be made in the manufacture of alum has led to the survival of many legal documents and patents from the sixteenth and seventeenth centuries all of which help to build up a picture of the industries.

Records suggest that 'alome' was being collected from the tertiary deposits around the Harbour in the early sixteenth century but, due to the inexact terminology of the day, it is more likely that the mineral referred to was native copperas in the form of melanterite – especially as alum is not known to occur naturally in England, in spite of named locations such as Alum Chine in Bournemouth. It was hoped that alum, the more valuable of the two chemicals, could be manufactured from the same raw materials on a commercial scale.

The earliest patent issued in connection with the search for alum and copperas was that granted to William Kendall in 1562. However, it was not until later in the decade that the quest began in earnest following the issue of a patent in 1566, originally to London merchant Cornelius de Vos, but later assigned to James Blount, 6th Lord Mountjoy.

James Blount had inherited two thirds of the Canford Manor Estate from his relative, the Marchioness of Exeter. In the sixteenth century the estate included a vast area of heathland between Wimborne Minster, Poole Harbour, and present-day Bournemouth. By exploiting the deposits of copperas ore known to exist on the estate, Lord Mountjoy was producing copperas on a commercial scale in the late 1560s, no doubt hoping to bolster his ailing financial position. Although at present the exact date is not known, the building of the first industrial scale copperas works is thought to have commenced around 1565. Contemporary records show that small amounts of alum were leaving the Port of Poole as part of the coastal trade at this time; much larger quantities were leaving for destinations as far away as London by the end of the sixteenth century.

Surviving documents suggest that the main works, and possibly the first to be in production, was *Okeman's House* situated in what is today the area around Lilliput. Within a few years the industry had grown and several other similar plants were in production along the coast between Boscombe and Brownsea Island. Later, in 1604, a further alum works was built west of the Harbour at Kimmeridge by Sir William Clavell.

Unfortunately, modern development masks the exact sites of the alum and copperas 'houses', but contemporary maps give an indication of their general locations. It is thought that a building recorded at the western end of Brownsea Island, as shown on Ralph Treswell's 1586 survey of Purbeck, may possibly be the site of the early works on the Island. An area marked as *The Mynes*, considered to be the extraction site of the raw material used in these works, is highlighted on an early seventeenth century map.

Ralph Treswell's 1586 'Survey' (see page 75) indicates a further location of *Mynes* that existed on the northern shores of the Harbour in the area stretching from Parkstone and Lilliput to Canford Cliffs, an area still recorded in the late eighteenth century as *Mines Heath*. It is likely that the *Haven House* mentioned in documents was located in the vicinity of Luscombe Valley, and the name *Alum Chine* fossilises its connection with the industry. Other houses existed further to the

James Blount, 6th Lord Mountjoy, part owner of Canford Manor estate and manufacturer of copperas.

east; *Merchants House* possibly at Durley Chine and *Bascombe Copperas House* at present-day Boscombe.

Alum was considerably more difficult to produce than copperas due to the high temperature required for the reaction between aluminium silicate and pyrites to take place. In the area around Poole Harbour at this time the main form of fuel was turf, which when burnt did not produce sufficient heat for the reaction to occur. Therefore, Mountjoy's attempt to produce alum on a similar scale to the copperas production proved costly and unprofitable. Unable to afford to run the works on his estate he was forced to lease them to his wife's kinsman, George Carlton, and to John Hastings. Rising debts also forced him to sell property that included his share of the Canford Manor Estate, which was sold to Henry Hastings, 3rd Lord Huntingdon. Mountjoy, however, retained the mineral rights of the estate for himself. This action prompted a lengthy legal battle between Mountjoy and Huntingdon to establish the ownership of both the Canford Manor Estate and its mineral rights. It was not until 1586, after Mountjoy's death in 1581 that the matter was finally resolved with the Privy Council deciding in favour of Lord Huntingdon.

Huntingdon continued the attempt to produce alum but met with as little success as Lord Mountjoy. He too lost a great amount of money in the endeavour and

Henry Hastings, 3rd Lord Huntingdon, was confirmed as owner of both Canford Manor Estate and its mineral rights by the Privy Council in 1586.

leased the works to Philip Smythe, citizen and merchant of London. The failure to produce alum on a commercial scale is echoed in the recorded shipments of both chemicals leaving the Port of Poole for the period 1591 to 1608. These show considerably more copperas being shipped than alum, mainly to London, no doubt to furnish the important textile trade there. The last shipment of alum from Poole was a small amount, '1 barrel', in 1602, whereas shipments of copperas continued until 1608.

By the time Smythe's lease ran out in 1608 production in the area had ceased. Later that year Henry Hastings, 5th Earl Huntingdon, made a brief attempt to restart operations on his estate. However, his venture proved unsuccessful after he came into conflict with local inhabitants over his attempt to enclose part of the common and waste lands to obtain sufficient fuel for the manufacturing processes. By 1609 the main focus of alum production had shifted to the north-east of England, where the necessary raw materials were more plentiful. The main centres of copperas production also moved to Deptford and Whitstable and, therefore, production of both chemicals in the area around the Harbour were commercially unsustainable.

After a short break, records show copperas exports from the Port of Poole re-commenced in the 1620s. At this time the shipments were to Rouan and Rochell instead of to London, and it is more probable that these were onward shipments from the east of England rather than locally produced materials.

Two further attempts were made to produce commercially viable materials on Brownsea Island. The first was by Sir Robert Clayton and his partner John Wildman when they recommenced production on the Island in 1677. Over time their enterprise also proved unprofitable and the works were finally closed down in 1704. The final attempt to produce alum was made in the nineteenth century when Colonel Waugh started to build a modern processing plant to utilise the *alum clay* deposits existing on the Island. However, he became bankrupt before the works could be completed, his ambitious plans remained unfulfilled and the Island was once again sold.

Today little remains around the Harbour to show these industries existed. Modern urban development has changed the barren *Mines Heath* to an area that supports some of the most expensive housing in England. Brownsea Island has reverted back to nature, a haven for red squirrels and other wildlife, its former industry all but forgotten.

SIXTEEN

Other Chemicals

ERIC STREET AND WILLIAM SHELDRICK

WITH THE DEMISE of the alum and copperas industries, there was little resurgence of chemical production associated with the Harbour until the nineteenth century. This resurgence began with Poole becoming one of the pioneers of the town (coal) gas industry, and continued in the twentieth century with the establishment of a nationally important Admiralty explosives factory and with a major British Drug Houses (BDH) production unit on the edge of Holes Bay. A number of smaller electro-plating, cosmetic, pharmaceutical, and fine chemical units were also established, but these have largely disappeared, and Poole and its Harbour no longer continue the tradition of chemical production pre-eminently established during the Tudor period.

The Town Quayside Gas Works was built around 1870 with an overhead coal conveyer from the quayside: also visible is the East Quay Pottery.

TOWN GAS PRODUCTION IN POOLE

The earliest record of industry in Poole is of a gas-making plant, dated 1819. In the 1830s there was a scheme to install gas lamps in the High Street using gas made in a unit close to the Town Quay. No notes have been found regarding the success and operation of this project, but the hazards involved must have been considerable.

The Bournemouth Gas and Water Co., founded in 1862 and incorporated in 1864, made 'town gas' by heating coal and distilling off the vapour, leaving the coke to be removed by hand whilst the gas had its tar removed from the coolers. About 13000 cubic feet of gas and 20 gallons of tar were produced from each ton of coal. A later development was to inject steam into the oven and raise the operating temperature which improved the quality of the products, a process that was incorporated into the Pitwines plant after 1923.

Before and during the First World War the plant expanded considerably, providing employment to a large

The Poole Pitwines Gasworks under construction. It opened in 1923 and closed finally in 1970. The site was then redeveloped with affordable housing.

number of Poole men, some of whom worked there for over 40 years. This plant was close to the quay, receiving coal from both South Wales and the North East. Several ancillary plants developed later – meter repair shops, a foundry, a machine shop – and some of these were used to make munitions for the war effort.

The company operated an excellent social programme, with an annual sports day, a band, cricket and football teams, a hospital fund, and a co-partnership scheme which provided an annual bonus together with a retirement pension.

In 1923 a major 'water gas' making installation was started at Pitwines, engineered by Messrs Woodall and Duckham, who were the Chief and Assistant Engineers

at that time. (Their company went on to build many plants throughout the world). Eventually there were 27 retorts; some of them continuous, with a consumption of up to 7 tons of coal an hour. By 1949 there were five Humphreys and Glasgow units with mechanical grates and completely automatic operation. Output of gas increased steadily from 1900, reaching some 5,000 million cubic feet per year and 180,000 tons of coke in 1946. From Poole, gas was supplied over an area ranging from Wareham in the west, to Wimborne, Blandford, Fordingbridge and Ringwood in the north, and as far east as New Milton and Lymington until the whole factory was shut down. The site has since been cleared and a supermarket and several large blocks of apartments and townhouses built on it.

This information was abstracted from *The Co-Partner*, a house magazine which was published from 1920 to 1950 and contains a remarkable record of

The Royal Naval Cordite factory with Poole Harbour in the background. It operated from 1915 until 1946. Part of it was reopened from 1950 until 1957 when it finally closed.

the technicalities of the process and of the local social life. Other documents are in the Poole History Centre including a copy of the annual reports of the company between 1863 and 1949, when it was nationalized. Further information was provided by Mr. R. Cherrett of Wimborne, who served more than 40 years with the company, as had his father and grandfather.

THE ROYAL NAVAL CORDITE FACTORY HOLTON HEATH

A factory, specifically for the production of cordite as the propellant for naval guns, was built during the First World War at Holton Heath on the north shore of the Harbour between Poole and Wareham. Its total area was about 500 acres. The explosive products were initially conveyed by sea from a jetty at Rockley to naval depots at Gosport and Chatham, and later by the main-line Waterloo to Weymouth railway that skirted its southern boundary.

It was built on the direct orders of Winston Churchill, then First Lord of the Admiralty, and was designed by Colonel Sir F. L. Nathan, who had previously been involved in the construction of a nitroglycerine plant in Scotland for the Nobel Company.

The principal ingredients of cordite are nitrocellulose and nitroglycerine. Both were produced on site, respectively from paper and glycerine using concentrated nitric and sulphuric acids, the last of which was also produced on site from iron pyrites (which was, incidentally, the raw material used for producing copperas around the Harbour in the sixteenth and seventeenth centuries, see Chapter 15). The final product was extruded into 'cords' of varying diameter, each with a calculated burning rate, for the whole range of naval armaments, from hand guns to guns for the largest battleships and, ultimately, for rocket-assisted naval aircraft.

A minor processing raw material was acetone which was also produced on site during the First World War by a process developed by Dr Chaim Weizmann of the

Nitroglycerine conveyor truck, especially designed to transport very sensitive materials.

Batch nitration plant for nitroglycerine production. In 1931 it was destroyed by an explosion that killed 10 people. It was replaced in 1937 by a continuously operated plant.

University of Manchester, who later became President of Israel.

The most sensitive of the raw materials was nitroglycerine, initially produced in two batch-process plants, one of which was destroyed in an explosion in 1931 with a major loss of life. This plant was replaced in 1936 by a continuous–process plant developed and constructed by the Meissener Company of Germany. During the Second World War it was capable of producing 24 tons per day of nitroglycerine. It, and the rest of the factory, was subject to a major air-raid on the night of June 3rd and 4th 1942 but fortunately survived (see Chapter 12).

Two high explosives – Picrite and Tetryl – were also produced during the Second World War but in relatively small quantities compared with the main output of cordite.

At the peak of the Second World War, the factory employed about 4000 people, many of them women. At the end of the War in 1945 the number of employees was progressively reduced until production ceased in 1946. The Picrite plant was restarted in 1950, and in 1952 the production of rocket propellant was resumed, but these plants were finally closed in 1956 and 1957 respectively. The whole site was progressively cleared and decontaminated and is now the Holton Heath Business Park.

MERCK/BDH FINE CHEMICALS

In 1946 the British Drug Houses Company (BDH), who were at that time owned by Glaxo in London, wanted to expand their range of processes and products, and came to Poole to take over the large sheds and grounds which had been used throughout the Second World War for builbing fast motorboats for the Air Sea Rescue Service, located between West Quay Road and Holes Bay. BDH were fortunate in being able to recruit experienced scientific staff released by the closing of the Holton Heath explosives factory. They expanded their range of AnalaR pure test chemicals and their specialised test materials which were world famous for their purity and consistency.

Effluents from the processes were treated in a separate

LEFT Two photographs of women munition workers in the Royal Naval Cordite Factory during the Second World War. Women were employed in the manufacture of nitrocellulose or guncotton and its admixture with nitroglycerine to produce cordite. In the lower photograph they are making the cordite, and vats of nitrocellulose can be seen in the background (bottom photograph IWM A24932).

BDH, West Quay Road (1946-1973), a processing plant for the manufacture of fine chemicals such as halogenated polyaromatics used for the manufacture of liquid crystals.

plant and the residual liquors were tested before being discharged into the Harbour. Any heavy metals were thus totally removed.

Initially, all activities were confined to the West Quay site – administration, production, quality control, sales, marketing, warehousing, distribution, workshops, and staff training. Chemical production was sectionalised to avoid cross-contamination because, for example, some AnalaR products had tested specifications of less than 0.02 parts per million of lead.

The categories were white chemicals (mainly inorganic), heavy metals, stains, dyes and indicators (for bacteriology and clinical microscopy), solutions of reagents, test kits, and special customer-requested reagents. The Biochemical Department produced high purity enzymes, complex active peptides, and other products either synthesised or derived from natural sources which were used in clinical research. These products were backed up by analytical methods devised on site. Other specialised products were bactericides and fungicides, as well as 'melt grown' crystals of lithium, caesium, thallium and halides which were sold into the optical industry. Later product ranges were in liquid crystals valued at up to £1m a ton, such as are now used for flat screen television sets, and thermo-chromic products.

In 1973 Glaxo sold BDH to E. Merck of Darmstadt, who continued the process of expansion and eventually opened their major packaging and administrative centre at the Broom Road site. The main factory continued as a major manufacturing unit into the 1980s. In 1991 there was a major fire in the warehouse at West Quay Road and although manufacturing continued afterwards, the whole factory was closed down about two years later, when Merck moved their main storage and distribution centre to the Midlands.

The whole site was sold, partly to the Sunseeker Company for the manufacture (once again) of motorboats. The remainder was sold to the R.N.L.I. for new training facilities.

OTHER CHEMICAL COMPANIES

A survivor and developer of the British Drug Houses processes is the Crystran Company who manufacture specialised optical products for many industries on the Broom Road Industrial Estate. Other chemical companies which have been started up and made brief appearances include Clodol Industries, Pallas Chemicals, Wessex Bio-chemicals, and Lantrec Chemicals. There have also been several electroplating plants set up in various places. The existing companies now are Sigma (office only), and Lush Ltd. who manufacture cosmetics on the Nuffield Estate.

SEVENTEEN

Oil and Gas

WILLIAM SHELDRICK

THE RESOURCES OF OIL that now support oil and petroleum gas production in Dorset come from reservoirs deep below Poole Bay, Poole Harbour, and the Purbeck lowlands and were laid down more than 200 million years ago. Today Dorset's oil and natural gas industry is based at Wytch Farm, where oil is processed from wellsites on the southern shore of Poole Harbour, Furzey Island, Kimmeridge, and Wareham.

Wytch Farm is western Europe's largest onshore oilfield and the sixth largest in the UK. It comprises three separate oil reservoirs, the Frome, Bridport and Sherwood reservoirs that lie under the Harbour and Poole Bay. Total recoverable reserves are estimated at 480 million barrels, of which 90 per cent are in the Sherwood reservoir.

HISTORY

Oil bearing rocks found in Purbeck have been used as a fuel since the Bronze Age. They were later used to fire the furnaces used in the alum and glass industries at

Map showing the wellsites and other facilities associated with the Wytch Farm oil field.

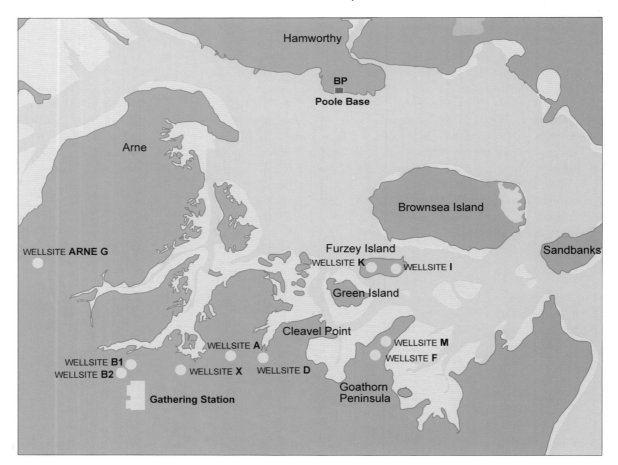

Kimmeridge at the beginning of the seventeenth century and, in Victorian times, gas produced locally from oil shale was used to light the streets of Wareham.

The first exploration well in Dorset was drilled near Kimmeridge in 1936 by D'Arcy Exploration, later to become British Petroleum (BP). This and other wells in Purbeck were initially unsuccessful. The modern Purbeck industry commenced in 1959 with the discovery of oil at Kimmeridge Bay and oil production began in 1960. More than three million barrels have been produced since and the well continues to produce about 100 barrels per day (bpd) of light high quality oil.

The Wareham oilfield was discovered in 1964 but was not brought on-stream until 1990. In 1973 exploration drilling commenced along the southern heathland fringes of the Harbour. Following exploration, licences were awarded to British Gas and BP and from a drill site near Wytch Farm, the Jurassic Bridport sandstone reservoir was located at a depth of 900 metres. By the end of the 1970's production started at a rate of 6000 barrels per day (BPD). Further drilling in 1978 revealed the deeper and more substantial older Permian Sherwood sandstone reserves at a depth of 1,600 metres. Production from the area lying directly under the Harbour is carried out from wellsites on Furzey Island, the Goathorn Peninsula, and other sites on the mainland north of Corfe Castle. The

An aerial view of Furzey Island: part of BP's Wytch Farm oilfield on the Dorset Coast.

extent of the Bridport and Sherwood reserves are shown in the illustration below. More recently, oil is being extracted from the Frome reservoir in a clay/limestone deposit at 750 metres, which extends eastwards from Sandbanks and Studland under the sea to the south of Bournemouth with estimated reserves of 7.5 million barrels.

Wareham is a separate reservoir located beneath the town and nearby countryside and is accessed via two wellsites to the west of Wareham. It has reserves of

Poole Harbour and Isle of Purbeck oil reserves showing the extent of the Sherwood and Bridport reservoirs.

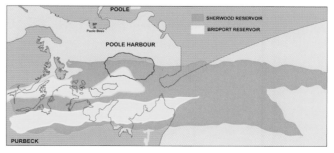

about six million barrels in Bridport sandstone, and an output of about 2000 bpd; it is small compared with its neighbours.

In 1984 BP became the operator of Wytch Farm following the divestment of British Gas interest to a partnership of new companies. Non-operator partners in the Wytch Farm oilfield are: Premier, Maersk, ONEPM, and Talisman.

ENVIRONMENTAL CONSIDERATIONS

Wytch Farm is situated in an Area of Outstanding Natural Beauty. The area also includes Sites of Special Scientific Interest (SSSIs), Special Protection Areas, internationally recognised Ramsar wetlands, National Trust land, UNESCO World Heritage Site coastline, and National Nature Reserves. In developing the oilfield BP Exploration Operating Company Ltd. aimed to maximize the recovery of oil and gas as economically as possible with the least disturbance to the environment.

This has been achieved though a unique partnership with the local authorities, statutory and voluntary environmental groups, and local communities, who all have a vested interest in ensuring that the characteristic beauty of the Isle of Purbeck and the Harbour as major tourist attractions remain unspoilt. The Wytch Farm development has been designed and planned with such care and thoroughness that visitors to the area are often oblivious to the presence of the oilfield. The policy has also benefited the environment through extensive scientific studies, greatly increasing our knowledge about the natural and social history of the area and its current ecology.

PROJECT DEVELOPMENT

The development of Wytch Farm began in the late 1970s and has taken place in three stages The first stage involved recovery from the Bridport reservoir with production of about 6000 bpd. Stage 2 began in the mid-1980s and involved the construction of two wellsites on Furzey Island, developing two more mainland wellsites on the Arne and Goathorn peninsulas, the expansion of an oil and gas processing plant, and the conversion of a crude oil rail terminal into a butane/propane handling facility. An underground oil export pipeline was laid from Purbeck to Southampton, where the crude oil is loaded onto tankers at BP's Hamble terminal.

A major development in the project was Stage 3, where innovative technology has enabled BP to recover oil from the previously inaccessible Sherwood reserves deep below Poole Bay. Initial plans included the construction of an artificial island – Hook Island – in the sea outside the Harbour, but after considerable evaluation and debate these plans were abandoned in favour of land-based extended reach drilling (ERD) operation. This was made possible by new drilling technology developed by BP's Research Unit at Sunbury. Since beginning Stage 3, BP has broken world records for extended reach drilling with the 11.3 kilometres-long M16 well to access the oil under Poole Bay at a depth of 1600 metres.

The development of this section of the reservoir from onshore on Goathorn Peninsula offered significant environmental advantages over the Hook Island proposal, as well as being more commercially efficient.

WYTCH FARM

The area of land managed by BP exceeds 310 acres of which 100 acres are occupied by development sites. BP also manages conservation areas comprising 64 acres, and more than 130,000 trees and shrubs have been planted around the oilfield and pipeline route.

There are currently 98 wells operating from 10 wellsites. Sixty-three of these are producers and 36 are water injector wells which help maintain the pressure in the rock formation. The wells and their associated facilities are located in recessed sealed wellsites, ranging in size between two and five acres. Wellsites K and L on Furzey Island produce a substantial proportion of the total oil production from the oilfield. Oil is pumped from the Bridport and Frome reservoirs by beam pumps while submersible pumps are used on the deeper more prolific Sherwood reserve.

Seawater is pumped into the injection wells to maintain pressure and manage the oilfields. About 85,000 bpd are taken from the Harbour at Cleavel Point, filtered, and pumped to the Gathering Station before being used.

The heart of the project is at Wytch Farm. This is the site of the Gathering Station, where the crude oil and petroleum gases from the reservoirs are separated. Oil and well fluids from the various wellsites are brought to the gathering station for processing via a network of underground flow-lines. Oil from Kimmeridge is transported to the Gathering Station by road tankers. At the Gathering Station, water and gases are separated from the oil and the water is re-injected into the reservoirs. The gas is cooled, metered, and separated before being passed through fractionation towers and separators. Butane and propane are stored in large underground vessels before being exported by road

tanker to the local distributors. The remaining gas is odorized, metered, and sold to British Gas who pump it by pipeline to Sopley where it connects to the national grid. The gas processing also produces fuel gas that is used on-site for power generation.

The oil that remains from these separation processes is cooled, metered and pumped to BP's Hamble oil terminal, on the eastern shores of Southampton Water, via a 16 inch diameter, 90 kilometres long underground pipeline. The oil takes 25 hours to complete its journey through four valve stations, which can be closed remotely if a drop in pipeline pressure is registered at the Gathering Station control room.

CONCLUSIONS

The recovery of oil at Wytch Farm in its primary stage from the Bridport Reservoir in 1980 was about 5000 bpd and this increased sharply when wells from the large Sherwood reservoir came on stream. Production peaked at about 110,000 barrels per day in 1997 and by 2002 had declined to about 50,000 barrels per day

The Wytch Farm Gathering Station where oil and gas products are collected, separated, processed and stored before transport.

as production entered its secondary enhanced stage. In 2007 production was around 23,000 barrels per day.

Economic and technical success is only half the story. The other half is that it has been achieved with a minimum impact on the environment and made possible by the collaboration of BP with local planning authorities, environmental organizations and the public. Wytch Farm has operated for more than 20 years in an Area of Outstanding Natural Beauty. It has achieved many environmental awards and is regarded as an industry model in preserving the environment.

The future of the field depends upon the following three key factors: oil price, technology, and regulatory approvals. Improved drilling techniques are continually being developed and the facility has a good track record, so Wytch Farm still hopes to continue to operate as a successful project for many years to come.

EIGHTEEN

The Clay Industry

THE EXTRACTION OF CLAY and its local fabrication have been associated with the Harbour from the earliest times. Locally-produced pottery like the Romano-British Black Burnished Ware illustrated below was widely distributed to other parts of Britain and the Continent from at least the Iron Age, but trade in the raw clay did not begin until the early seventeenth century. From that time onwards, the industry became more specialised, responding to both changing public demand and to the types of clay available.

Broadly, the pattern that developed was that high-quality ball clay from the Isle of Purbeck was both exported to other centres of fabrication and used locally for the production of high-quality products.

Lower-quality clays from the north of the Harbour and Brownsea Island continued to be used for less-critical applications, and this part of the industry received a considerable boost during the nineteenth and twentieth centuries in response to a growing population and increasing housing demand. Such production units were located on or near their respective clay source, since it was not economic to transport lower-quality clays long distances.

Clay Production

BEN BUXTON

THE CLAYS AROUND THE HARBOUR originated from sediments deposited in the lagoons of a river flowing from the west around 40 million years ago. The clay occurs in 'lenses' consisting of layers of different colours and having different properties.

Demand for high-quality clay from the Isle of Purbeck received a boost from the new fashion for tobacco smoking which led to a demand for clay pipes from the early years of the seventeenth century. Tea drinking also created a demand for the production of teacups and teapots. Clay was dug from pits in the Arne, Furzebrook, Norden, Rempstone, and Creech areas and was transported by packhorses and carts to Wareham Quay and to quays on the west side of the Arne peninsula. In 1669 clay was being shipped from Russel Quay at Arne. A century later, Thomas Hyde built a quay to the south-west of Russel Quay, and in 1771 Josiah Wedgwood contracted Hyde to supply him with ball clay.

Hyde went bankrupt in 1792 and other suppliers stepped in, amongst them the family of Joseph Pike, who had been digging ball clay in Devon, and had started working at Furzebrook in about 1760. Benjamin Fayle began operating at Norden in about 1795; competition was fierce, and Fayle decided to get ahead

Benjamin Fayle's horsedrawn Middlebere Plateway opened in 1806 and was Dorset's first railway.

by revolutionising the transport of the clay from the pits to the Harbour. He commissioned a railway line from pits at Norden to a new quay on Middlebere Lake. The line opened in 1806. It was Dorset's first railway, and only the second in southern England after the Surrey Iron Railway which had opened in 1803 (for a map showing the Purbeck rail and tramways see page 213). Technically it was a 'plateway' which differed from the 'edge' railway that became the norm, in that the flanges retaining the truck wheels on the line were on the rails (called plates) rather than on the wheels. The Middlebere Plateway, as it is known, was horsedrawn throughout its 100-year life. Clay was taken by barge from the quay to Poole for transhipment to larger vessels.

Fayle constructed a line in 1854 from clay pits at Newton, east of Norden, to a new pier on the Goathorn Peninsula, and from 1870 steam locomotives operated on it. In 1907 the company extended the line west to Norden, thus replacing the Middlebere Plateway. This line – Fayles's Tramway – was built despite the fact that the Wareham-Swanage branch of the main line, which opened in 1885, passed through Norden, and exchange sidings had been built which enabled clay to be transferred to trucks on the main line and exported.

Meanwhile, the other clay company, Pike Brothers, had built a tramway in 1840 from clay pits at Furzebrook – including the pit now known as Blue Pool – to a quay at Ridge Wharf, on the River Frome between Wareham and the Harbour. Originally horsedrawn, the first of a series of steam locomotives operated on it from 1866. As if in anticipation of a growing family it was named *Primus*;

subsequent purchases being named in numerical order up to *Septimus*. The narrow-gauge network expanded to serve clay pits and mines to the south and west, as far as Povington. Furzebrook became the focus of processing the clay, and from the early twentieth century exchange sidings from the main Wareham-Swanage line enabled clay to be exported that way.

The clay tramway network gradually closed down between 1930 and 1970. The Goathorn line stopped carrying clay in about 1930 and closed altogether about seven years later. From 1928 to 1934 the line had also carried tons of Purbeck stone used in constructing the 'training bank' which helps to keep the entrance to the Harbour clear of sediment. Pike's line to Furzebrook closed in 1940, when the area was taken over by the

Fayles's Tramway. The engine was the *Tiny*, built by Stephen Lewin at the Poole Foundry in 1868 (see Chapter 20).

Ridge Wharf, 1911, the terminus of the Pike Brothers' narrow guage railway. From here clay was transported by shallow-draught sailing vessel (as on the left) or in barges pulled by steam tug to Poole Town Quay.

Army for military training. The remaining Pike's lines closed in 1956-7. Thereafter, lorries were used for transport. Short lengths of track remained in use in the Norden area until 1970, in later years using diesel engines. Pike Brothers and Fayle merged in 1949 and Pike's Furzebrook works became the processing centre.

The clay pit and mine at Cotness near East Creech in about 1950, with the Purbeck Hills in the background.

The combined Company was taken over by English China Clays (ECC) in 1968.

The best clay is found not on the surface but under layers of sand or gravel. This 'overburden' can be several metres thick and has to be removed to get at the clay. Until the 1970s, when mechanical excavators were introduced, the clay was dug by hand using spades called tubals; from the 1930s pneumatic spades were used. The technique was to create a series of working faces from the top to the bottom of the pit, giving the pit sides a step-like appearance. The men would throw the cubes of clay directly into trucks below, and the rails were frequently moved to keep up with the changing working faces.

From the middle of the nineteenth century, mines were sunk to extract the clay from deep deposits. An inclined tunnel was dug down and clay was dug from

A drawing by Alfred Dawson of 1882 showing the Norden claypits worked by the Fayle family.

Clay barges alongside a larger vessel at Town Quay in about 1900.

galleries radiating out. The sides and roofs of all tunnels had to be fully shored up. The mines were served by their own underground railway systems, the loaded trucks being winched out into transhipment sheds where the clay was tipped from the trucks into bins which then emptied into the trucks of the tramway system, or, from the 1950s onwards, into lorries. During the twentieth century, mines became more common than pits, but, with increasingly costly safety regulations, they became uneconomic and the last one closed in 1999.

The raw clay has to be weathered before being supplied to customers. In the past it was left outside in 'weathering beds' for up to a year, but in more recent times the weathering process has been done artificially at the processing works at Furzebrook

Today, clay production is concentrated in four open pits, and the operator is Imerys who took over from ECC. Production is currently at the rate of 160,00 tons a year.

The Clay Trade
from the Seventeenth Century
DAVID COUSINS

'I must now trouble my Dear Friend to procure me some clay to work upon, or we must give over work, or make bad ware, which is worse … It is Poole Clay I want … let the price be what it will, I must have it.'
Josiah Wedgwood, in a letter of 1771.

THE OUTLET which gave rise to the beginnings of significant trade in the highest quality clay from the Isle of Purbeck was not Wedgwood-type pottery but tobacco pipe production (hence the term 'pipeclay') following the introduction of tobacco into Britain at the end of the sixteenth century.

Whilst the production of tobacco pipes in the seventeenth century, and of decorated tiles and high-grade pottery in the nineteenth and twentieth centuries,

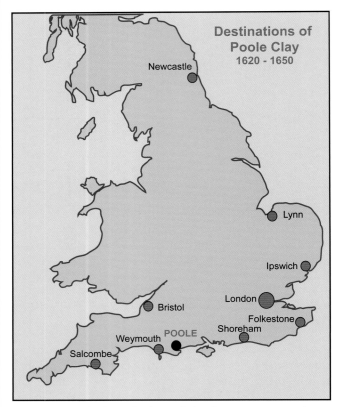

Destinations of
Poole Clay
1620 - 1650

The ports to which Poole shipped clay between 1620 and 1650. Most clay went to London, with smaller amounts going to ports on the south and east coasts.

○ Port taking clay from Poole
○ Port taking clay from Exeter
○ Port taking clay from Bideford

The ports to which Poole, Teignmouth and Bideford shipped clay between 1720 and 1760. Teignmouth (Exeter) and Bideford tended to ship clay to the west, whilst Poole tended to ship it to ports on the east.

became important local industries – the first of these in Poole and Wareham and the second around Poole – the largest element in the high-quality clay business in the seventeenth and eighteenth centuries was its export to other centres of fabrication which could justify the transport costs and where fuel was more readily available. Certainly, neither Wedgwood, nor any other Staffordshire potter, made any attempt to produce pottery in Dorset, preferring to pay for transport of the clay to their factories in Staffordshire.

Ball clays in economically significantly amounts exist in only a few places in England – The Isle of Purbeck, North and South Devon, and the Isle of Wight. Clay shipped from Poole has, from the beginning, encountered competition, particularly from Devon, with Poole tending to serve ports on the east coast – particularly, London – while exports from ports in Devon such as Bideford tended to serve the west coast.

The first recorded shipment of clay from Poole seems to have been in 1626 when a total of 122 tons were shipped to London for tobacco pipe manufacture with one shipment of 20 tons to Newcastle. From this small beginning the clay trade expanded until, in 1796, nearly

10,000 tons a year were shipped from Poole, rising to over 30,000 tons in 1831, 44,000 tons in 1836 and over 70,000 tons in 1878. Details of such shipments together with the names of ships used and of their masters are contained in the Port Books of the period. From the beginning until at least 1760, the export of clay to foreign ports was prohibited.

Until 1640 there was also a ban on making clay tobacco pipes outside London, and a monopoly, held by several persons in succession, on the sale of tobacco pipe clay in London.

Until about 1670, most of the clay was shipped from Poole by Thomas Cornell, but entries in the Port Book for 1676 show that by this time his hold on the market had declined, and the trade was shared with George Carew, Edmund Hayter, and Robert Hunt.

The rise in tea and coffee drinking in the latter half of the seventeenth century together with the influence of imported Chinese porcelain, led to a demand for more refined tableware. Potters needed clays which were both plastic and white firing, and which they could use either by themselves, or in mixtures with other clays. Ball clays had all of these properties so it became economic

Merchant	Years of operation	Total clay shipped
Austin, John	1720	147 tons
Austin, William	1726-1743	1,950
Austin , Thomas	1754-1758	460
Brown, John	1707-1743	5,835
Brown, Dennis	1743-1754	634
Brown , Robert	1741-1759	2,744
Brown, Robert and Dennis	1754-1758	1,419
Cornell, Thomas	1636-1666	1,534
Cornell	1672	402
Cornell, William	1676-1683	2,818
Gould, Richard	1679-1691	218
Gould, John	1681	11
Gould, George	1691-1713	4,321
Gould, William	1713	110
Hayter, Edmund	1676-1738	8,156
Hayter, John	1738-1743	514
Hunt, Robert	1676-1681	2,068
Hunt, Jeremiah	1681-1683	600
Hyde, Thomas	1691-1720	5,727
Hyde, Elizabeth	1720	318
Hyde, George	1726-1743	6,918
Hyde, George and son	1754-1759	4,597
Sarjeant, John	1677-1683	343
Smith, Dennis	1676-1707	4,792
	Total	63,537

The table shows some of the main families of clay shippers in Poole between 1636 and 1759. It shows the periods when different members of the families were active and gives an indication of the weight of clay each shipped over that period. The figures are not precise, but they do show how one generation of a family succeeded another as each retired.

Men working in the South Western pottery claypits. This scene, photographed in about 1912, shows men cutting clay in a large pit using spades. It gives a good idea of what a working claypit in the seventeenth and eighteenth centuries might have looked like.

to transport clay by sea, from Poole and Devon, to the traditional pottery-making centres elsewhere in Britain.

The first pottery of this type was tin-glazed earthenware, which needed a white body, so that the white glaze (in imitation of Chinese porcelain) was not discoloured. Important tin-glaze potteries in the seventeenth century were at Southwark, Rotherhithe,

A clay barge at Ridge Wharf in about 1900. In the years around 1670, clay was being shipped from Poole and Russel Quays in small sailing boats similar in size to this barge.

Use	Period	Notes
Clay tobacco pipes and wig curlers	From around 1590 to the end of the 19th century. Initially in London and Bristol then later in other locations around the UK.	Inland manufacturers commonly used local pipe clay as opposed to ball clay.
Tin-glazed earthenware	In London and other locations in the UK from around 1600 onwards.	------------
Brown salt-glazed Stoneware	Around 1670 onwards in London, later in other parts of the country.	Ball clays (pipe clay) important constituent for brown salt-glazed stoneware.
White salt-glazed stoneware	Around 1670 onwards in London, 1720 onwards in Staffordshire.	Ball clays (pipe clay) important constituent for white salt-glazed stoneware.
Creamware and other fine white earthen wares	ca 1760 onwards	Ball clays important constituent in clay mix for creamware. Refined by Wedgwood and other Staffordshire potters.
China	ca 1780 onwards	Ball clay a constituent.
Porcelain	ca 1760 onwards	Ball clay a constituent.
Coade Stone	ca 1760 – 1810, London	Possibly local pipe clay rather than ball clay.
Floor Whiting	18th – 19th century	Possibly local pipe clay rather than ball clay.
Whiting of military equipment	ca 1650 onwards	Possibly local pipe clay rather than ball clay.
Crucibles	17th century onwards	Thought to have been used in the glass industry.
Saggers	18th – 19th century	Supports for china etc in kilns during firing.
Drain pipes and sanitary ware	19th – 20th century	Brown salt-glazed stoneware drainpipes and white earthenware sanitary ware.

and Lambeth in London, which were situated close to the Thames since they were dependent on coastal traffic for supplies of clay.

Production of stoneware in England started with the factory of John Dwight at Fulham in about 1672, and the tobacco pipeclay he used to produce this stoneware came from Poole. The demands of the London potters for tobacco pipeclay resulted in an increase in the clay shipped to London from about 1,000 tons in 1660 to over 2,000 tons by 1683, and over 3,000 tons by 1713.

Today, much of the clay extracted from the Isle of Purbeck is shipped to Spain, Portugal, and Italy, where it is used to manufacture ceramic tiles, many of which are then exported back to Britain.

ABOVE A summary of the uses of ball and pipe clays.

BELOW A basket of ball clay, from a display in Poole Museum.

NINETEEN

Pottery

WILLIAM SHELDRICK

THE HARBOUR has provided materials for a pottery industry since prehistoric times and is a tradition that has continued, in various forms, around the Harbour until recently. The most important potteries of the area developed as a result of the ceramic and housing boom during the nineteenth century and are described below.

BRANKSEA (BROWNSEA) POTTERY

Colonel William Waugh bought Brownsea Island in 1853, a decision apparently influenced by his wife, an amateur geologist, who noticed the white clay deposits below the surface. Waugh engaged the services of a geologist who assessed the merit of the high-grade clay and the significant deposits of coloured clays. Waugh, anticipating a profitable return from the exploitation of the clay, purchased the Island for £13,000.

Waugh invested heavily in the infrastructure and no expense was spared in building the new pottery on the south-west corner of the Island. The Pottery was a three-storey building containing seven large kilns and three engine rooms containing a 13 horsepower beam engine, a 16 horsepower horizontal steam engine and a steam brick-making machine. There was also a smaller building, known as the Terracotta and Architectural Pottery Works, equipped to manufacture chimney pots, fire bricks, and more ornate ware.

Clay from the Seymour Pit area on the north of the Island was transported by horse-pulled wagons on a 1¼-mile-long railway to the main potteries, with sidings to the Seymour Pit Pier, the New Pier and Pottery Pier. A small village grew up to house the more than 200 workers.

Although every technical facility had been provided it proved impossible to produce the fine porcelain which Waugh had hoped for and by 1857 he was bankrupt, owing his bank £250,000. He and his wife fled to Spain, which then had no treaty for the extradition of fraudulent bankrupts. The workers left the Island and for the next 13 years the courts deliberated over its ownership. In

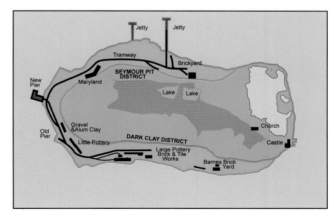

LEFT The main evidence of Colonel Waugh's Pottery Works is the sherds of broken pottery on the south-west corner of Brownsea Island.

BELOW Brownsea Island, showing the areas associated with the clay industry.

A general view of the pottery works on Brownsea Island in about 1880.

1870 Brownsea was sold by the London and Eastern Banking Corporation to George Cavendish-Bendink, who formed the Branksea Island Company Limited and continued to run the brick and tile industry until 1887. By 1901 the pottery buildings had all disappeared.

The Patent Architectural Pottery, Hamworthy, in 1855.

THE PATENT ARCHITECTURAL POTTERY

The Patent Architectural Pottery opened in Hamworthy in 1854 to make coloured glazed bricks, mouldings and tiles. The excellent design and quality of its products were soon well-known and it won awards in London and Paris. The Prince Consort is reported to have recommended its wares. The firm continued in business for more than forty years before it was taken over by a rival firm, Carter and Company.

CARTER AND COMPANY

In 1861, the chief pottery technician at Hamworthy Architectural Pottery, James Walker, left the company and set up a pottery on the East Quay to make red tiles. This business did not prosper and in 1873, after it had gone bankrupt, it closed. The part-derelict pottery was taken over by Jesse Carter, a building merchant and ironmonger from Surrey. Carter moved to Poole, restarted the business as Carter and Company and increased its range of building products to include cement, produced from Purbeck limestone. He re-established the red tile business and increased the range of glazed and painted wall tiles.

By the early 1880s the business was flourishing and was not only challenging its local rival in Hamworthy but also some of the Staffordshire producers. In 1895 Carter and Co. acquired Hamworthy Architectural Pottery and more land was acquired at East Quay to become the major part of Poole Pottery works.

In 1902 Jesse Carter retired and handed control of the potteries to his two sons, Charles and Owen. It was mainly through the work of Owen as the Art and Technical Director, together with Radley Young, head of the Design Department, that the company was able to establish itself in a pre-eminent position in the increasingly popular field of art ceramics. At the same time the demand for tiles, mainly white and cream, was outstripping the capacity of the East Quay works. A large works was purchased in 1912 in Hamworthy which left the East Quay works to concentrate on the art products. Despite a setback in production during the First World War the design and product range increased and in 1921 the company of Carter, Stabler and Adams (CSA) was formed as a subsidiary of the Carter Company

Hand-decorating pots at Poole Pottery in the 1930s.

ABOVE LEFT The three storey East Quay pottery, bought by Jesse Carter in 1873.

ABOVE An 1896 advertisement for Carter & Company.

to produce ornamental and domestic pottery. Over the next 20 years the new company produced a wide range of decorative tiles and stoneware in many different colours, decorations and finishes.

A Poole Pottery tile panel of about 1930, painted with a map of Poole designed by Edward Bawden.

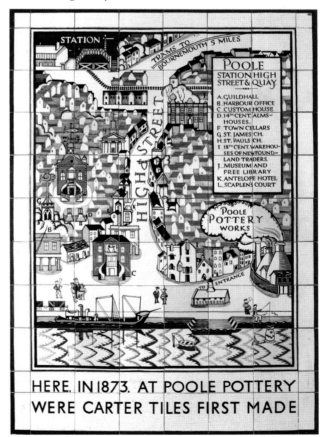

A tile panel made by Carter & Company in the 1950s and now in Poole Museum.

The Second World War was a difficult period for CSA with little demand for their high-grade decorated products, but they survived. Harold Stabler died in 1945 and with John Adam in poor health the responsibility fell to Charles Carter's son Cyril to revive the business. A new kiln was built and by 1948 the pottery was at full production again. Although much of this production was based on the highly regarded pre-war range, contemporary hand-thrown and hand-painted pieces of excellent quality were also introduced – many of which are now collectors' pieces. Other ranges such as Delphis and Aegean were very successful. In 1964 Carter, Stabler and Adams became part of the Pilkington Group and the name of the company was changed to Poole Pottery Limited. A management buy-out took place in 1992 and the new company expanded its activities in the area. Although some design work is still done in Poole, the production is now based at Burslem, Stoke on Trent.

SOUTH-WESTERN POTTERY

George Jennings was born in Southampton in 1810 He was trained as a plumber and aged 21 he went to London to further his career. A few years later, using a small legacy received from his grandmother, he set up his own business, first in Lambeth and then in Blackfriars, where he prospered. He was hard working but, more important, inventive in applying his increasing experience and skills in the new sanitation industry. After several of his new inventions had been accepted by industry, he was awarded the Medal of the Society of Arts, personally presented by the then Prince Consort. He later received a medal for arranging the sanitation facilities for the Great Exhibition of 1851. He also constructed the sanitary fittings for the British Hospitals in the Crimea, which were fitted by his own workmen. He conceived and patented an improvement in the construction of stoneware drainpipes but, unable to secure its introduction by London potters, he decided to do so himself.

In 1856 he secured the leases of three clay beds near Poole and founded the South Western Pottery, which became famous over the next century for the manufacture of stoneware pipes. A large quantity of coal was required to fire the kilns and initially this was imported by ship from Newcastle, via Town Quay. The stoneware products were then exported again to Jennings's factory wharf in Lambeth. Jennings was not happy with these arrangements, or with the amount of harbour dues he was paying to use Town Quay, so he constructed his own pier into the Harbour at the Salterns, Lilliput, which had the advantage of being much nearer to his pottery. The pier was a solid embankment about 500 feet long, and extended another 100 feet into the-then Main Channel

ABOVE An advertisement for the South Western Pottery.

BELOW Map showing the location of the South Western Pottery and its rail links.

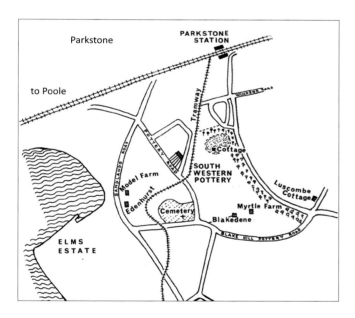

A general view of the Kinson Pottery in about 1885.

them with houses and a school for their children. He died in a road accident in 1882 but his sons continued to run the pottery until 1903 when it was taken over by Thomas Wragg & Sons Ltd. It continued until 1969 when the site was sold, the pottery demolished, and a housing estate built.

THE KINSON POTTERY

A pottery had been established on a site on the Ringwood Road about two miles north of Poole before 1850 but had not been successful. A new company took it over in 1856 and established it as the 'Kinson Clay Fields Pottery Company' to exploit the extensive deposits of clays on the site and produced a range of pottery ware, fire goods and bricks. By the 1860s the works had twelve kilns operating and was exporting its firebricks as far away as Canada.

In 1884 the business was acquired by William Carter, the son of Jesse Carter who owned the pottery on East Quay. The main product line of stoneware, drain pipes and terracotta goods sold well and the business continued to prosper. In 1908, William Carter retired and was succeedsed by his son Herbert Carter who ran the company successfully until he died in 1956: he was a well-known and much respected citizen of Poole with a fine record of public service.

THE SHARP JONES AND CO.
BOURNE VALLEY POTTERY,

The first clay was dug on the Branksome site in 1873, serving the pottery situated on the present John Lewis site at the junction of Ashley Road and Bournemouth

by a timber pier. The goods were transported by a horsedrawn tramway which was replaced, in 1872, by a steamdriven railway.

George Jennings also built up a business as a sanitary engineer, particularly in the design of public lavatories, during the period he was making sanitary pottery. He posthumously won for his firm the Grand Prix in Paris in 1890 for his symphonic pan, a major development in lavatory design. He was remembered as a good employer who looked after his workers well, providing

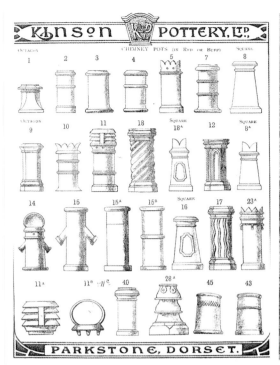

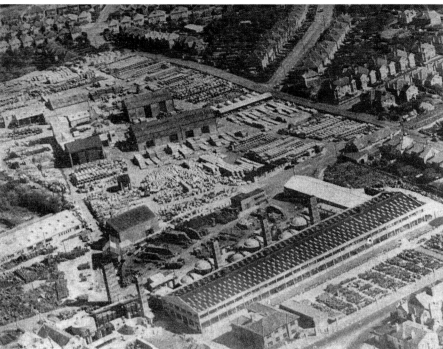

Road. In 1886, additional clay deposits were acquired at Bourne Bottom, and two sites connected by a standard-gauge railway line.

The products were stoneware, tiles, and bricks, but in 1875 the Company was one of the first in the UK to produce concrete pipes for drainage. During the Second World War most of the Company's pipes were used in the construction of airfields, and some products were used in the construction of the Mulberry Harbour.

After the War, the operation of the clay pits became uneconomic and, in 1948, the pits and the railway were closed, the factory then concentrating wholly on the production of concrete pipes. In 1961 the operation was taken over by Redland Pipes and the range of products increased to include spun glass-fibre pipes.

Production ceased in 1981, the Bourne Valley works closed and the whole site has since been redeveloped.

SANDFORD POTTERIES LIMITED
(COLVILLE, SANDFORD AND ALSTON LTD)

Sandford Pottery, located to the north of the Harbour between Poole and Wareham, was built in 1856 on the same site as the Victoria Brick Works which had started some years earlier, and whose bricks had been used in the building of the Crystal Place for the Great Exhibition in 1851.

The pottery was built to produce high-grade china ware. Unfortunately, after two or three years the

ABOVE An aerial view of the Sharp Jones and Co. Bourne Valley Pottery in the 1950s, a site now occupied by John Lewis and other retail outlets at the junction of Ashley Road and Bournemouth Road, Branksome.

ABOVE LEFT The range of chimney pots made by Kinson Pottery, many of which can still be seen on houses in the area today.

available clay was found to be unsuitable for making china, and production ceased. Little information is available on the history of the pottery over the following three decades, except that a succession of companies attempted to run the business, most of which ended in failure and bankruptcy. One of these ventures was an attempt to convert the pottery into a works to extract oil from Kimmeridge Oil Shale, but this was unsuccessful due to the high sulphur content of the result and its obnoxious smell when burning.

Colville, Sandford and Alston Ltd revived its fortunes by producing architectural pottery from 1882 to meet the demands of the building boom in the Bournemouth and Poole area.

In 1920 there was a further change to the Sandford Pottery Company. While apparently prospering, unfavourable trading conditions in the 1960s forced the company to close. The plant was demolished in 1979.

THE BRICK INDUSTRY

The earliest references to brick-making around the Harbour are in Taylor's map of Brownsea Island (1770) showing Barnes Brick Works, and Parkstone (1765). Greenwood's map of Dorset in 1825 shows brick production at Kinson, West Howe, Upton, Broadstone, and Hamworthy. In addition to the six major potteries that started up in the second half of the nineteenth century around the Harbour, most of which also made bricks, it is estimated that by 1900 there were about 20 smaller brick producers operating. Their main markets were the expanding towns of Poole and Bournemouth, and increased construction associated with the introduction of the railway to the area.

By 1930 many of the small brickyards had closed or had been integrated into the operations of the large producers. In 1950 ten were still operating but by 1972 all clay-based brickworks had closed, although the manufacture of calcium silicate bricks continued in one or two locations. The long-established Upton Brick Company, which had been making hard common bricks for almost a century, closed in 1969.

THE END OF THE POTTERY INDUSTRY

In 1960 there were seven pottery companies (listed below) within the Dorset Stoneware Pipe Manufacturers Association, and a number of independent brick companies still operating – within a decade all but one had closed: E. A. Elliot & Sons, West Howe Pottery (Dorset) Ltd, Sandford Potteries Ltd., George Jennings's South Western Pottery (Thomas Wragg & Sons Ltd),

ABOVE The Alder Road claypits in about 1912.

BELOW The remains of the eighteenth century Barnes Brick Works on Brownsea Island.

Sharp Jones & Company Ltd., Kinson Pottery Ltd., Dorset Clay Products Ltd., and W. Sykes and Sons Ltd..

Most of these companies had been operating for more than a century. Dorset Clay Products with a relatively modern works completed in 1939 was taken over by the Admiralty and did not start pottery production until 1948. The only company not to close its operations was the Dorset Brick and Stone Company (W. Sykes and Sons Ltd) whose products were mainly based on sand and cement. Today, virtually nothing remains of the industry except the pottery-related place-names on housing and modern industrial estates.

TWENTY

Mechanical Engineering

WILLIAM SHELDRICK

A NUMBER OF significant mechanical engineering companies were established in Poole from the middle of the nineteenth century onwards. Whilst not exclusively Harbour-related interests, all of them had products serving maritime outlets, both locally and nationally and, in some cases, internationally.

THE POOLE FOUNDRY

The business on which Poole Foundry was based was founded in Poole by William Pearce, who in 1842 purchased some land in Baiter Green to expand his agricultural implements business. Further land was acquired in 1844 and 1860 and a foundry was established. During this period Pearce's business expanded steadily and in 1850 he was displaying more than 30 different agricultural implements at local and national exhibitions and was employing more than 40 people. An engraving made by George Branning in 1855 indicates the extent of the foundry. In 1863 Pearce sold his business to Lewin and Wilkinson.

Stephen Lewin, an established merchant in Boston, moved to Poole in the early 1860s to support his younger brother Charles a timber merchant. William

The Poole Foundry, an 1855 engraving by George Branning.

An 1876 advertisement for the Poole Foundry.

Wilkinson was also a businessman from Boston who had engineering experience of agricultural machinery. In 1863, Lewin and Wilkinson became partners and bought the business of William Pearce. Part of the agreement was that Wilkinson would run the business in Poole. The partnership was dissolved in 1868 and Wilkinson left the company. Lewin then appointed James Welman, an engineer from Plymouth, to manage the foundry. During a period when British agriculture was thriving to provide food for both sides of the Franco-Prussian War there was a great demand for steam-driven agricultural machines from the Poole Foundry. This was a period of prosperity for Stephen Lewin who generously reduced his staff's working day from 10 to 9 hours. Unfortunately the boom in agriculture was short-lived and Lewin's business declined with it.

In 1874 James Welman retired and Stephen Lewin appointed a young engineer named William J. Tarrant to manage the foundry. Tarrant was experienced in the manufacture of traction engines and it was under his leadership that the products of Poole Foundry for which the Lewin's company is mainly remembered today – locomotives – were built. These new products found

A Poole-built Lewin engine supplied to the Seaham Harbour Dock Co.

A steam tractor built for the Anglo-American Oil Co. by the Dorset Iron Foundry Company Ltd.

many customers and the factory workforce increased to about 200. By 1876 the foundry was able to offer a large range of steam-driven equipment including that for maritime outlets.

Unfortunately, in 1876, a fire broke out in the yacht building shop and considerable damage was done. Much equipment, estimated at more than £12000 was lost, of which only part was covered by insurance. Stephen Lewin suffered further misfortune when a few months later his factory manager William Tarrant resigned to manage another smaller foundry in the town, the Dorset Iron Company Ltd, then owned by Charles Stone. Stephen Lewin was able to persuade his previous manager, James Welman, by offering him a partnership to return to his previous position in the damaged factory and try to restore the business.

After the serious fire Lewin reduced his production of agricultural equipment and concentrated on locomotives and marine work (see the steam yacht on page 150), but was unable to weather the trade depression of the early 1880s. He had to give up the freehold and lease back part of his property to carry on work at the foundry, with James Welman as his partner. Unfortunately the financial situation became worse and the final day of the Poole Foundry came in December 1884 when the remaining stock in trade was put up for auction and sold. It was not until 1890 that a new tenant could be found for the foundry, when the Albion Engine Company, later to be known as the Atlas Engine Company, leased the site to develop its new gas engine. Work was started on the extension of the foundry and the premises were to be known as the Poole Engine Works and employ 300 men. Unfortunately, for reasons not fully known, within 12 months the works closed and that was the end of the Poole Foundry.

THE DORSET IRON FOUNDRY

The Dorset Iron Company was set up in 1859 by the partnership of Munden and Stricken in West Quay Road and around 1870 the business was acquired by C.J. Stone who in 1879 decided to sell off his business. William Tarrant who had only just taken over the job as manager a few months earlier, was able, with local support and financing, to take over the foundry as a going concern with himself remaining as manager. In 1880 a new company was formed, the Dorset Iron Foundry Company, with T.S. Richardson as the first director and Tarrant as shareholder and in charge of the business. Tarrant, who had been successful in the Poole Foundry, was able to use the experience and contacts he acquired there to help develop the production of locomotives and other steam engines by the Dorset Iron Foundry. It is known that two locomotives built by Tarrant were shipped to New Zealand, one in 1881 and

Inside the works of the Dorset Iron Foundry Company Ltd in about 1935.

the other in 1882.

Although the iron foundry of Stephen Lewin ceased production in 1984, the Dorset Iron Foundry Company managed by Farrant carried on for many more years. Ironically part of their work was to help maintain and repair equipment that Tarrant had produced when working for the Poole Foundry. There are records of the Dorset Iron Foundry continuing its business in West Quay Road until 1964.

THE SALTERNS – LILLIPUT

Houses close to the Harbour's edge at Lilliput are now some of the most expensive in the Borough; yet few of their owners appreciate that they are built on disused industrial land. Industrialisation of the area started around 1564 when Lord Mountjoy, owner of the Canford Estate built a works to produce copperas from alum shale mined locally using peat as fuel (Chapter 15). This operation lasted for about 50 years and was followed about 100 years later by a commercial salt works, also owned by the Canford Estate, with peat-fired boiling houses crystallising salt from seawater drawn from ponds within what is now known as the Blue Lagoon (Chapter 14). Afterwards, for more than a century, there was a substantial brick kiln on the Elms Estate.

In 1867, George Jennings of South Western Pottery constructed a 500 yard long pier from the Sandbanks Road out into the main channel of the Harbour. The pier was for bringing in coal to fire the kilns, and to ship out the finished products. Soon Jennings connected the pier to the pottery with a railway line, extending through to Parkstone Station (Chapter 19) which was in use until the 1920s.

The First World War required increased industrial production, and the connections to both the railway network and coastal sea routes made Lilliput an ideal location. Factories were erected in what is now Salterns Way and Dorset Lake Avenue. One of these involved the making and repairing of railway wagons, another built timber-framed buildings, including aircraft hangers, for the Air Board. Near the end of the War came two separate initiatives to develop the lagoon and Jennings's pier into major shipbuilding works which would have changed the character of the area forever.

First, and most ambitious was a 1917 proposal by The Dorset Shipbuilding Company to construct a shipyard which would have employed 10,000 men and required raising £2 million in capital. Both Poole Council and the Harbour Commissioners supported the proposal. This failed, it is believed, because existing shipbuilding interests in Tyneside and Scotland, fearful of southern competition, lobbied the Treasury to limit the amount of capital to be raised.

In 1918 came a second, more realistic scheme spearheaded by one of the manufacturers already on the site, a Mr Alban Richards. He purchased the lagoon, pier, and surrounding land from Lord Wimborne, formed a company [Salterns Ltd] with several well-respected local directors, published a prospectus explaining his development proposals and went to the Stock Market to raise more than £100,000 capital.

The main purposes of Salterns Limited, as outlined in its prospectus to raise capital for the project in November 1919, were to establish a shipyard and ship-repair base and engineering works and to further develop the existing general engineering and woodworking factory existing at the Salterns to include the building and repair of heavy transport vehicles for both road and rail.

For reasons which are not yet clear, within four years the company had failed and the land was sold off. The only reminder today is the inner basin of Salterns Marina, (see page 232) built in 1922, but had Salterns Ltd succeeded, the Harbour frontage at Lilliput would have changed beyond all recognition.

HAMWORTHY ENGINEERING

The history of Hamworthy Engineering goes back to around 1912 when Percy Hall and his brother Sydney Hall formed the company, taking its name from where the original works was located. With only six employees originally, the business eventually grew to employ more than 2000 in 1955 when it moved to its new premises in Fleets Corner.

The company initially made a variety of products, including air compressors, oil engines, and hoists and winches, but plans to develop this range were halted during the First World War when the company was involved in military and armament production. In 1915 Hamworthy Engineering set up its own foundry to produce high grade castings. Unfortunately, in 1938 a fire in the pattern shop destroyed engine patterns and effectively ended the production of the engine business. During the Second World War the company maintained its normal line of pumps and compressors which were needed for the war effort. In 1954 in association with the Hydreco Division of the US Company, New York Air Brake, Hamworthy Hydraulics, a 50 per cent owned subsidiary of Hamworthy Engineering was formed to produce and sell hydraulic equipment.

In 1962 Powell Duffryn acquired the interests of

Hamworthy Engineering and the 50 per cent share of Hamworthy Hydaulics, and in 1993 the David Brown Group purchased Hamworthy Hydaulics and Hamworthy transmissions. In 1995 the Hamworthy Hydraulics business changed its name to David Brown

ABOVE A Harveys 'Skylark' pleasure boat, built in Poole, passing the original Hamworthy Engineering works, probably in the 1920s.

BELOW An aerial view of the Hamworthy Engineering works at Fleet's Corner in 1955.

The growth of engineering and manufacturing works, together with an increasing population, led to the building of the Poole Power Station in 1949/50 alongside Holes Bay in Hamworthy. It was demolished in the early 1990s.

Hydraulics.

In 2000 Powell Duffryn PLC was acquired by Nikko Principal Investments. Hamworthy Engineering, now known as Hamworthy, has since sold certain low growth activities and developed new products. The company specialises in innovative and customised designs for marine gas handling, pumping and waste treatment systems, as well as compressors and rudders. Hamworthy employs over 1,100 people. It still has its headquarters at Fleets Corner and has design, development, and production facilities in the UK, Norway, Denmark, Singapore, and a modern assembly plant in China.

The once familiar motif of British Seagull.

BRITISH SEAGULL

The manufacture of British Seagull outboard engines was an important and well-known industry in Poole for nearly 60 years. The earliest engine to carry the Seagull name was the Marston Seagull, first produced in the early 1930s by the Sunbeam Motor Cycle Company. The original engine was designed by Marston Engineers from whom John Way-Hope, a former employee, and Bill Pinninger, a design engineer, purchased the manufacturing rights and patents and developed the engine further. In 1938 they moved to premises on Poole Town Quay and the name was changed to British Seagull. The engine, proclaimed as the best outboard engine in the world, was essentially the model 102 introduced in 1935 and which continued until 1979. During the Second World War large numbers were produced for light assault craft, barges, and pontoon bridge building.

The experience gained during the War helped British Seagull develop a range of robust new engines. By the mid-1950s the company moved to new premises at Fleets Bridge and in the 1960s and 1970s production reached a yearly rate of nearly 80,000 units.

In 1982 British Seagull moved again, to Newtown Business Park, and in 1987 launched the 'QB' series including the 6 hp Kingfisher, followed by the 5 hp Osprey, and the 4 hp Curlew. Sadly, production finally ceased in 1996, by which time more than one million engines had been built. Fortunately, responsibility for the British Seagull name was taken over by Sheridan Marine on the River Thames in Oxfordshire who continue the manufacture and supply of spare parts.

TWENTY-ONE
Brewing

RAYMOND FARLEIGH

ORIGINALLY A HOUSEHOLD ACTIVITY, the origins of commercial brewing around the Harbour are likely to remain lost in the mists of time. Given the role of beer as a staple foodstuff one would imagine the family trade to have been its early mainstay, but Poole's maritime connections would have created an additional demand for the product for ship's stores, as well as providing an incentive to acquire or build public houses to cater for 'Jack ashore'.

A history of the brewing industry in Dorset. which includes exports of ales and malt from Poole, is included in volume two of *The Victoria County History of Dorset* (1908). A considerable amount of hops was being imported into Poole from the Netherlands in the reign of Edward IV, indicating a changing taste to hopped liquor. The export trade in ale to the Channel Islands was also considerable in the fifteenth century, with records not only of ordinary ale but 22 casks of 'byre' worth £22. Malt was also exported and in September 1467 the *Mary of Poole* included in her cargo 12 quarters of malt valued at 4 shillings per quarter. The export trade in beer with the Channel Islands continued to thrive during the reigns of Elizabeth and James I, involving the brewers in litigation with the corporation who levied tax of 1d per kilderkin on all beer thus exported.

In the following centuries some named brewers appear, albeit with their locations uncertain and their importance conjectural. This picture comes a little clearer from the mid eighteenth century with the Dolphin Brewery in Market Street operating by the 1750s and Dean's (later Miller's) in Hill Street by the 1780s.

The nineteenth century dawned with the area's major breweries all established and the tied house system of pub ownership beginning to entrench. But there were also a number of minor brewers and a handful of home-brewing houses still active, and the production and sale of beer positively encouraged by the authorities as a perceived remedy for the evils of excessive gin drinking.

As the Victorian age wore on, the business became

The remains of Panton's Brewery, Wareham, in 2007.

increasingly sophisticated with advances in engineering and more particularly in chemistry, but at the same time moved further from the economic mainstream. Such improvements as safe drinking water, and more affordable Indian tea, meant that beer was no longer Hobson's Choice on the nation's table, and the brewers became ever more closely identified with their public houses. Fortunately for the two big Poole breweries this change coincided with the phenomenal rise of neighbouring Bournemouth, where many of their larger pubs were to be built.

Of the three major breweries operating around the Harbour in the nineteenth century probably the largest was that of H.J. Panton and Co. in Pound Lane, Wareham. In their heyday they ran two subsidiary breweries in Swanage and Ringwood but, although they owned a number of pubs in Poole and round about, their main presence was on the Isle of Purbeck and in a wide

On the left is Marston's Dolphin Brewery on West Quay Road, with the offices of the Hants and Dorset Mineral Water Co. on the right. Photographed in in 1968, six years before its demolition to make way for the St. Aubyns Court development.

area through Ringwood to Southampton. Bought out by Strong's of Romsey in 1892, this Wareham brewery was closed and dismantled in 1989 but most of the buildings survive as residential accommodation.

The older and larger of the two in Poole itself was the Dolphin Brewery with its counting house in Market Street and the brewery buildings bordering on Levets Lane. Claiming to be established in 1745, it is certainly recorded as a malthouse by 1751 and a

Bottles from Poole's breweries.

brewhouse by 1773. Originally constructed by the Strong family whose memorial tablet survives in the gallery of St. James's Church, it became Adey's in 1818 and Hickman's c.1839. It went through a difficult period in the 1860's as did so many Poole businesses, and in 1862 was unsuccessfully put up for sale as a valuable 15-quarter plant worked by steam power with two malthouses and 16 public houses. About this time the commercial (as distinct from the in-house) malting side was sold off to become the genesis of another Poole dynasty, Christopher Hill's. The brewery recovered under a partnership which included one John Taylor Marston of Sleaford, who became sole proprietor in 1887 by which time it was firmly re-established. When it was incorporated as Marston's Dolphin Brewery Ltd in 1897 it had grown into a 40-quarter plant with 59 tied houses. In 1913 the former Balston's twine works on West Quay Road was acquired and turned into a new malt house served by the Quay railway line.

In 1926, Marston's, like Panton's before them, were taken over by Strong and Co. of Romsey (there is no connection with the family of the brewery's first owners, nor between the Marston's of Sleaford and Poole and those of Burton). Brewing stopped, but Strong's continued to use the brewery as a bottling and distribution depot and to work the depot until 1935. Poole Corporation purchased the brewery in 1940, partly for conversion into an air-raid shelter. Ironically, it was severely bomb-damaged but was sold after the war to Wessex Industries Ltd. for a fork-lift truck factory. It was demolished in 1974 to make way for the St. Aubyns Court development, and the West Shore malthouse followed suit a year later. Surviving reminders are the tiled frontage of the former Swan Inn in Lagland Street and assorted dolphin motifs on the Goat and Tricycle, the Dolphin in Holdenhurst Road and the Ensbury Park Hotel, all in Bournemouth (the last currently obscured), and the former George Inn in New Milton.

The second Poole concern, Styring's Poole Brewery on Towngate Street advertised itself as 'Established 1795'. At that time its founder, Joseph King, was landlord of the Angel and owner of the old Bull's Head in the High Street, but whether he brewed at either, or elsewhere, remains to be discovered. In 1818, however, he acquired an eighteenth century malt house in Dear Hay Lane which had been operated by Miller's brewery (see above) and built a new brewery alongside, which was run from the outset by his sons Joseph II and James. They acquired at least three inns through the 1820s and a second brewery in Christchurch in 1832, to where James King moved. The brothers both died in 1852 and the Christchurch trade passed to James's children. The

Poole Brewery estate passed into trust for Joseph King II's natural children and was leased. In 1856 it was sold to Frederick Styring and Martin Forrest Kemp-Welsh, who died young, two years later, leaving Styring the sole owner. He built up an extensive tied estate in Poole and Bournemouth as far east as Lymington, and extended the brewery complex across Dear Hay Lane and northwards along Towngate Street. Always one among many of his business interests, Alderman Styring in 1879 leased and in 1881 sold the brewery and 35 houses to George Pope (brother of Alfred and Edwin Pope of the brewery then rising up in Dorchester) and Robert Walmsley. They continued to trade as Styring, modernised the brewery in 1882, and continued the northward extensions culminating in 1883 with the malthouse, backing on Nightingale Lane, which was to be a Poole landmark for the next 70 years.

In 1900 Styring's were taken over by Eldridge Pope and the brewery building to the south of Dear Hay Lane was sold to wholesale grocers Mundell and Bollam who reputedly smoked bacon over oak chips in the old malt kiln and boiled ham in the brewing copper – certainly the latter was not taken out until between the wars. They relocated to Fleets Bridge and by the 1960s the old brewery had become K.E. Goddard shoe warehouse and was subsequently Weston's DIY Timber supplies until demolished in 1981. Today the Job Centre Plus stands on the site.

ABOVE J.T. Marston and the staff of Marston's Dolphin Brewery in about 1880.

BELOW Styring & Co in about 1885.

Eldridge Pope retained the northern buildings as a distributive depot and bottling stores and continued to work the maltings and to use Styrings bonded warehouse (Poole No. 4 Bond) on West Quay Road for maturing

ABOVE Styrings Brewery from the air in the 1930s.

BELOW The Pure Drop Inn in East Street was originally built as the East Street Brewery in 1831, hence the hoist and the louvred shutters just visible above the flag on the left.

whiskies in cask prior to removal to Dorchester for blending. Malting was discontinued in 1955 and bottling in about 1959, when the distribution side went to Eldridge Pope's Boscombe depot. The corner shop was kept on and the extensive vaulted cellars used for storing wine. The bonded warehouse was relinquished in 1969 and the remaining buildings were demolished in the late twentieth century and replaced by the Malthouse Flats.

So is there anything left to see? In Wareham there are the extensive, if heavily converted, remains of Panton's Brewery in Pound Lane, with a row of the workers' cottages in St. John's Hill, and the malthouse (similarly converted) of the smaller Bennett's Brewery by the bridge on Abbott's Quay. In Poole Old Town the Pure Drop Inn in East Street was built in about 1831 as the East Street Brewery and ceased brewing in 1860, the louvered brewhouse shutters and hoist beam are the giveaway and the functions room is the old malthouse (and the functions room of the Royal Oak and Gas Tavern next door was another). The Quay Advice centre in Hill Street preserves the façade of the old Whitbread bottling stores, converted from a corn store by the celebrated London brewers in 1897 and later enlarged, hence the

Poole's pubs included the Shipwrights Arms on the quay at Hamworthy and the Poole Arms on Town Quay. The Shipwrights Arms was first mentioned in 1500 as an ale house, and was originally a passage house for passengers waiting to board ferries for the Purbecks. It was demolished in 1978. The facade of the Poole Arms is covered with tiles made by Carters, and bears the coat-of-arms of the borough – a dolphin and three scallop shells.

'erected 1905' datestone – everything behind was pulled down and rebuilt in 1998.

Finally, and further along Hill Street, 'The Old Brewery' was the premises of the Poole (micro) Brewery, which having started in Sterte Avenue in 1980 moved to the rear of the newly opened Brewhouse pub in 1983, staying until 2002 when it was taken over by the Milk Street Brewery, another micro brewery of Poole, and converted into apartments. The present building is basically the result of a rebuild in 1991 to which it has remained remarkably faithful despite the raising of the roof to insert a third storey.

TWENTY-TWO
Ship and Boatbuilding

JEAN SUTTON

THE DEVELOPMENT OF shipbuilding through the ages is a fascinating story that can be broken down into four types of hull construction, all of which are represented in the story of shipbuilding associated with

Poole's 33 foot long Iron Age log boat is hollowed out of a single long and dates from about 300 BC. The top photograph shows as it was when first brought ashore in 1964, the lower photograph as it is today displayed in Poole Museum.

the Harbour:

- Carved from a single piece of timber.
- Fabricated from planking assembled in various ways.
- Constructed from sheet iron/ steel.
- Cast from materials such as concrete or more polyester/glass fibre.

The first of these is well represented by the Iron Age log boat that dates from about 300 BC and is now in the Poole Museum. Such vessels would have been used for transporting people and goods within the Harbour and possibly for short voyages outside it.

Little is known about subsequent types of construction used around the Harbour until after the Norman Conquest when shipbuilding became an important element of the local economy. Planked construction was known from the Bronze Age, and ships trading with the Harbour during later prehistory would have been of this type with construction on the Continent or in Britain.

The conditions necessary for building vessels, from the simplest inshore craft to the largest naval ship of the line, remained the same from prehistory until the development of iron ships in the mid-nineteenth century: a firm base, a 'hard', on which to lay the supports for the keel; an incline to launch the vessel; and a channel of sufficient depth and width to ensure it did not go aground. Few permanent structures were needed: a forge to make the small amount of ironwork, a fire for the pitch, a pit for the bottom sawyer to stand in and a mouldloft floor on which to draw the frames to scale. The *Elephant* onboard which Nelson raised his telescope to his blind eye during the Battle of Copenhagen was built by Poole shipwright George Parsons on just such a hard on the banks of the River Hamble in Hampshire in 1786. Poole and Hamworthy were both resilient

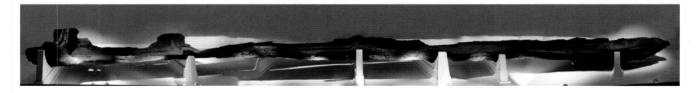

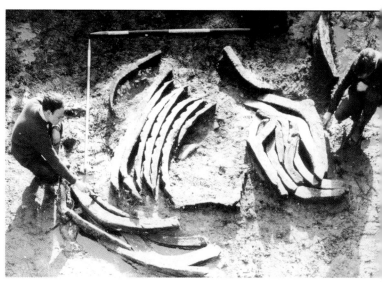

ABOVE The Seal of Poole of 1325 shows a fairly large merchant ship, a 'navis', suggesting that Poole was a prosperous port.

BELOW This sketch depicting the ship on the seal shows a vessel with a distinct bow and stern, as opposed to the normal double-end for the period, and an integral quarterdeck, both recent innovations at that time.

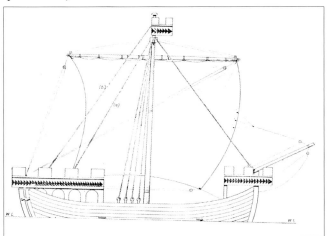

David Watkins (left) by the store of late fourteenth, early fifteenth century boat timbers which he unearthed in 1986/7 on what was then the shore, where they would have been regularly immersed at high tide. The timbers would have been used to construct a small working boat. There was a long tradition of boatbuilding on this site until reclamation overtook it.

peninsulas of harder rock not too far from the Harbour entrance. From its development as an important port soon after the Norman Conquest, Poole shipwrights were able to build vessels required for all purposes, from ferries to foreign traders.

Like most ports round the coast, Poole's governing body chose a vessel to portray the port for its seal in 1325, indicating, no doubt, the best the shipwrights of Poole were capable of at the time. They had much to be proud of. This 'navis', or ship, represented the final development of the medieval trading vessel: it combined the great cargo carrying capacity of the 'hulk' with the speed and seaworthiness of the 'snake' or Viking ship and had an integral quarterdeck. Its single sail probably sported the heraldic device of Poole's overlord, the Earl of Salisbury, prominently displayed as a shield on the seal.

In 1986-7 a store of new and salvaged boat timbers was unearthed during excavations on what had been the western shore near St James's Church, where they would have been regularly immersed with the tides. There were some fifty-three timbers, most of them large cut knees but also V-shaped timbers, notched out for clinker planking. They appeared so fresh that the chisel marks could be seen on the timber. They show that the vessels of the late fourteenth and early fifteenth centuries were built using similar materials and construction methods. On an elm keel, frames were erected, each made up from a series of curved oak timbers on to which overlapping oak planks were riveted and sealed with moss. These particular timbers would have been used to construct a boat up to 30 feet long with a beam of ten or twelve feet for coastal work or fishing, but the principles remained the same.

The great increase in Poole's foreign trade, with its dominance of the Newfoundland fishing trade, demanded improved technology in sails and rigging, but the construction of the hulls varied little. The hull of the brig, the most popular foreign trading vessel and the workhorse of the eighteenth century, differed from that of the 'navis' only in being longer in proportion to width, and having flush planks instead of overlapping; that is, it was carvel rather than clinker built. After the launch the best seamen the port could produce set up the standing and running rigging and bent the sails. The brig had two masts, square-rigged on both fore and main mast, each with mainsail, topsail, and royal.

Old maps and charts, supported by documentary evidence, show that shipyards occupied the western shore of Poole itself and the Hamworthy shore, generally referred to as Hamside, opposite. The records are silent on the builders of most of the early vessels. Meadus & Co. emerge briefly in the 1760s and re-emerge a century later, continuing in business for three decades under various names: Thomas Meadus, Thomas Meadus & Sons, W. Meadus and W. & T. Meadus. Manlaws appear in 1820 and, after inter-marriage with the Wanhill family, carry on business under various members of that family until the end of the century. Chislett & Lewis and Musselwhite, both small boat builders, appear briefly in the records before the end of the nineteenth century and various members of the Allen family built small boats from the mid-nineteenth century until the end of the twentieth. Ashton & Kilner were very productive in the first two decades of the twentieth century, and Newman operated for the major part of the century.

In some cases members of the same family built and owned the vessels: the 87 ton brig *James* was built in 1834 by Robert Slade for the Slade family business, and traded between Poole, Newfoundland, and North America. The 146 ton brig *Love and Unity* was built in 1817 by Cox & Slade, again for the family business. In 1875 the 82 ton ketch *Triumph* was built by W & T Meadus for themselves. She holds the unique position of being the only vessel recorded as 'never heard of more' after leaving Gioga with a cargo of palm oil. Ships were wrecked – surprisingly few – but no others foundered. In 1848 J and J. M. Wanhill built the 88 ton schooner *Heroine*, (see page 153) and in 1820 built the 74 ton schooner *Thomas* for the family coasting trade between Poole and London. The fishing families, Greenslades and Wills, always built their own vessels.

Old maps show both shipbuilding yards and timber ponds, or 'cambers', where all timbers to be used in ship construction were immersed until about 1800, and masts only thereafter. Although most of the vessels engaged in Poole's staple trade, the Newfoundland cod trade, were 'plantation built', that is built in Newfoundland where the leading merchants had their own extensive shipyards, production increased rapidly in Poole shipyards from the middle of the eighteenth century – sloops for coastal trade and short foreign trading voyages were as popular as brigs – with the greatest growth in the 1760s and

Following the Second World War cruising yachts were built at Newman's boatyard to Len Cox's design, contributing to Poole's growing reputation for building the best yachts in the country. In this view from left to right are *Quest II*, *Baluta*, *Fiona*, and *Theodora*.

This sketch by Leslie M. Ward (1851-1922) shows a boat being repaired at Kilner's Yard, Hamworthy, which built mainly small vessels during the early years of the twentieth century.

1780s, gradually decreasing from the early decades of the nineteenth century. We know from a government survey in 1804 that there were five shipbuilding yards in Poole employing 23 shipwrights and 43 apprentices, but these figures do not include the large numbers of sawyers, caulkers, carpenters, and unskilled labourers. This comparatively large workforce reflects the advantage gained by Poole shipbuilders from the spurt of trade with Europe brought about by favourable conditions following the renewal of the war with France in 1803. Several merchants imported the timber used in the Poole shipyards from North America and the Baltic. Three rope-walks at what is now the bus station, Baiter, and the southern tip of the Hamworthy peninsula provided the cordage, while at the same time meeting government contracts. All over Dorset, cottages with rows of large windows on the upper floors survive, indicating where sails were woven from the flax and hemp grown in the

Brit valley. The records of several vessels state specifically 'sails by Pipler', a local sailmaker.

Building the vessel was only the start. Most of the work in a shipyard concerned the maintenance and repair of vessels which returned to their home yard at regular intervals. The splendid charcoal drawing of Kilner's Yard by Poole artist Leslie Ward on this page demonstrates this. Two men are engaged in replacing a rotten plank while a third man burns off the accumulated growth on the other side of the hull. This latter process could be done in the careening dock, clearly marked on most early maps, conveniently sited near the ballast quay. Here, after the ballast had been removed, a vessel could be hauled over on one side by means of tackles leading from the masts, and caulking and repairs carried out as well as cleaning the bottom. Some vessels returned to their yards for major structural work.

When trade expanded, shipowners sometimes opted to increase the size of their vessels instead of commissioning expensive new ones to obtain greater tonnage. Robert Slade & Co. had their brig *Mars*, built in 1825, lengthened and almost rebuilt in 1830 to take advantage of the improving trading prospects in the

The brig *David*, 138 tons, built in Poole in 1850 by Miller & Meadus for Thomas and David Slade, represents the most popular type of vessel employed from the mid-eighteenth to the mid-nineteenth century. She traded mainly between Labrador and Leghorn. This is another painting by Michele Renault (see page 152).

The 87 ton two-masted schooner, *Mountaineer*, built in Poole in 1836, was totally wrecked off Ramsay in the Isle of Man in 1873.

longhaul trade between Liverpool and South America. The tonnage of the brig *Bridport*, built in 1773, was more than doubled to 290 tons five years later. From the 1780s, many vessels were 'coppered', covered with sheets of copper to protect the hull from the 'worm'– *teredo navalis*. The 192 ton brig *John King*, built in 1838, was

lengthened in 1839 and returned to the yard at ten-year intervals to be part copper-sheathed, have yellow metal fitted, and to be doubled and sheathed and part-felted. She traded to South Africa and South America and was classed as A1 at Lloyds in 1860.

Shipowners frequently decided to change the rig of their ships to adapt them to different trades or save on manpower. The 180 ton scow *Flora*, built in 1764, was lengthened to 250 tons in 1770 and re-rigged as a ship with a third mast. Typical was *Waterwitch*, built by Thomas Meadus in 1871 as a 206 ton brig, one of the best quality built vessels ever launched from a Poole yard. Her Portsmouth owners bought the timber from redundant stocks in Portsmouth Dockyard. It must have been very old and well seasoned as all except the beams

The Poole Foundry (see Chapter 20), which stood on the site of an old rope walk where the present South Road School stands, began production of steam launches in 1874. By this time wealthy people considered them a status symbol.

DAVID LEWIN, POOLE, DORSET,
Near the Isle of Wight.
FAST STEAM
LAUNCHES & YACHTS
For River or Sea Service,
Of Wood, Iron, or
Steel,
And Machinery adapted for
same;
Excellent References and
Best Work guaranteed.
H350a

Town Quay from Hamworthy in the late nineteenth century, photographed by Ernest Coney.

ABOVE A small locally-built lugger off Town Quay in the early twentieth century.

BELOW 'Gondolier' pleasure boats built by Newman & Sons in the 1920s.

OPPOSITE PAGE TOP The 88 ton topsail schooner *Heroine*, built by J. and J. M. Wanhill in 1848 and part-owned by various members of the Wanhill family, traded between Poole, the Mediterranean and the Azores. She is depicted entering Leghorn in this watercolour by Michele Renault, who painted many of the Poole ships

OPPOSITE PAGE BOTTOM The 156 ton schooner *A La Mode* was built by Cox of Poole for Cox & Co. in 1833 and sheathed in copper to the low water mark between 1836 and 1841. Engaged mostly in the Newfoundland trade, she is shown here entering Leghorn Harbour in 1853.

were 'salted'. Her owners proudly claimed that she was copper-fastened, held together with copper bolts, which was relatively rare. In 1884 she was converted to a barquentine, retaining her labour-intensive square rig on the foremast only, her mainmast being replaced by another mainmast and a mizzenmast, both carrying fore and aft rig. After fifty years as a humble coastal collier she enjoyed a brief spell as a training vessel for Trinity House pilots, who had to serve up to twelve months on a square-rigged ship. She carried her last cargo of coal in 1836, the last square-rigged vessel to sail under the red ensign, but later traded under the Estonian flag and was still afloat in 1944.

Most of the vessels built in Poole followed an honest trade. Few appear to have engaged in questionable activities. The small sloops *Friendship* and *Chesterfield* seized and condemned for unlawful trading were

As well as eight Motor Fishing Vessels Bolson & Sons built for the Royal Navy (bottom right), they also built assault landing craft in their yards during the build-up to D-Day, and the photograph on the right shows the 100th dressed overall.

unlucky: anecdotal history points to many more engaged in smuggling, but not undue numbers. Only two Poole vessels, the *Anne* and another *Friendship*, both belonging to Pike, sailed in about 1740 for Africa to load with slaves for America.

Uniquely, Tito Durrel amongst all the shipbuilders of the seventeenth and eighteenth centuries tendered to build vessels on contract for the Navy. In 1746, during the War of the Austrian Succession, he secured a contract to build a fourteen-gun sloop, 270 tons, the *Viper*, which did convoy duty before sailing for the West Indies. Renamed *Lightning*, she served as a fireship for a brief time before sailing for North America during the Seven Years' War, finally ending her days as she had begun, in convoy and cruising. Her moment of glory came in a Hornblower type attack on a battery at Cedeyra, Cape of Ortegal, where she silenced and dismantled the battery and took and burned 33 coasters. During the long French wars from 1795-1815, while most of the small yards from Bristol to Ipswich sought Navy Board contracts to build brig sloops and gun boats to enforce the blockade of French ports, Poole shipbuilders had sufficient commercial business. Only after the

This 500 ton wooden minesweeper, built by the Dorset Yacht Co., was one of many built there and at Bolson's Yard in the mid-1950s for the Admiralty.

resumption of peace in 1815 did they began to feel the cold blast of international competition.

After 1815, with the increasing liberalization of trade, merchants needed hulls capable of carrying larger cargoes further afield. The schooner, the barque, and the ship – not the 'navis' of earlier times but specifically a vessel with three masts, square-rigged on all masts – rose on the stocks round Poole and Hamworthy shores to meet the challenge of the era of free trade. When the last great monopoly, the East India Company, was removed, multi-masted barques were built for the Far East trade: *Canopus*, 400 tons, launched from Pinney's yard in 1841 and the *Earl of Durham*, 462 tons, built by Willis, were among many which traded to India and New Zealand. But these large vessels traded out of Liverpool, not Poole.

The launch in 1838 of the *Great Britain* steam-powered iron ship from Bristol heralded a decrease in wooden shipbuilding in small south coast ports. But Poole shipbuilders had not been burying their heads in the sand. David Lewin embraced the new age with his wooden or iron steam launches which he sold to men as powerful as the Czar of Russia. Wealthy local gentry were taking to the waters for pleasure and grasped the status symbol a steam-powered vessel offered. Sir Florence Bysshe Shelley, the poet's son, owned three steam-powered cutters, while others preferred the challenge of pitting their skills to harness wind and tide in a sailing craft. The 1860s proved to be a great period for British yacht building, and Poole gained a reputation for building fast boats. Wanhill's, which employed a large number of men, became one of the best-known builders of yachts in Britain. *Egeria* was the yard's largest and most successful yacht.

Poole shipbuilders in the twentieth century more than made up for any lack of patriotic activity in the two preceding centuries. In 1918 concrete barges were built in Poole to fetch armaments and supplies back from Europe. Between 1941 and 1943 J. Bolson & Son built eight motor minesweepers for the Admiralty, all of 165 tons. The Dorset Yacht Co. built Motor Gun Boats, and, with Newman's, motor launches. As the allies prepared for the invasion of Europe all these yards began making assault landing craft. To increase Bolson's output Norton's timber yard on West Quay Road was requisitioned and with improved methods the workforce managed to produce one a day. In the final year of the war Bolson's built eight 50 ton Motor Fishing Vessels for use as auxiliary craft by the Royal Navy.

Early in the Second World War it was agreed that a number of high speed launches would be built by the British Power Boat Company in Poole for dispersal reasons. A yard was opened on the site of former timber merchant Sherry & Haycock in West Quay Road where a hangar was constructed and twenty-one 68 feet long target-towing vessels were built. As the invasion of Europe became imminent construction ceased and the 300-400 strong workforce re-engined and repaired all US and Canadian coastal craft round the clock. Newman's and Dorset Yacht Company built the longer 72 feet Harbour Defence Motor Launches.

In August 1945 three of Bolson's landing craft were adapted to the happier function of excursion boats,

ABOVE The Dorset Lake Shipyard Company in the 1970s.

BELOW A general view of the Sunseeker Yard at Hamworthy from Town Quay. The company was founded in the 1960s, and today employs over 2,500 people working on seven different sites.

returning the firm to its pre-war business. As well as meeting the tourist demand for cruising in local waters the firm started building in steel, producing working boats for the local sand and gravel company, tugs for Shell Tankers Ltd and the United Africa Company and many others. The Admiralty defence programme kept both

Bolson's and the Dorset Yacht Company yard busy in the 1950s: both yards built minesweepers of the 'ham' class and others, but the contracts were not renewed. Bolson's sold its main site and turned to repair and maintenance at its Hamworthy yard, eventually closing that, too, in 1993. The Dorset Yacht Company, which became the Dorset Lake Shipyard Ltd, produced every type of small vessel for a world market before, like Bolson's, limiting operations to repair and maintenance.

With increasing demand for leisure craft in the late 1950s and 1960s, a number of boatyards started up over a wider area, some of which are described further in Chapter 32.

Outstanding amongst these is Sunseeker Ltd, founded in the 1960s from small beginnings by Robert Braithwaite and now pre-eminent as a world–class producer of luxury motor yachts up to 130 feet in length and with plans to develop even larger vessels. With a never-ending choice of navigation and communication equipment, Sunseeker yachts can now operate virtually anywhere in the world.

Hull construction is wholly polyester/glass-fibre supported by wood and other materials of the highest quality. Construction and assembly take place at several sites in and around Poole, currently employing 2500 staff. A network of independent distributors allows Sunseeker to provide a fully-integrated sales and service programme throughout the world.

ABOVE One of Sunseeker's most recent models, the Predator 130.

BELOW Robert Braithwaite at the helm of one of the earliest Sunseekers, the Hostess 17.

The Harbour has thus maintained its position as an important centre of shipbuilding appropriate to the requirement of the time and to the available technology – from the earliest log boat, to the ocean-going vessels of the Middle Ages, to the national requirements of wars from the sixteenth to the twentieth centuries, and now to the most advanced pleasure craft.

TWENTY-THREE

Fishing

DAVID GRANGER

T HE SHELTERED WATERS of the Harbour have
provided valuable fishing for thousands of years.
Certain local geophysical features favour the fisheries.
The combined and conflicting gravitational pull of the
moon and sun on the oceans produces oscillations in the
Atlantic, which are transferred to the English Channel
causing spring and neap tides. The total effect of tidal
movement is a standing wave, the lower component of
which is called a nodal line. In open ocean the nodal
line is reduced to a point, called an amphidrome, by
the rotation of the earth. The tidal oscillation rotates
around the amphidrome. There are no amphidromes in
the English Channel, but the tides along the Dorset coast
behave as though there were an amphidrome situated
inland of Bournemouth. The result of this is that the
Harbour is micro-tidal; having a tidal range less than
two metres, in contrast to twelve metres on the French
coast opposite.

A further consequence of this effect is that the
Harbour is blessed with double high water, in common
with the coast between Portsmouth and Lulworth. The
main low water is followed by the flood tide causing the
main high water. There is then a minor ebb followed by a
second, lesser, high water preceding the main low water.
This produces a relatively long 'stand' of high water in
the Harbour every day, during which the mud flats are
covered. For 16 out of 24 hours the water level in the
Harbour is above mean tide level. Whilst a disadvantage
to the important population of over-wintering waders,
this stand increases the feeding time for the filter-feeding
invertebrates of the mudflats upon which the finfish
depend for food, and hence enriches the fishery.

A lobster fisherman and his family off Town Quay in 1833.

A modern Poole crabbing boat, the *Karen Marie*.

EARLY DEVELOPMENTS

The recent discovery of an Iron Age jetty and workings at Cleavel Point indicates extensive maritime activity in the Harbour at that time, which must surely have included fishing. The Romans sent pickled Poole oysters packed in amphorae back to Rome in exchange for oil and wine. Fish paste was a popular condiment with the Roman legionaries. Black Burnished Ware from Poole found at Hadrian's Wall might well have contained fish paste or salt.

A history of the fisheries of Poole from the Middle Ages until the beginning of the twentieth century is included in the second volume of the *Victoria County History of Dorset* (1908). The *Inquisitiones Nonarum* for 1340 show that Poole fisheries were considerable. Corfe Castle fisheries are mentioned in the Doomsday book and in 1342 the tithes of the fishery at Corfe Castle (mainly herring) were valued at 12d and Studland at 2s. Wareham herring were of great repute in the mid-1300s and Wareham tenants of the manor of Shaftsbury paid their rent in herring. The fishermen of Wareham claimed the right to fish in the Harbour on payment of a nominal fine to the Lord of Corfe Castle.

In 1468 the *Mary of Poole*, with Robert Jackson as master, is recorded as having landed a large catch of herring, on which duty of £1 9s 3d was paid. In 1503 the *Peter of Poole* is recorded as landing a mixed catch of conger, 'breems, couners, and whytyings'. Cod, whiting, rock salmon, grey mullet, and the occasional lobster were the main catch. Seine netting and baited line fishing from the shore also took pilchard and flatfish. These were hawked through the local countryside by fisherwomen, each with her own beat. Fresh fish packed in Dorset – 'dorsers' – was transported to London by fish-jobbers by means of dogcarts drawn by teams of Newfoundland

The *Eclipse*, a Poole fishing boat owned by John Edward Wills coming into the main channel off Studland under full sail.

Part of the Poole fishing fleet under sail in 1912. There were then about 40 boats in the fleets, none of them with an engine.

dogs. By council order, all fish had first to be displayed for sale on the quayside for one hour before it could be sold elsewhere.

In the 1470s, Cornish fishing fleets, and ships from Normandy, the Netherlands, and the Channel Islands traded into Poole. The *George* from Fowey, in 1467

A group of Poole fisherman in about 1900.

brought fish worth 30 shillings. Poole-caught fish, salted and barrelled were sold in London, Spain, Portugal, and Italy. Brownsea Island was noted for crab and shrimp in the seventeenth century.

Poole oysters were famous in the seventeenth century, and were reputed to contain the largest pearls to be found in English waters. According to a long-standing custom the last day's catch of the season was scattered in the Harbour channels to breed and maintain the beds. However, it was not until 1885 that the oyster fishery was officially regulated by licence. In 1887, 200 acres were granted to a local company in Wareham Channel.

Poole oysters, pickled and barrelled, were in great demand in Spain and Italy and as far afield as the West Indies. In 1905 landings valued at £3464 were made. Oyster shells were, by bylaw, dumped on the strand; eventually reaching such a mound that even today many warehouses find their foundations in layers of shells. Oyster shells were also used for making cement.

NEWFOUNDLAND

Following John Cabot's 1479 voyage in the *Matthew* from Bristol, which reported great shoals of huge cod over the Grand Banks off Newfoundland, the adventurous fishermen of Poole established annual trading excursions there (see Chapter 27). This trade was of great value to the Poole shipbuilding industry; Poole being famous for 'Leith smacks'. Poole-built ships of up to 150 tons, some 80 in number, carrying provisions, clothing and cordage, accompanied by smaller ships made regular spring trips to Newfoundland.

The smaller ships fished the Grand Banks. This fishing was hazardous and extremely arduous. It was carried out by a fleet of small dories launched from the mother ship. In the notorious Grand Bank fogs these small boats were often out of touch with the ship for days together.

The Poole fishing fleets set up a triangular trading pattern. They returned to Newfoundland three times a year, coming back with oil, salted cod, skins, and furs. In the autumn, these they exported to Spain, Portugal and Italy. In 1791, 78 Poole ships, totalling 9528 tons set out for Newfoundland. Throughout the eighteenth century this triangular trade by the Poole Newfoundland fleet was the most important commercial venture in the county. At the end of the Napoleonic Wars, however, Poole Newfoundland fisheries greatly flagged.

PRESENT-DAY FISHERIES

The Poole Harbour Aquatic Management Plan (Harbour Commissioners, 2007) gives a good up-to-date description of fishing in and from the Harbour. The Harbour has a commercial fishing fleet of about 100 registered fishing boats and also provides landing and marketing facilities for boats from Mudeford and Swanage.

Regulations made by the Local Sea Fisheries Committee, which the Southern Sea Fisheries District (SSFD) under legislation implemented by the Environment Agency control, include both finfish and bivalves. Their authority extends to six nautical miles

Harry Matthews holding an eel spear in a Poole punt, 1910.

offshore. Additionally, the Harbour is subject to many conservation designations. Flatfish, sole or plaice, taken by trawl or gill net provide a major part of the fisherman's income. Round fish, taken both by hand line and gill net are also profitable, especially bass because of its fine flavour. Pollack and mullet make up the balance.

Some craft work out as far as mid-Channel. Grey mullet, bass, flounder, sole, and plaice constitute most of their catch using fixed, drift, seine, and trawl nets. Skate and cod are fished by long line with multiple hooks. Eel fishing is also of local importance. This is carried

Unloading sprats at the Quay in the 1960s, a period when the catches were often so large that some were sold for 6d a bucket and the rest taken away to be processed for fertiliser and animal feed.

The old Fishermen's Dock in 1948.

out with traps fitted with special otter guards to stop them entering the trap to eat the eels and drowning. The industry as a whole is worth some £2 million per year to Poole.

The Harbour is an important shellfish ground where Licensed Seasonal Aquaculture has been maintained since 1915. It is now administered under the Poole Fishery Order 1985 by the SSFD Committee, who in turn lease the Harbour floor from the Crown Estate. This order allows the Committee to lease sections of the seabed to individuals or companies for cultivation of

shellfish, and to regulate the fishing for oysters, clams, and mussels in the remainder of the Harbour. The leased beds are used to grow on and fatten stocks of mussels, clams, oysters, and cockles.

Harvesting is by means of dredging using a pump-scoop unique to Poole. The dimensions and mesh-size of the dredge are closely regulated to ensure that juvenile infauna and spats are not taken. The catch has by regulation to be sorted immediately it is on the boat so that undersized bivalves and other fish can be returned to the water at once, unharmed. Some sorting and cultivation is also done in the former Sandbanks ferry, moored off Brownsea Island. All fishing activity

The former Sandbanks ferry is now moored off Brownsea Island and used by the Harbour shellfish industry.

Map showing some the areas within the Harbour reserved for growing shellfish.

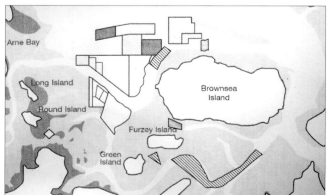

is monitored by District Fishery Officers. About 100 tons of cockle and about 2 million each of Manila clam and Pacific oyster are laid to fatten and breed in the aquaculture beds each year. This industry alone produces landings worth more than £1 million a year. In addition to shellfish taken within the Harbour, lobsters, brown crab, spider and velvet crab, and whelks are also landed by boats fishing in the English Channel.

The facilities for the fishing fleet at Poole were greatly improved with the completion of the Town Quay Boat Haven in 2001. The pontoons provide permanent floating moorings with access by foot to each individual boat. Landing facilities have been placed along the quayside to improve access when offloading or loading vessels.

There is also considerable recreational fishing in and outside the Harbour. A charter fishing fleet of some 35 boats, one of the largest in the UK, attracts recreational fishermen from all over the country. Hobby fishing, mainly for flounder, from the shoreline, is popular. There is also unregulated cockle fishing and bait digging, both manually and by dragged dredge. Limited prawn fishing also takes place. There are 19 angling clubs in the Poole area.

The Local Sea Fisheries Committee, in liaison with the SSFD governed by the Fisheries Regulation Act, seeks, by means of bylaws, to protect the marine environment and to secure a profitable and sustainable fishing industry in the Harbour.

ABOVE The new Town Quay Boat Haven.

BELOW Waiting for a bite. The *Girl Friend* just outside the Harbour entrance.

Poole Quay from Hamworthy, Bernard Gribble (1872-1962).

PART FIVE
Transport, Trade and Recreation

TWENTY-FOUR

Introduction

CHRISTINE WIDDOWSON

After the initial development of Poole Harbour, some form of waterborne transport would undoubtedly have been important to its further development. The Harbour gave direct access to the English Channel and meant that navigable communication with other parts of coastal Britain and the rest of the world were possible. With the increase in settlements around the Harbour, and as communities and trade developed, the ability to use the Harbour for transport would have become increasingly important. Projects such as the Green Island-Cleavel Jetties were undertaken to improve links between the Harbour, the local area, and beyond.

Other forms of transport, whilst competing with the Harbour's waterborne traffic, have also served to reinforce it. Paths between the settlements, and landing points, around the Harbour would necessarily have developed into recognisable trackways, and later into roads.

Wareham's importance, particularly in the Middle Ages, was because it was the lowest bridgeable point in the river system connecting with the Harbour.

Major roads came with the Romans and their need to link their landing site at Hamworthy with the rest of the country. The road network serving the Harbour developed further in the following centuries, and continues to develop. Tramways were used during the eighteenth century and local rail transport developed during the nineteenth century culminating in the arrival of the mainline rail link to Hamworthy, Poole, and Wareham.

Air transport associated with the Harbour followed closely the growth and subsequent decline of flying boats immediately before, during and after the Second World War.

The growth of recreation has been much less specific and has instead followed the more gradual development of utilitarian activities associated with the Harbour, improved access, and increasing leisure time and wealth. This is because the most important recreational activities have their roots in what were initially necessities. Competitive yachting, for example, can be traced directly to the ambition of the owners of sailing ships to be the first into port with their cargoes. Fishing, originally a necessity for the food it could supply, can now be indulged as a *pure* recreation.

The features underlying the Harbour's trade, transport, and recreation are considered in the seven chapters that follow.

TWENTY-FIVE
Charting the Harbour

ANDREW DAVID

The first maps to include the Harbour were concerned more with the surrounding land than the Harbour itself. Ships were of relatively small draught, and great reliance was placed on local knowledge. It was not until well into the eighteenth century that the Admiralty commissioned detailed surveys of ports such as Poole.

This late seventeenth century map of the Harbour is an early attempt at charting the main channels, and predates Murdoch Mackenzie's chart by nearly a century.

On 24th May 1771 Lieutenant Murdoch Mackenzie was appointed Admiralty Surveyor in succession to his uncle, Professor Murdoch Mackenzie with orders to survey the whole of the coast of the British Isles starting at the entrance to the Bristol Channel and continuing roughly anti-clockwise around Britain.

Serving initially as a supernumerary on the *Peterel*, a 71 foot sloop, with an assistant, his cousin, Graham Spence, he was given command on 11th June 1780. His pay was one guinea a day when actually employed on

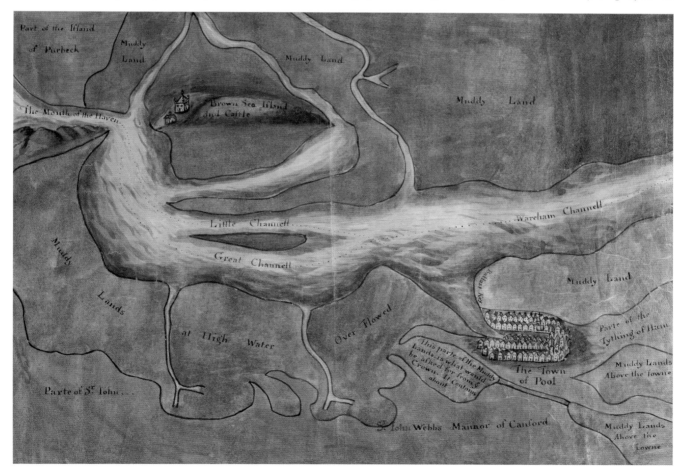

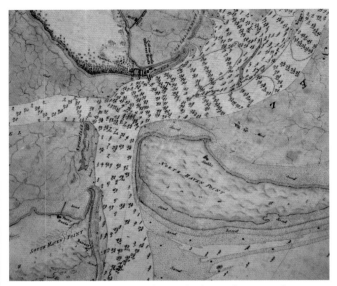

A detail from the original of Murdoch Mackenzie's chart showing the Harbour entrance. Note the gun battery and Ferry House shown on South Haven Point.

his survey, and half a guinea a day when refitting.

Having been refitted and re-provisioned, the *Peterel* left Portsmouth on 10th May 1785. Among the provisions on board were 21 bags of bread (i.e. ship's biscuits), 46 gallons of brandy, 2 barrels of beef, 2 barrels of pork and 170 lbs of cheese. He reached Poole Harbour on 12th August 1785, where he anchored off Brownsea Island, adjacent to the Customs House, which he used as a base for the next few months.

Surveying equipment included a theodolite, sextants, a Gunter's chain, poles for survey marks, and tents. Each day began at 5.00 am and continued until 4.00 pm, seven days a week. His first task was to measure the tidal range, for which a tide pole was erected in mud adjacent to the sloop 'to observe the rise and fall of the tide', so that the height of the tide could be subtracted from the soundings to reduce them to low water.

Mackenzie began his survey by sounding the bar. He then measured a base along the sands of Studland Bay from Studland to South Haven Point, which he then extended by triangulation to cover the whole of the Harbour. Next, the two surveyors would have erected a series of marks around the Harbour, fixing their positions from the various triangulation stations. As the survey progressed, which was on a scale of 6 inches to a nautical mile, Mackenzie or Spence would have walked along the high water mark to fix its position and the positions of various objects on land, in considerable detail, including the positions of various batteries. One of these batteries, a small redoubt of three guns for the defence of the entrance to the Harbour, was near the

Ferry House on South Haven Point. Mackenzie also noted on his survey that, at its narrowest, the peninsula leading to Sandbanks was only 240 feet wide between the High Water marks. As a result of his painstaking work, Mackenzie's survey shows much more detail than the corresponding sheets of the one-inch Ordnance Survey map, published almost 30 years later.

Simultaneously, either Mackenzie or Spence would have been away in one of the sloop's boats to sound out the Harbour, the depths being obtained by lead line and their positions fixed by horizontal sextant angles rather than compass bearings. The evenings were spent 'inking in', either subtracting the height of the tide from the soundings and plotting the amended depths on a specially prepared sounding board, or plotting the coastline.

Even with the approach of winter the survey continued, except when bad weather made working impossible. January 1786 was very cold. On one occasion drift ice fouled the small bower anchor cable, causing it to part. Even when conditions were too bad to leave the sloop, the surveyors were kept busy plotting the results of their observations. In January, Spence was confined to bed on board, but Mackenzie was still out in the Harbour taking soundings from an open boat. On 17th February Spence was sufficiently recovered to work on the draughts, but there is no indication that he was able to resume fieldwork. On 3rd April Mackenzie moved the *Peterel* to a shipbuilder's wharf, perhaps an even more convenient place for obtaining provisions and fresh water, where she remained until 6th April when Mackenzie moved the *Peterel* once more to his old anchorage off Brownsea Island. The survey was now complete and on the 15th April 1786, Mackenzie took his departure and made his way back to Portsmouth.

Mackenzie's next task was to draw a fair copy of his survey on linen-backed paper, for forwarding to the Admiralty, which clearly took some time. It is a massive document measuring 145 x 150 centimetres, beautifully drawn in pen and ink with colour washes; it is held in the United Kingdom Hydrographic Office in Taunton. It was accompanied by at least one view, which sadly does not appear to have survived, and a comprehensive memoir, which was brought up to date in about 1808 by Graham Spence. In the unpublished memoir, Mackenzie noted that vessels drawing 22 feet could cross the outer Poole bar and anchor as convenient in the outer Harbour, but no vessel drawing more than 17 feet could enter the inner Harbour, where the whole of the Newfoundland trade was carried out.

On receipt of Mackenzie's survey in the Admiralty it was added to a large collection of surveys already held there, where it remained unpublished for the next

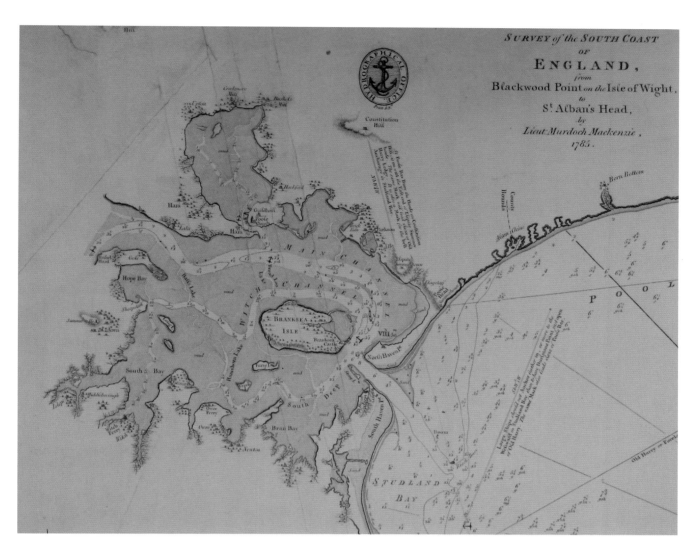

twenty years. It was not until 1st September 1810 that Mackenzie's survey of the Harbour was finally published by the Admiralty and then only as part of a small-scale chart titled 'Survey of the South Coast of England, from Blackwood Point on the Isle of Wight to St Albans Head, by Lieut. Murdoch Mackenzie, 1785', on a scale of one inch to 1½ nautical miles. On it are printed directions for ships approaching Poole Harbour:

> 'At Poole Bar Buoy the House on Constitution Hill, is on with the East End of Elipute [Lilliput] Summer House. The same Mark will lead clear of Old Harry Ledge. It is also the mark for the best Anchorage in Studland Bay', with a warning that 'Large Ships should not anchor further in, or more to the West in Studland Bay than to have Durlstone Point just open of Old Harry. The same Mark also leads clear of Poole Bar'.

When they were first published, Admiralty charts were only issued to ships of the Royal Navy and it was not until 1821 that they were offered for sale, thus enabling

A detail from the published version of Murdoch Mackenzie's survey of Poole Harbour, 1810.

the general public to make use of Mackenzie's survey. In 1836 the Admiralty published a large scale chart of Poole Harbour on a scale of 2¼ inches to a nautical mile, based on Mackenzie's survey and which had been brought up to date by soundings on the bar taken in 1829 by Lieutenant Thomas Spark, who was serving at the time in the Water Guard (i.e. he was a Custom House Officer). Mackenzie's charts were withdrawn from sale between 1852 and 1864.

Due to failing eyesight Mackenzie was forced to retire in 1788. He died on 27 January 1829, at the age of 85, in Minehead. He was buried in St Mary Magdalene Church, Exford, next to his second wife, where there is a memorial tablet to them both. There is also a stained glass window erected to his memory in St Mary's Church, Chiddingfold.

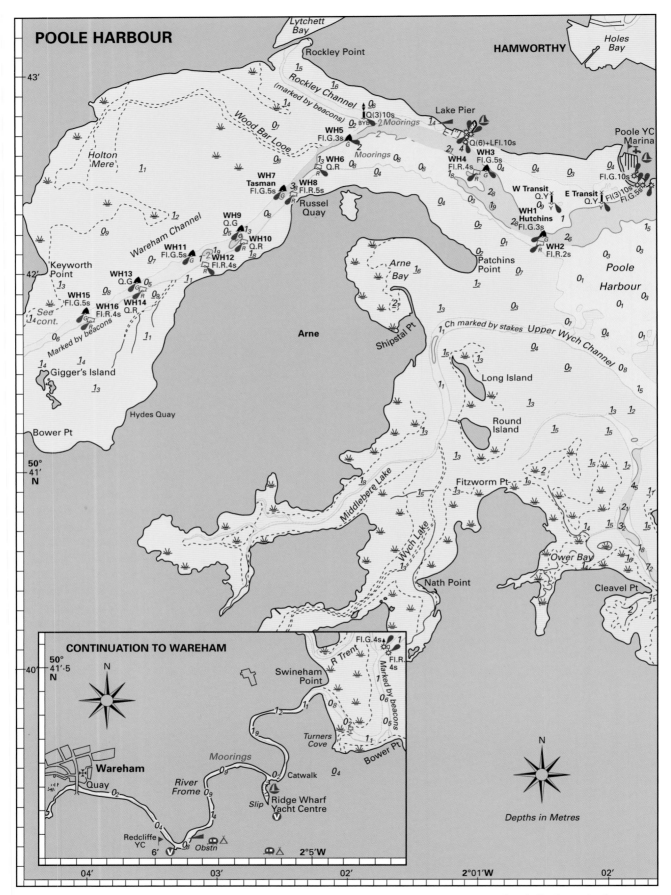

POOLE HARBOUR

HAMWORTHY

Lytchett Bay

Rockley Point

Rockley Channel

(marked by beacons)

Holton Mere

Wood Bar Looe

Q(3)10s
BYB 2 Moorings

Lake Pier

Poole YC Marina

WH5 Fl.G.3s

Moorings

WH3 Fl.G.5s

WH4 Fl.R.4s

Fl.G.10s

WH6 Q.R

WH7 Tasman Fl.G.5s

WH8 Fl.R.5s

Russel Quay

W Transit Q.Y

E Transit Q.Y

Fl(3)10s Fl.G.5s

WH1 Hutchins Fl.G.3s

WH9 Q.G

WH10 Q.R

WH2 Fl.R.2s

Patchins Point

Poole Harbour

Keyworth Point

Wareham Channel

WH11 Fl.G.5s

WH12 Fl.R.4s

WH13 Q.G

WH15 Fl.G.5s

WH16 Fl.R.4s

WH14 Q.R

See cont.

Marked by beacons

Arne Bay

Arne

Shipstal Pt

Ch marked by stakes Upper Wych Channel

Long Island

Round Island

Gigger's Island

Hydes Quay

Bower Pt

Middlebere Lake

Wych Lake

Fitzworm Pt

Ower Bay

Cleavel Pt

Nath Point

50° 41' N

50° 43'

42'

41'

40'

CONTINUATION TO WAREHAM

50° 41'.5 N

N

R Trent

Fl.G.4s

Fl.R. 4s

Swineham Point

Marked by beacons

Turners Cove

Bower Pt

Wareham Quay

Moorings

River Frome

Catwalk

Slip

Ridge Wharf Yacht Centre

Redcliffe YC

Obstn

2°5'W

N

Depths in Metres

04' 03' 02' 2°01'W 02'

The current chart of Poole Harbour published by Imray Laurie Norie & Wilson in *The Shell Channel Pilot* by Tom Cunliffe and included by kind permission of Imray Laurie Norie & Wilson and the Controller of Her Majesty's Stationery Office and the UK Hydrographic Office.

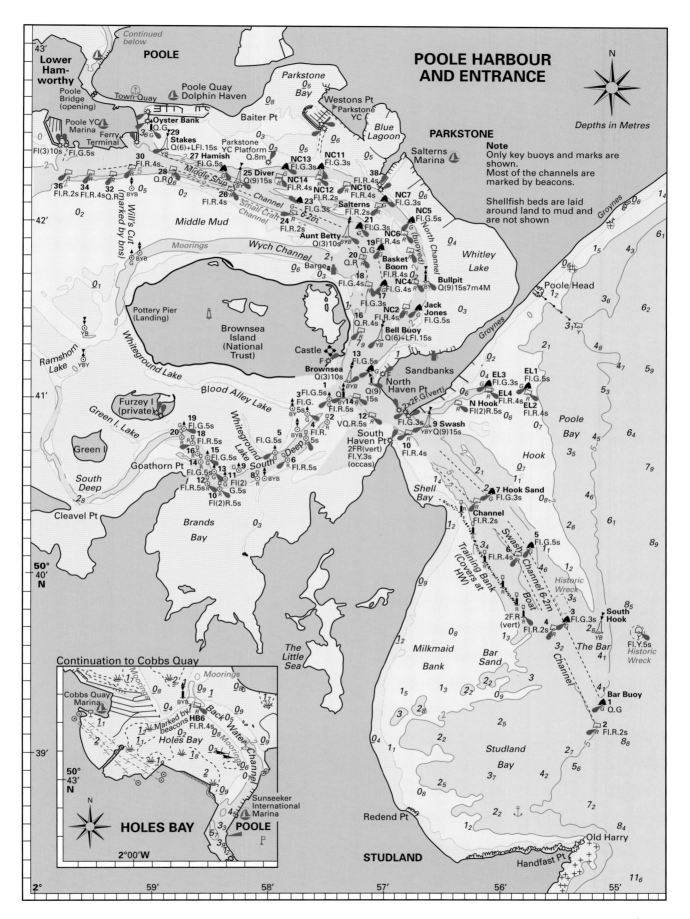

POOLE HARBOUR
AND ENTRANCE

N

Depths in Metres

Note
Only key buoys and marks are shown.
Most of the channels are marked by beacons.

Shellfish beds are laid around land to mud and are not shown

PARKSTONE

Continuation to Cobbs Quay

HOLES BAY

2°00'W

STUDLAND

TWENTY-SIX

Shipping

JEAN SUTTON

Tourists spilling out of comfortable cars and coaches to stroll along Poole Town Quay see the Harbour as a beautiful stretch of water, ideal for sailing. A different view prevailed in former centuries when it was the main local highway for the transport of people, goods, and raw materials in all seasons and all weather. Before the Roman conquest vessels carrying exotic cargoes converged on a port in the south of the Harbour. It was on the northern shore, at present day Hamworthy, that the Romans developed a port to supply their conquering army. Later military forces used the Harbour. Part of King Alfred's new fleet carried troops to attack

Town Quay from the air in the 1920s, with Hamworthy in the foreground.

the occupying Danish force in Wareham. Vessels carried soldiers of Stephen and Mathilda's opposing forces to fight for control of the imposing castle there.

About this time boats transported Purbeck marble, partially fashioned by the marblers of Corfe, across to the nascent port of Poole for transhipment and distribution to London and elsewhere. Vessels laden with highly prized English wool later sailed for European woollen cloth centres from a now confident Poole, raised in 1433 to the status of Port of the Staple. Later, in Elizabeth I's reign, locally mined and processed alum and copperas, essential for dyeing, were carried in some of the 20 or so vessels of up to 70 tons belonging to the port.

A network of ferries connected the local communities in the Isle of Purbeck with Poole. Passage houses

The *Jubilee* alongside Hamworthy Quay in about 1900.

provided shelter and basic comforts at various points round the Harbour from which the ferries sailed. At Goathorn and Wytch people from Corfe Castle and other villages embarked for the market at Poole. A good night out ended tragically for the passengers whose ferry went aground in the mud on the return passage on a wild night in 1759:

'In this storm 19 passengers in a passage-boat from Poole to Wareham were forced upon the beach, 13 of whom perished in endeavouring to reach the shore. Nothing could be more dismal than to see the poor souls half-buried in the mud, with the seas breaking over them, without being able to afford them any relief, and the piercing cries were terrible.'

When another passage boat sank in the Wareham Channel in 1806, 18 of the 20 passengers who were drowned were women, farmers' wives on their way home from market.

At the passage house at South Haven wildfowlers moored their punts and joined revelling smugglers. Only two small locally built vessels, the *Chesterfield* sloop in 1791 and the *Thomas & Mary* smack in 1787, were condemned for unlawful trading. This gave credence to the suspected complicity of the officer in charge of the revenue cutter moored in Brownsea Road. The most frequented of all the passage houses was that by Customs House steps serving the manually operated ferry which carried workers across the narrow channel to the many shipyards in Hamworthy. From here, too, in the later nineteenth century, a large number of workers had to be ferried to the New Pier on the south-west corner of Brownsea Island serving a large pottery. It produced mainly sewage pipes which were transported by sloop to the fast developing new town of Bournemouth. Single sailing boats and later chains of barges hauled by steam

The ferry between Customs House steps and Hamworthy in about 1900. Despite the bridge, it continued in operation until well into the 1970s.

The Portsmouth Hoy pub on the Quay recalls the regular weekly service by two large hoys which sailed from Poole to Portsmouth every Monday, returning Saturday. The hoy changed over time and varied from place to place, but performed a similar function to the Thames barge – and indeed, despite the name, it is a Thames barge that is now illustrated on the sign outside the pub!

tugs carried the fine white pipe, or ball clay, from piers at Ridge, Russel Quay and Goathorn to Town Quay for transhipment to the Staffordshire potteries. Thames barges loaded some of the clay at the piers and carried it direct to some of the London potteries. Boats with apt names like *Ceres* and *Wheat Ear* regularly brought flour from Belben's Mill in Portsmouth to supply a fast-growing population in Dorset while from the western ports and creeks boats came loaded with rich dairy produce.

People in all the Dorset towns and villages depended on James Manlaw's weekly schooner service to bring goods from London, and on the twice-weekly deep-hulled hoy service from Portsmouth for more local carriage. The distinctive square-rigged brigs, and later the larger barques and ships, dominated the vessels heading for foreign ports. During the long French wars many were fitted with gun ports to accommodate armament for offensive or defensive purposes. The 276 ton ship *Eleanor* carried 12 nine-pounder carronades and 2 six-pounders for her voyage to Antigua and Jamaica in 1800 while the *Anna* snow, 222 tons, bound to Buenos Aires in 1807, carried a similar main armament. Occasionally the merchants of Poole, exasperated by huge losses at the hands of French privateers, sought Letters of Marque from the Lord High Admiral and armed their own vessel to retaliate.

All vessels entering and leaving the Harbour needed the services of the men who knew the vagaries of the narrow channels and the sand bar just outside the entrance: the pilots. Pilot cutters, owned and manned by rival families, were always a feature of Harbour life. After 1808 pilots were required to register with Trinity House and seek a licence. The new regime fostered cooperation and a more professional attitude to ensuring the safety of vessels entering and leaving the Harbour.

Notice of James Manlaw's regular service between London and Poole is a reminder of the role played by sloops all round the coast.

The Working Harbour
A portrait in pictures

ABOVE The TS *Royalist*, a sail training ship belonging to the Sea Cadet Corps, moored alongside the Quay.

BELOW A fine study by Ernest Coney of a schooner drying its sails alongside Burden's, a ship's chandler that closed in 1970.

A Baltic timber boat alongside Sydenham's yard.

The *Alberge* at Town Quay in 1910.

The Age of Sail

The *Will Everard*, built in 1926, was probably the most famous of the many Thames barges seen in Poole Harbour over the decades. The four *Everard* barges were reputed to carry the greatest area of sail, 5,600 square feet, all managed by skipper, mate, and third hand.

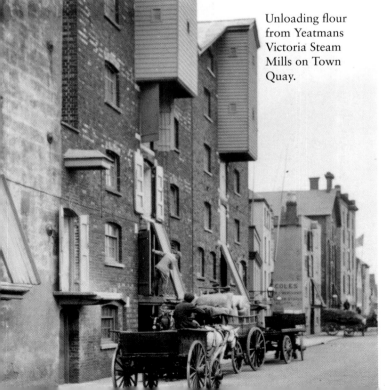

Unloading flour from Yeatmans Victoria Steam Mills on Town Quay.

A brigantine dries her sails prior to sailing with a cargo of clay loaded from the barge moored alongside.

A group of people waiting for the town ferry look across to
Town Quay where two Thames barges, a brigantine, and a
paddle steamer are moored. A tug tows a topsail schooner
out into the Harbour. Wagons carrying coal on the rails along
the quay can be seen in the background, as can the kilns of
Poole Pottery.

This is one of the fine photographs by Ernest Coney (1859-
1937) included in this book. Coney lived over the Shipwrights
Arms, Hamworthy, and flourished as a photographer at
the end of the nineteenth and beginning of the twentieth
centuries.

The Age of Steam

A Baltic timber boat, the *Garlstorf*, being towed towards the lifting bridge by the *Wendy Ann 2*, probably in the 1960s.

A Hull collier unloading coal at Town Quay in the 1930s.

ABOVE These photographs are reminders of when Town Quay was a working quay and goods were loaded and unloaded by the big crane near what was then Poole Pottery. The cargoes shown are caravans (probably made by Bluebird), timber, livestock, and fertilizer from Smolensk. In 1964 400,000 tons of cargo were unloaded from the 1,500 ships that docked in Poole.

LEFT Pipler & Sons, which opened in 1866 and is still a chandlery today.

ABOVE In about 1900 the Harvey family started a fair weather rowing-boat ferry service from Sandbanks to South Haven, which they called Shell Bay to attract the trippers. Even though the oars gave way to engine, the service was put out of business by the opening of the Sandbanks Chain Ferry in 1926.

BELOW The third Sandbanks Ferry, built by J. Bolson & son Ltd was given an affectionate send-off by nostalgic regular passengers when she was withdrawn from service in 1994 after 35 years' and replaced by *Bramble Bush Bay*. It still survives, moored off Brownsea Island for use by the shellfish industry in the Harbour.

Harbour Memories

ABOVE *Poole Harbour, Dorsetshire,* by Edmund Gouldsmith (1852-1932). Note the second of Poole's bridges in the background.

RIGHT Harry Reeves, the Poole Harbour postman, setting out on his round in the early 1970s. This painting, by David Cobb, was issued by the Post Office as a poster to draw attention to postal codes, which had just been introduced.

THE HARBOUR COMMISSIONERS

The Harbour and the Port of Poole are managed by the Poole Harbour Commissioners, who were originally given responsibility to conserve, regulate and improve the Port and Harbour by Act of Parliament in 1895.

Today, the Harbour Commissioners employ a staff of about 100. Their main responsibilities are to maintain the shipping channels by dredging and providing navigational aids such as lights and buoys, provide a pilot service for ships visiting the Harbour, allocate moorings, maintain and develop the Port facilities such as cargo handling, license works around the Harbour, co-ordinate resources in the event of any pollution, provide a 24 hour Harbour Control Office, and enforce the Harbour byelaws.

Harbour Control is now exercised from the Harbour Office on Hamworthy.

ABOVE The Harbour Master's launch and the inshore lifeboat pause to exchange news.

BELOW The Harbour Master's personal watercraft enables him to reach any part of the Harbour at great speed.

BOTTOM These four vessels are a familiar site. The 18 metre tug *Herbert Ballam*, honouring the former councillor, Mayor and Harbour Commissioner for 31 years, was built by Bolson's and launched in November 1997. She is the most powerful tug in the Harbour. With her are two pilot cutters and, on the extreme left, a Harbour Master's launch.

The Harbour Today

ABOVE The move of the Port from Town Quay to Hamworthy took place in stages from the 1970s. Initially 8 acres of land were reclaimed, and this has gradually been extended to 44 as more has been required.

BELOW Loading gravel in the Port of Poole.

After the Second World War the landing craft base at Hamworthy and HMS *Turtle* were handed over to the Royal Marines to become their amphibious warfare training centre. At the same time, an abandoned clay pit found a new role as a training lake for the Special Boat Squadron.

In 1972 the Corps of the Royal Marines was granted the Honorary Freedom of the Borough of Poole. They saw action in 1982 during the Falklands War, and the open space leading into the Dolphin Centre was renamed in their honour.

In recent years both the Royal Marines and Special Boat Squadron have seen service in Iraq and Afghanistan, and their landing craft remain a familiar sight in the Harbour.

ABOVE A cruise liner entering the Harbour.

RIGHT Competition amongst ferry operators to take tourists round the Harbour, across to Brownsea Island and up to Wareham is unrelenting. Behind Brownsea Island Ferries' *Maid of Poole* is *Purbeck Gem*, one of Greenslade's three cruisers run by a member of the old Poole fishing family since fish stocks were trawled out in 1970.

BELOW RIGHT Indispensible to the safety of vessels navigating the channels in this largely shallow Harbour are the buoys, here receiving a new coat of paint at Yard Quay, the Harbour Master's store and maintenance depot.

BELOW The old Harbour Office stands on the site of a Meeting House built in 1727. The tablet commemorating this and the sundial were incorporated in the present building of 1822. It now houses H.M. Coastguard.

THE SWASH CHANNEL WRECK

The wreck of what is probably a seventeenth century merchant ship was discovered in 2004 during a survey prior to dredging to deepen the approach to the Harbour. The wreck has yielded some remarkable remains, including cannons, barrels, copper, pewter, musket balls, and apothecary jars. Analysis of timber samples suggest a felling date after 1585 and it is likely timber came from Germany or Holland. The wreck is now administered by English Heritage and is being investigated by the maritime archaeology group at Bournemouth University.

The carved merman from the bow or quarterdeck of the ship, and which was recovered in 2008.

TOP The Brittany Ferries *Condor Express* passes Brownsea Island, outward bound for Cherbourg.

BOTTOM The pilot boat turns away from the Brittany Ferries *Barfleur,* which until recently operated between Poole and Cherbourg. Brittany Ferries decision to move the *Barfleur* to Portsmouth is a good example of the ways in which circumstances beyond the control of Poole Harbour Commissioners can have a significant impact on the Harbour Commissioners revenue.

TWENTY-SEVEN

Newfoundland
'A Plantation of Poole'

IAN ANDREWS

IN 1497, a year after he had visited Poole, King Henry VII agreed to pay a reward 'to hym that founde the new Isle' (John Cabot) – the sum of £10!

Over the next century trade between Poole and Newfoundland gradually developed. The Table of Quayage Rates in 1579 lists among the other items, 'Fyshe of Newfoundland drye'.

Large quantities of salt were also landed at Poole; a necessary ingredient for the salt-fish trade. Another cargo passing through the port was 'train oil', derived from cod livers. Though an evil smelling cargo it was carried by a vessel with a much sweeter sounding name, the *Primrose*.

The earliest evidence of a direct link between Poole and England's oldest colony (and Canada's newest province) dates from 1583 when the Senior Bailiff, Christopher Farwell, was fined £30 for his contempt in

Split cod (green fish) laid out on flakes (stages covered with wood) to dry in the air before being salted down into barrels.

absenting himself from his duties in the town by 'going a long voyage towards the Newfounde Land' without the consent of the Mayor and Burgesses. Within two years, however, he must have purged the contempt, for he was chosen Mayor of Poole.

In August 1583 twenty British ships were in St John's, Newfoundland, when Sir Humphrey Gilbert claimed the colony for England. It would not be unreasonable to surmise that Poole men were among the seamen present. These seamen ran the serious risk of attack from foreign vessels, then principally Spanish, which far outnumbered the English fishermen.

Once established, the trade flourished. In 1595 the trade revenue of the Port of Poole was over £3,000, yet seven years earlier, at the time of the Armada, if one believes the reply given, the town had been unable to furnish any ships for the defence of the realm and the Lords of the Council 'being credibly informed of their dishabylyte – they are eased of this burden'.

One of the typical vessels of the Poole fleet, then numbering 30 or 40, was *The Flying Harry*. She was of 30 tons only, perhaps only 50 feet long, and among her cargo was 'three hundred of newland fyshe, 26 fisshes to every hundred'. Poole (but no other) vessels were exempted from quay dues at Poole on their Newfoundland imports, to encourage the trade.

After the Armada, ships were regularly requisitioned for the King's purposes to suppress the Spanish, but Poole owners, in defiance, preferred to send their ships to Newfoundland, leaving others to patrol the coastal waters and afford them protection on their return. In 1594 Sir Walter Raleigh wrote to the Secretary of State informing him that 100 ships were to return in August 'and they must not be allowed to be captured or it would be the greatest blow ever given to England'.

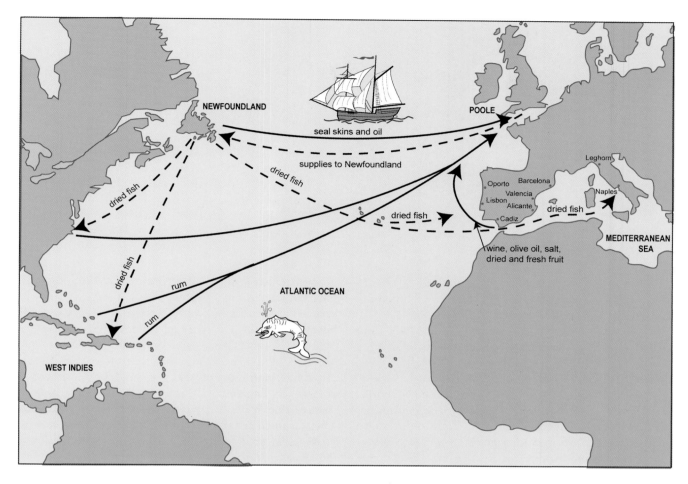

Map showing the triangular trade. Poole boats sailed to Newfoundland laden with supplies, then carried dried fish to America, the West Indies and the Mediterranean, finally returning to Poole with rum, wine, olive oil, and other goods.

SEVENTEENTH CENTURY

By 1616 the traditional wealth of the town, the cloth trade (for it was a Port of the Staple), had been overtaken by the fishing voyages 'to the New Found Land and soe home' as a letter to the Council of State described it. It was a business full of risk. In 1628, for example, it was recorded that in four years 20 ships, of a total tonnage of 1,465 tons, valued at £13,400, had been lost, leaving only 16 ships of a total of 838 tons. The State Papers of Charles I record that the Newfoundland fishing grounds were an open resort for pirates in need of men and victuals.

Whether as an excuse or a reason, when the town was asked to contribute to the repair of St Paul's after the Great Fire in London it rustled up only 10 guineas. The note forwarding this explained that Poole was very small and poor,

> 'much decayed by late times of hostility, and the death of divers of the chiefest of the inhabitants, the greater part whereof are mariners, now at Newfoundland and gone to sea....not to return till March.'

The usual pattern was for the ships to carry out a seasonal trade, for Newfoundland's climate was unattractive for settlers. In the spring there would be sealing in the Northern Ocean and in the autumn fishing on the Grand Banks for cod. Settlement was not encouraged but in the seventeenth century some pioneers (known as planters) remained there between voyages, erecting shore establishments for storage and building ships. Later they were joined by individuals who lived by catching fish and selling to the merchants. In 1675 Trinity's population had been 41. By 1787 it grew to 1,000 and was double that in 1823. This required provisions as well as men to be taken out and there was a growth at this time of trades to support their needs. Nearly all of West Street, for example, was taken up by boot and shoemakers and there was a tannery at Tatnam.

The seasonal visitors resented the settlers and took their grievances to the Star Chamber in 1618, claiming

The Mansion House in Thames Street (now the Hotel du Vin) was built by Isaac Lester and his brother Benjamin, who grew wealthy on the trade between Poole and Trinity, Newfoundland.

Benjamin Lester (1724-1801).

the settlers took the gear and burnt their store buildings and took the small boats (dories or skiffs) they had left on the shores awaiting their return in six months. The settlers, too, were unhappy, as they had no protection from foreign raiders and the government showed no intention of garrisoning the colony, relying only on protecting the fleet at sea.

The settlers were regarded as 'loose and useless', and captains of vessels sailing for Newfoundland were required under bond to bring back all the men they took out. It was also declared illegal for inhabitants to burn or destroy any stage before the arrival of the fishermen from England. Evasion of these rules was commonplace and for all the fine words the parties were left to sort themselves out, which by 1680 they appear to have done, for the Mayor of Poole and 24 merchants signed a petition against a proposal to remove the planters, prophesying ruin to traders and settlers alike if the project was carried out. Repeated requests for naval support were refused. In 1652, for example, the Council of State refused a convoy and advised the merchants that 'if they can dispose of themselves so as to forbear that trade this year, it will most consist with their affairs at present'.

Despite this official discouragement, trade flourished and attitudes changed. By the end of the seventeenth century the principal concern was protection of the now valuable trade from the French. Convoy captains were instructed to collect statistics and furnish reports. In the 1675 census of ships there were only 150 English ships to 400 French in the trade to the Island.

Poole's main rival port in the trade was Dartmouth but the towns united in seeking protection from French attacks, both on land and by sea. The convoys accompanying the fleet and the defences in

The fillets of dried cod carved above a fireplace in the Mansion House, the Lesters house in Thames Street.

Newfoundland were strengthened, even though the support fell short of actual attacks on the French ships. Poole's sailors seem, though, to have taken the law into their own hands, for the French complained to the Privy Council of the acts of piracy committed on their ships returning from Newfoundland by ships taking refuge in Poole – selling the goods taken from them to inhabitants of the neighbourhood of Poole.

To keep justice among the fishermen, as well as dispense justice to the settlers, a system of appointing 'Admirals' of the fishing fleets was established, usually the captains of the first fishing vessels to arrive at the drying grounds. As they had no qualification they were subject to the influence of their backers, the merchants, at best, or the merest bribe, at worst.

EIGHTEENTH CENTURY
THE GOLDEN AGE OF POOLE

By the Treaty of Utrecht (1713) Newfoundland was ceded outright to Britain and the French were banished from the eastern towns, where the interests of the Poole merchants were paramount, like Trinity and Carbonear. In some cases these towns had been named after their native area – Purbeck Cove and Old Harry in Bonavista Bay, Cape Ballard, and perhaps Round Island and Green Island. Later, in Trinity, familiar street names appeared, such as Garland Road, High Street, West Street and Church Road.

The 1700s saw the growth of the 'seven strong firms' of Poole (the Lesters, Jeffereys, Spurriers, Garlands, Slades, Whites, and Jolliffes), and in 1726 Daniel Defoe wrote that Poole was 'the most considerable port in all this part of England' and had been 'particularly successful' in Newfoundland fishing.

Apart from the cod fishery (symbolised in the fillets of

The Lester fleet of over 60 ships in Trinity Harbour, Newfoundland.

dried cod carved in the fireplace of the Mansion House in Thames Street, built on the wealth of the trade by the Lesters and the trade in seal skins) there was a fine salmon trade developed by the hardy adventurers.

Between 1713 and 1764 the resident population of Newfoundland increased fivefold, from 3,000 to 16,000, mainly due to the fishing being left to the settlers, the adventurers relying on transporting their produce to lucrative Mediterranean markets and on the truck system of payment, supplying the settlers' needs for domestic, agricultural, and fishing implements. Each employee was allowed credit in the company stores of half his probable earnings, whereby a further profit accrued to the merchants, for the price of the goods was often double the price paid at home.

The restored house of Lester Garland (left) in Trinity, and the company store. The house duplicated the design of a Lester family house in Lytchett Minster and is the oldest brick building in North America. The materials, including the glass, were carried to Trinity from Poole on cargo vessels.

The brig *Venus* entering Leghorn in 1862.

The *Expedient* entering Naples in 1867.

The *Constance* entering Leghorn in 1876.

The *Superb* entering Naples. The *Superb* was built in Poole by Cox & Co in 1824 and plied the Newfoundland trade between 1863 and 1875.

The wealth created by the trade sustained a living directly or indirectly for many people in Poole when general economic conditions in England were depressed. Ropewalks for cordage and nets, sailmaking, shipbuilding and iron foundries flourished. The real fortunes were shared by a small number of merchants, many to become interrelated by marriage. For example Joseph White employed 198 English and 15 Irish servants in Newfoundland in the summer and 30 in the winter. When he died in 1771 he left £150,000 – a considerable sum in those days – and Young in 1788 left £20,000; Green in 1791 left £40,000 and Slade in 1792 £70,000. When Benjamin Lester died in 1801 he left property worth over £100,000 in Newfoundland, ships worth perhaps £20,000 as well as property in England. He had owned over 60 ships (brigs, brigantines, schooners etc) in his career, built either in Poole or in Newfoundland.

The trade consisted of three voyages (triangular) – to Newfoundland, then to the fish-eating Catholic countries in the Mediterranean and then the return to Poole (see the map at the start of the Chapter). From the Mediterranean the vessels that had traded fish and skins transported salt or wine or goods from the spice routes to Poole, before setting out to Newfoundland again next season with fresh provisions for the settlers and the salt to preserve the fish. The English rights to the shores enabled them to dry and cure the fish and transport it dry in barrels. Other countries had to catch and gut the fish at sea on 'bankers' and transport it wet (green) to their home port. Many of their ships foundered as a result of the amount of water swilling round the holds. A secondary trade in refuse (inferior) fish to feed slaves in the West Indies developed, with return journeys laden with sugar, molasses, and rum. For many men (few women made the voyage as settlement was still not encouraged) the rum was a further cause for running up debts that prevented them paying for a passage for their return at the end of each season. Early missionaries were shocked at the drunken and dissolute lives they led.

During the latter part of the eighteenth and early nineteenth centuries the trade suffered from lack of government protection of the fleets. French and American privateers inflicted great losses on the shipping. In 1760 one merchant, Joseph White, had been reduced from owning 14 ships to one only, and the following year that too was lost to a French vessel, though retaken by a Guernsey privateer who brought it into Poole and claimed 1/5th of its cargo for his prize.

In 1762 the Lesters (brothers Benjamin and Isaac) resorted to self-help against the French in the absence of Government support. Benjamin arranged to invite the French admiral to dinner in Trinity and persuaded other merchants to answer 'This is Lester's' if asked about their property and landings. He persuaded the French admiral to spare his property, in return for supplying the French fleet with provisions. This appears to be the only time French intentions were thwarted other than by force in their battles against the English. Benjamin Lester was an ingenious man. When bait collected by 15 men ran out, he purchased further supplies 'from an old man who knocked down 300 puffins a day with poles' to provide bait for the fishermen.

Soon after this time the Lesters brought more than goods to the Island, for John Clinch (1749 – 1819) was taken out to Trinity as a minister, having previously acted as surgeon to the community. He had returned to England at the residents' request to be prepared for ordination by the Society for the Propagation of the Gospel. Whilst in Poole he founded its first Sunday School (at Skinner Street). He had known Edward Jenner in his youth and as a result Clinch is famed for introducing smallpox vaccination to North America.

Weather took its toll on the fleet and its crews. It was a risky trade, involving a three week to three month 3,000-mile-long hazardous crossing – with the fogs, icebergs, and rocky Newfoundland shore to contend with. Total losses were regularly reported. A feature of the Poole trade was that the merchants carried their own risk and did not insure in the emerging London market. Notwithstanding this, the value of the trade can be judged from a report in 1788 that the exports from Poole were valued at £100,000 annually and the fish caught on the Banks by Poole vessels amounted to just under half the total annual trade, being more than 700,000 quintals of cod – an average of 50,000 fish being taken by each vessel. Three ships in the same year were reported to have on board 17,000 seal skins and 350 tons of oil.

At the close of the century the Napoleonic War scaused many ports to withdraw from the trade – many for the Carolina or Virginia coast – but those remaining, and particularly Poole, benefitted greatly from the high prices they obtained for embargoed goods, trading with the Portuguese and Spanish towns blockaded by Napoleon. The contraband goods were brought into Poole after successfully running the blockades.

One of the risks of the 1700s was to be met by a press gang and recruited into the Navy, for fishermen had always been regarded as a nursery for the Royal Navy. To counter the attempts at compulsory recruitment, Poole Corporation put up £200 in 1793 as bounties for men entering the Navy of their own free will, but even this, coupled with the reluctance of mayors to back the press warrants, did not afford complete protection, and so while gangs were busy, many of the Newfoundland seamen got off their vessels on the Purbeck shore, hiding there till word was sent that the coast was clear and they could safely rejoin their ships for another journey.

One noted Mayor of Poole, John Masters, was a Newfoundlander born at Silly Cove (now renamed Winterton). His father came to England and lived for a while in Poole before returning to Newfoundland, where he was killed by the native Beothicks (Newfoundland's original inhabitants). John was educated in Wimborne and, like many a lad of his day, apprenticed to a master in the Newfoundland trade. By 1715 he became a ship's master and in 1740 married the daughter of the master who had introduced him to the trade. In 1742 he thought of putting up as one of the town's two MPs (in the unreformed system MPs were elected by the powerful merchants to represent their interests, not those of the town at large) but settled in 1748 for the office of mayor – an office he held again in 1752. He died in 1755 and his memorial tablet is in St James' Church, Poole.

NINETEENTH CENTURY
COLLAPSE OF THE TRADE

The dependence of the town on the trade was absolute. Poole's population was perhaps 5,000, and produced at least one firm (the Slades) which had made a million pounds from the business. Some part of these fortunes was invested in the town. The fine townhouses and mansions built by the wealthiest merchants are all that remain today as evidence of the 'Golden Age', but they also controlled banking and other related businesses. It was little wonder that bankruptcies, ruin, and poverty befell the town when the main trade collapsed.

After the Napoleonic War ended in 1815 trade slumped. Cod, which fetched 20/- a quintal, dropped in price to 10/-. Unemployed agricultural labourers, eking out a miserable existence, fled to the towns and finding no work, took their chance of a new life in the New World and went out to Newfoundland from Dorset ports. In Newfoundland they found that life was not easy – food was rationed, supplies were limited and when they landed from England it was feared there would be riots. The relief from support by the parish this outlet offered to Poole had its advantage to the town – which was full of stores, 'a well stocked fish shambles for fresh fish, sometimes too obviously in the act of becoming stale fish'. 'Yet among seaports', Philip Gosse wrote, it was 'one of exceptional sweetness and cleanliness'.

One account describes conditions for the settlers in Newfoundland in 1833. Slades and Kelson's diaries

An engraving by Arthur Bell of a fish store on Town Quay.

revealed of their rivals, J.B. Garland & Co., that their bell rang at 7 p.m. for the end of the day's work, having started at 5 a.m. This regulation was partly the result of stopping issues of grog. 'Their servants insisted on fewer hours of labour in consequence thereof and Mr Garland has given in to their demands.' The diary continues, 'It is dangerous work to meddle with the old customs of the fishery. By and by, no doubt, the servants will insist on the bell being rung to strike work in the evening at 6 o'clock'.

By the 1830s the Banks of Newfoundland supported only 10 British ships. Giant American vessels of up to 300 tons, with their mile-long dragnets, put the older small British boats out of business. Restrictions placed by the King of Spain on the

ABOVE West End House, St James's Close, was built by the Newfoundland merchant John Slade in about 1740.

BELOW Thomas Slade the Younger (1824-1887).

import of fish were the final blow, It was only a matter of time before the merchant firms which had established Poole, to the exclusion of other ports, as 'the Metropolis of the Newfoundland trade', went bankrupt. Once their power was broken, formal arrangements for civil government in Newfoundland, which they had resisted, were established, with an elected House of Assembly.

Because of poor prospects in England, youngsters were still seeking to be apprenticed to the trade for periods of 2 or 3 years. In 1844 there was a waiting list of 34, yet the number of ships in the merchant fleet was a fifth what it had been 30 years earlier.

Many Poole men achieved distinction in Newfoundland. Among these, Philip Gosse, the naturalist, sailed from Poole to work as a junior clerk in a Poole shipping firm and John Bingley Garland (Benjamin Lester's son-in-law) was elected Speaker of the first House of Assembly in 1833. Among his acts of benevolence Garland gave Poole its cemetery and some almshouses.

THE TWENTIETH CENTURY

Today the visible evidence of the trade can be seen in the mansions built by the merchants, who vied with each other to build the most impressive houses (e.g. Mansion House and Poole House, Thames Street; Jolliffe House, West Street; West End House, St James Close; Beechurst, High Street and Upton House in Poole and Stone House, Wimborne; Post Green, Lytchett Minster, and Leeson House at Langton Matravers). The hovels of the seamen have been swept away. The Church of St James in Poole still has the pine columns brought over as deck cargo from Twillingate, Newfoundland, and St Peter's in Twillingate has the discarded brass chandeliers from St James given to them in 1845. Lester (or Garland) House, built by Benjamin Lester in Trinity c.1750, now restored by the Trinity Trust and used as a museum of the links with Poole and an educational base, is Canada's oldest brick building – the materials having been shipped there from Poole.

Attempts were made to revive trade in the 1920s following a visit by Lord Morris, Newfoundland's Premier, to Poole in 1918. It was proposed in 1924 that a trade in salt cod, transported in 200 ton vessels between May and December each year, then carried through Bristol, should transfer to Poole – but the question which defeated it was whether there was a market for the fish.

Though the discussions came to nothing, the twentieth century saw continued contacts. The links extend to a shared place in radio history, for not only

St James Church, Poole, showing the pine columns imported from Newfoundland by the Slade family when the church was rebuilt in 1819.

did Marconi make his first experiments from the Haven Hotel and his yacht *Elettra*, but it was to St John's that he sent the world's first transocean signals from Poldhu in Cornwall. Another modern link is the shared interest in oil: at Wytch Farm and the offshore field under Poole Bay and from the Hibernia project off the shores of the Province.

The foundation of a Wessex Society in Newfoundland and of the Wessex Newfoundland Society in England in the 1980s has done much to remind people of the centuries-long links and to bring today's peoples together in close bonds of friendship and common heritage. Three out of four of Newfoundland's inhabitants can trace their ancestry to the West Country. Even so, in 1949, a narrow majority of 51 per cent to 49 per cent voted to join Canada as its newest Province.

The Borough of Poole and the City of St John's have joined in a declaration of friendship prior to discussing a formal twinning arrangement. Bournemouth University, with a campus in Poole, has been twinned with Memorial University in St John's (MUN), and scholarships established for a number of its students to study in St John's.

CONCLUSION

In 1901, the *Morning Post* of London wrote (and it is still true):

> The Newfoundlanders are wholly Anglo-Saxon and Celtic stock, and nowhere in the Colonies is there a population more British in their appearance, manners and sentiment. Living in this climate, so similar to our own, the people have the fresh complexion of our own West Country men and the hardy look of our deep-sea fishermen.
> Newfoundland has ever kept itself closer in touch with the Old Country than with the mainland of America. It is an island in which the Englishman soon finds himself at home, and he cannot fail to love these people among whose leading characteristics are an unaffected heartiness, kindliness and hospitality.'

TWENTY-EIGHT

Unofficial Trade

Piracy

DAVID WATKINS

IN THE POPULAR IMAGINATION pirates evoke images of the Caribbean, cutlasses, and canons. These images derive, often inaccurately, from the so-called 'Golden Age of Piracy', the period from the 1650s to the 1720s.

Poole's golden age of piracy was some 300 years earlier. An early reference occurs in 1338 in the records of Edward III. An enquiry is ordered in

Plate made by Poole Pottery and painted by Karen Hickisson in 1977.

Southampton and Poole concerning ships that had conveyed the King's forces over the seas and then had plundered shipping off Flanders.

The most notable Poole pirate was Harry Paye, also known as Henry Paye, who first appears in the royal accounts in 1402. An enquiry is ordered into the capture of a richly laden Spanish ship by Henry Paye of Poole together with another ship of Poole and one of Guernsey. In the following year the Sarjeant at Arms was commissioned to bring a number of men before the King and Council for an enquiry into the capture of a French barge – the *Saint Anne* with its cargo of wine. Most of the men are from Dartmouth but second in the list is 'Henry Paye of Poole'.

Paye developed a fearsome reputation amongst the French and Spanish. 'This Arrypaye had burnt Gijon and Finisterre and carried off the crucifix of St. Mary of Finisterre... and he wrought much other havoc in Castille.... And although other armed ships came forth out of England he was the most famous.' This fame cost Poole dear when a squadron of Castillian and French galleys raided the southern coast in 1405. The raiders attacked the town, meeting valiant resistance from the people of Poole. The fighting was fierce with many killed on both sides, including Harry's brother. Eventually the Poole people were forced to flee to the heath, leaving the raiders to burn the town.

Two years later, in 1407, Paye's ship and 14 others swept the English Channel capturing French and Spanish cargo vessels. A contemporary account states that 120 ships were captured loaded with valuable goods including vast quantities of good French wine. To help to recompense the people of Poole for their sufferings Harry brought the captured ships back to Poole. According to local tradition the town feasted and drank the captured wine for many days.

At other times Harry Paye appears as a patriotic warrior in the King's service. The Augustinian Friar, John Capgrave, describes the attacks of Harry Paye, in the

Poole celebrating Harry Paye Day in 2007, the 600th anniversary of his capture of 120 French coasting vessels in 1407.

company of Lord Berkely and Sir Thomas Swynborne, on the French fleet sent to aid the Welsh revolt led by Owen Glyndwr.

The line between piracy and patriotism was often vague. Harry Paye often acted as a licensed pirate. In 1404 Henry IV licensed Harry Paye as follows

'Know ye that we have granted and given leave to our well-beloved Henry Paye to sail...the seas with as many ships, barges and ballingers of war, men-at-arms and bowmen properly equipped...to do all the hurt he can to our open enemies...and for the safety of our realm'.

Harry Paye ended his days in Faversham in Kent. There is strong evidence that he married Isobel de Tonge, daughter of the wealthy Simon de Tonge of Faversham. He died in 1419 and was buried in the Parish Church of St Mary of Charity.

There were many other pirates in medieval Poole. In February 1408 at Westminster a commission was issued to bring certain men from the south coast before the King to answer charges that they had captured a great number of ships from Brittany. This was in effect a warrant for the arrest of suspected pirates amongst the names of which are:

Thomas Canawey, Mayor of Pole
James Hogge of la Pole
John Gervys of la Pole

Thomas Caneway is the earliest known Mayor of Poole and we only know about him because he was a suspected pirate. We know little else about him except that, like Harry Paye, he was licensed to carry pilgrims across the Bay of Biscay to Spain where they went to visit the shrine of St James at Compostela. Thomas Caneway and Harry Paye must have known each other and were, perhaps, brothers-in-arms.

Smuggling

IAN ANDREWS

IF PIRACY or privateering provided lucrative opportunities for shipowners and captains, smuggling was (and still is) a temptation for a wider circle with access to the coast.

The earliest British legislation dates back to King Edward I when the export of wool or cloth (and later live sheep) was made dutiable, albeit under legislation designed to suppress piracy (defined as 'robbery, kidnap or violence at sea without lawful authority'). The very word 'smuggling' did not enter the English language until the late 1600s, but covered an offence of 'conveying goods clandestinely in order to avoid payment of legal duties'. The intervening years do not imply that 'free trade' did not take place; human nature certainly attracts rogues. Poole was at the time treated as one of the principal ports of the kingdom with Cinque Port status under its Winchelsea Certificate of 1364. Indeed, under Edward IV, while relaxing restrictions on customs officers acting as merchants, a greater degree of supervision was introduced and a special 'surveyor' was appointed to Poole – whose district included Exeter, Bridgwater, Fowey, and Dartmouth – no mean task, even if provided with a boat!

In Poole in 1486 a smuggling ship named the *Rose* was rummaged and 1,200 pounds of 'best paper, considerable amounts of ginger and cloves, bales of silk and a quantity of diamonds' were seized – not from a local, but a Spanish merchant. For Poole the trade associated with the legal business of exporting Poole-brewed beer to the Channel Isles, followed by a return journey carrying at least some of the goods not available in Britain due to the lengthy periods of war with France – such as wine, lace, or silk – was not unknown. That detailed records of this or other seizures do not exist is the product of the absence from Poole's archives of its first book of Admiralty Court jurisdiction, for the collection of excise due had been farmed out here to a water bailiff as it was to contractors (often corrupt) elsewhere and

Poole Custom House, the scene of the attack by the Hawkhurst Gang in 1747. The present Custom House was built in 1813, after its predecessor had burnt down.

was not directly conducted by the Revenue until 1671.

In the 1700s the list of goods dutiable was greatly extended to about a thousand items, and dues were vastly increased as the needs of the country for greater revenue to meet war costs and colonial expansion grew. A Parliament almost exclusively composed of landowners elected by landowners was unlikely to increase taxes on land. The most popular in demand was (despite James I's strictures) the newly discovered tobacco from the East Indies, tea and spices as well as spirits from the West Indies. Even playing cards were dutiable, with the excise-paid stamp needing to be affixed to the Ace of Spades.

To improve efficiency, collectors were appointed, Custom Houses built, boats (usually cutters) purchased, and Searchers, Tide Waiters and Riding Officers employed to combat evasion. Poole's Town Beam for weighing goods imported and exported situated outside the Custom House (built originally in about 1788 but burnt down and rebuilt in 1813) is a survival of this period. It is of note that for the purpose of promoting the Newfoundland trade predominating in the town at this time, the import and export of salt, vital for the dried cod trade, otherwise heavily dutiable, was exempt if reexported.

A combination, at the height of the trade in the 1700s, of resentment (even today it is said rates are paid in sorrow but taxes in anger), need, demand and supply, profit, opportunity and adventure made smuggling as acceptable to all classes of society as minor motoring infringements today, despite the severity of penalties for those caught. At a time of depression in agriculture an agricultural labourer needing to feed, clothe and house his family and earning 7/- a week was in receipt of only 70 per cent of the wage estimated to survive at subsistence level. In the motto of the age, a farmer would 'turn a blind eye' to the 'loan' overnight of his work horses to the organisers of gangs. Innkeepers, carriers, and landowners would receive a reward 'in kind' for overlooking the activities of the many involved in the distribution of the smuggled goods to recipients throughout the surrounding counties and as far as London. Even the parson and the lord participated in return for 'sweeteners'.

Furthermore, once goods had been landed there was no police force to deter the landward distribution of the booty. Even the passing of the Smugglers Act of 1836 which introduced rewards and pardons for 'informers' was a resounding failure. Magistrates and juries were reluctant to convict, and 'bent' customs and excise employees conniving with smugglers appear to have been the rule rather than the exception. One of the most trusted Customs officials was William Culliford, son of Wareham's MP, and his investigations for the Board exposed local corruption by the majority of the Custom House staff in Poole and described how masked smugglers, such as John Carter's gang in 1682, travelled around in Poole armed with clubs and swords that they did not hesitate to wield. John Carter was actually one of the town's magistrates and merchants with friends in high places and stores all over town! All in all he concluded, the smugglers held the reins in the town and their trade was booming at a time when we went to war with France in 1689, which had severed a lot of the town's legitimate cross Channel trade.

'If Poole was a fish pool and the men of Poole fish,
There'd be a pool for the Devil and fish
for his dish!'

Not for nothing was the couplet current in the eighteenth century.

What made Poole such a leading hotbed? The answer lies not at the Quay, but partly in the uninhabited littoral between Studland and Christchurch, studded with chines, providing concealed pathways ashore, and more importantly in the large and intricate inland coastline of the Harbour. Here the many shallows and inlets on a heathy shore made it unlikely that few, if any, would

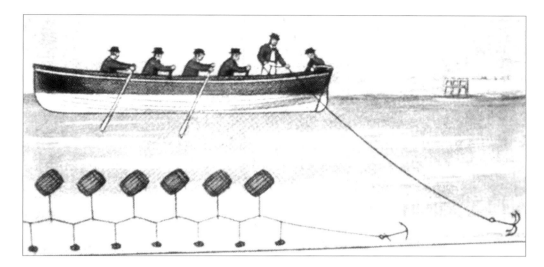

Revenue officers dragging for barrels, sunk by smugglers, and which they recovered when the coast was clear.

notice the landings from tub-boats and small dragger boats.

Many devices were employed to conceal cargoes, including false bottoms to boats and devices to haul barrels etc underwater to the hidden landing spots, where transfer to waggons and thence to 'safe' houses (or even natural hidey holes such as Coy Pond) could be achieved. In later years devices were sometimes more sophisticated and detailed involving forged documents, credits and reimportation somewhat akin to the VAT import and export devices of the later twentieth century! Discoveries of tunnels in the oldest part of the town are often popularly attached to the trade having taken place under the noses of vigilant Custom staff, but the present writer believes these were more likely the foul sewers and drains to carry away detritus and night soil from the overcrowded town, given so many other secluded bays and creeks being available along the 25 miles of shoreline on both the Purbeck and Poole Harbour shores, where any nearby riding officer could easily be distracted to a possible landing further away.

Customs staff worked with their hands tied behind their back, in the sense that they received no support for their vessels at sea from the Navy and on land it was only in the Napoleonic period that Ranger or Volunteer Forces were, depending where they were stationed, available to assist the few tackle large numbers of miscreants. Not that there were not clashes. In November 1797 a violent fracas between a gang and the crew of a Custom House cutter took place. The cutter crew had come ashore to seize a large cargo of tobacco and other contraband that had been landed, 'whereupon much mischief ensued' and several of both parties were very dangerously wounded. The smugglers gained the advantage and carried off their goods. They were later overtaken by additional officers aided by a party of dragoons 'and the conflict becoming

morer dreadful, several lives were lost'.

An even more notorious and outrageous event had taken place in 1747, but was not the work of the men of Poole. The daring deeds of the notorious Hawkhurst gang of Sussex (who claimed they could assemble a gang of 600 in an hour if necessary) culminated in an armed attack made by them on the Poole Custom House. It arose from the success at sea of the *Swift* – a Poole revenue cutter given a 'tip-off'. It had captured a consignment of 37 cwt of tea, valued at £500, with 40 barrels of brandy and rum and 'a big bag of coffee' shipped from Guernsey, and lodged it in the Custom House on Town Quay with Collector William Milner (an ancestor of Virginia Woolf). This capture meant a great financial disaster for the smugglers, who had already paid the Guernsey shippers for the consignment and were intending to 'run' the goods to Sussex. They determined not to lose their property, if by any means they could recover it. Accordingly, a body of no fewer than 60 of them, armed and mounted, set out through Lyndhurst and Fordingbridge for Poole, posting half of their number on the roads to keep watch. The other 30 pushed on, and reached Constitution Hill on the night of October 6th. After sending two of their number to spy out the Quay, they advanced to take the Custom House officers wholly by surprise; broke open the building, found it deserted and seized all the tea stored there, with the trifling exception of one bag, weighing five pounds.

The next morning this audacious band returned at leisure, back through Fordingbridge, in sight of hundreds of people, and safely distributed the tea in their usual channels of business. Here we are done with them, except to note that it was 18 months before any

ABOVE The Hawkhurst Gang from Sussex, who in 1747 stormed the Custom House to liberate the tea confiscated by the Revenue men.

BELOW The murder of one of the two informers on the Hawkhurst Gang, a luckless shoemaker called David Chater. Chater was thrown into the well when still hanging from a rope, which when they let go sent him plunging to his death.

of the gang were apprehended. In the meantime they had murdered two 'informers' they had captured. Eventually 10 of the gang were executed. And all this took place in daylight! Collector Milner was later dismissed for various malpractices in 1758 – mainly on information from his ambitious deputy that he was too close to a firm of Poole shipowners, whom he joined as a partner later and then sought revenge on his deputy, but that is another story!

One other seizure worth note was fought not with clubs or swords, but words. In 1790 after a seizure by the commander of the revenue cutter *Speedwell*, Captain George Bursac, he received a forthright letter,

Sir,

Damn thee

and God damn they two Purblind Eyes thou Buger and they Death looking Son of a Bitch O that I had bin there (with my company) for thy sake when thou tookes them men on Mine on board the Speedwell Cutter on Monday ye 14 Decr. I would drove thee and all thy Gang to Hell wher thou belongest thou Devil Incarnit Go Down thou Hell Hound into thy Kennell below and Bathe thy Serlf in that Supherous Lake that has bin so long Prepared for such as thee for it is time the World was rid of such a Monster thou art no Masn but a Devil thou fiend O Lucifer I hope thou will soon fall into Hell like a Star from the Sky; there to lie (unpitied) and inrelented of any for4 Ever and Ever Which God Grant of his infinite Mercy Amen

J. SPURRIER
Thou Damn'd Bursack
I'll Break thy Back
When I see thee again
And if I don't
Depend upon it
I kill one of they men*
*Dick – - – n

Forceful stuff, indeed – he certainly makes his intentions clear!

One way those apprehended could escape the consequences of their crimes was to volunteer for service as a seaman in the Royal Navy, but the numbers taking this option were the exceptions rather than the rule.

Not all the trade was inward bound. Wool that traded for £7 in England was worth up to £18 in France. In October 1806 a riding officer in Poole seized a cargo of contraband wool valued at £250 destined for this trade, together with a wagon and a horse, valued respectively at £20 and £45.

One of the best known of the smugglers, who largely unloaded his contraband cargoes at the then lonely Branksome Chine, was the 'gentle smuggler' Isaac Gulliver and his 'White Wigs'. Gulliver was typical of many smugglers in that his cargoes were carried long distances from a fleet of luggers used exclusively for contraband, with complex inland organisation (adapted houses and farms) required and not to the town of Poole itself. Even the Poole Customs Collector, asked to report on him in 1788, described him as 'a person of great speculating genius' but 'we find that he is not known at present to be concerned in any kind of merchandise'. One can but wonder the truth of this at the time, but in later years (he died in 1824 and is buried in Wimborne Minster, where he was a churchwarden) he was regarded as genuinely respectable, having accepted a free pardon, set up a legitimate wine merchant's business and married well into the local Fryer banking family.

Local involvement in Poole's smuggling created reputations. The Brougham Commision of 1835 reported on Hampreston; 'It is a most wretched place, the principles of morality of the major part are so contaminated with smuggling that it is despaired of reclaiming them.'

The famous Lymington wildfowler, Colonel Hawker,

A nineteenth century engraving, supposedly of Isaac Gulliver and some members of his gang, on one of the chines where they landed their contraband.

recounts in his diary how he found himself holed up overnight with a revellous, but congenial, band of smugglers as he stayed overnight at the inn at South Haven on one of his excursions to Poole.

From 1822 for 30 years Poole shipbuilder Richard Pinney (of Pinney and Adams) was one of the select private contractors entrusted with building cutters for the Customs Board. Richard Pinney was Mayor of Poole in 1841 and for the next 10 years built virtually all the small revenue cutters required up to 70 tons, at a standard fee of £11 5s per ton.

And today? The Custom House is now a restaurant and café, while Customs and Excise (the two separate services were not united until 1906) operate from the commercial ferry port in Hamworthy. Yes, of course there is still smuggling, of people, drugs, and tobacco. And there is still voluntary community vigilance in the regular Harbour Watch. Technology has moved on from a pair of binoculars to new technology. And one twentieth-century smuggling run from Cherbourg was intercepted solely because of intelligence that the miscreants had drawn from naval stores there without heeding the custom of paying their respects to the Admiral!

TWENTY-NINE

The Lifeboat Service in Poole

ANDREW HAWKES

AFTER SOME DRAMATIC rescues near Poole Harbour it was decided that some form of life saving at sea was required. The Royal National Instruction for Preservation of life from Shipwreck (RNIPLS) was tasked to provide a lifeboat in the area to serve Poole Bay and Poole Harbour. The first lifeboat was provided by the RNIPLS in May 1826, and stationed on the beach at Studland where it could be crewed by the local fishermen. The fishermen disliked the boat, allowing it to become unseaworthy and using their own boats in an emergency. In 1854 the RNIPLS was reformed as the Royal National Lifeboat Institution (RNLI) and they took over the task of providing a lifeboat in the area.

In 1864 the RNLI said if the some of the cost of a new lifeboat could be raised locally they would provide another lifeboat to Poole. Some £40 was collected, Lord Wimborne gave a plot of land so a building could be built at North Haven, Sandbanks, to house the boat, and, it was hoped that a crew of fishermen to man the

Poole's first lifeboat, the *Manley Wood*.

boat could be found from Sandbanks and Poole. The boat was named *Manley Wood* after its benefactor, a Devon clergyman. It arrived in Poole in 1865 and served until 1879, during which time it was was launched 10 times and saved 62 lives.

The *Manley Wood* was renamed in 1867 to the *Joseph and Mary*, and again renamed to the *Boys Own No 2*. In 1882 because of the difficulty of finding crew at Sandbanks the boat moved to a new Lifeboat Station at the end of Town Quay. She was credited with saving another 12 lives, launching 28 times.

In March 1897 the crew were asked to try a new lifeboat. They liked it so much they asked if they could keep it; their wish was granted and the new boat was given the name *City Masonic Club* and became the Poole lifeboat until 1910. She saved 16 lives and attended 26 incidents.

By 1910 it was recognised all lifeboats should be self-righting, so the boat was replaced by the longest-serving lifeboat; she was the *Harmer*, who served Poole for 29 years saving 40 lives with 60 launchings.

In 1939 Poole was given its first motor lifeboat, the *Thomas Kirk Wright,* a lightweight boat of 32ft suitable for the shallow Harbour and the calm seas outside in the Bay. The Swanage lifeboat gave cover in stormy weather. In 1940 she was one of 19 lifeboats sent to Dunkirk where she was put to work ferrying troops off the beach to larger offshore boats, thus saving an unknown number of British Expeditionary Force and Canadian troops

The crew of the *City Masonic Club* pose for the camera just off the Lifeboat Station (now a Museum) on Town Quay.

from certain capture by the Germans. She saved 15 lives in Poole and launched 64 times. She was sold into private hands in 1962. In 1974 the *Thomas Kirk Wright* was purchased by the National Maritime Museum and became an exhibit in the old Poole Lifeboat Station.

The *Thomas Kirk Wright,* one of 19 lifeboats sent to Dunkirk in 1940 to help ferry troops off the beaches.

The American-built *Augustine Cortauld* was launched over 100 times and saved 32 lives during its nine years on station in Poole.

Poole's two current lifeboats. The inshore *Bob Martin* and the Tyne class *City of Sheffield*. Poole's Lifeboat Station is the busiest on the south coast.

From 1962 until 1974 Poole was served by a succession of reserve lifeboats, the *Bassett Green* from 1962–1969, *George Elmy* from 1969–1971, and *J.B.Cooper* from 1971–1974.

In 1964 the station's first inshore lifeboat arrived. Initially it was an inflatable with an outboard motor on the stern, and there has been a succession of other inshore lifeboats since. The present one one is an Atlantic 85-class lifeboat named *Bob Martin*.

In 1974 the RNLI closed their London office and moved to Poole, setting up a new headquarters along with a boatyard and warehousing all on one site. Here they could hold reserve stock ready to replace any lost or broken item – from a complete lifeboat to the smallest screw – and dispatch it to anywhere in the UK immediately.

After a succession of various reserve lifeboats it was decided that Poole required a new boat. The *Augustine Courtauld*, an all-weather 44 feet steel American-designed lifeboat with a top speed of 16 knots, arrived in Poole in 1974. A new lifeboat station was built within the Marina at Poole Harbour Yacht Club to accommodate her. She covered Poole Harbour and Bay between 1974 and 1983, saving 32 lives and launching 106 times.

Another new lifeboat arrived in 1983. The *Inner Wheel* was first stationed at Poole Harbour Yacht Club,

ABOVE The Lifeboat College in Holes Bay from the air.

RIGHT A sea survival training day at the Lifeboat College.

but later moved to a new lifeboat station on Town Quay next to Hamworthy Bridge. She served until 2001, saving 176 lives and attending 813 incidents.

The present boat arrived in 2001 and is an all weather 47 feet Tyne class lifeboat with a maximum speed of 17.6 knots. To date the *City of Sheffield* has launched 374 times, saving 42 lives and recovering £9½m worth of property.

When the British Drug Houses closed their factory next door to the RNLI headquarters the land was made available for redevelopment. The RNLI acquired it, building a state of the art residential Lifeboat College to serve as a centre for training lifeboat crews from all of the United Kingdom. The College opened in 2004 and includes conference facilities as well as operations training rooms, bridge simulators, and engine workshops.

On the site opposite stands a modern warehouse for supplying stores and spares to service all the lifeboats around the British coast. The old store was converted to aid the development and repair of the lifeboat fleet.

THIRTY

Road and Rail

BEN BUXTON

As quays, communities and industries were established around the edges of the Harbour so it became necessary to have a network of tracks to allow the free flow of people and goods to and from the shore. Over time these tracks became roads, some of which still exist today, either as roads, byways, or footpaths. As rail transport developed it was also used as the most efficient way of transporting materials to and from the ports around the Harbour.

ROADS

There must have been tracks of sorts, or routes at any rate, linking settlements, industrial centres and quays on the Harbour with the hinterland from early times. Pottery made in the area in the Iron Age has been found over a wide area in Dorset and Hampshire. There must

A watercolour of the cottages at Ower Quay, 1910. The figures are all members of the Churchill family, who then lived there.

have been a route to the Harbour and to the massive jetties or piers at Cleavel Point and Green Island, dated to about 250 BC.

The earliest road, in the sense of a built structure, was the Roman road linking the depot on the Hamworthy peninsula to the fortress at Lake Farm, near Wimborne. It was built during the conquest of Dorset in the years following the Roman invasion of Britain in AD 43 (see Chapter 9). It was presumably maintained for civilian use throughout the Roman period, and part of the southern section, north of Upton, appears on maps from the seventeenth century onwards. It was important enough in the 1840s to be bridged by the Southampton and Dorchester railway, and is now used as a bridleway.

There may have been an early Roman fort of the conquest period at Wareham, which would have had road links to other military bases at Lake Farm and Dorchester. There was certainly a settlement at Wareham later in the Roman period, which likewise would have had road links to other settlements. There was also a major pottery east of Wareham at Bestwall (Swineham Farm) (see Chapter 9). This was presumably, as now, close to the River Frome which was used for importing raw materials and exporting the finished products. On the south side of the Harbour there must have been roads linking settlements such as that at Ower, and industrial centres such as that at Norden.

Most of the Roman roads would have disappeared through lack of use and maintenance after the end of the Roman period. Little is known of the road system in the Harbour area in subsequent centuries. Wareham was the most important town and port on the Harbour from Saxon times until the fourteenth century, and it must have had road links to inland towns such as Dorchester and Corfe Castle. The Purbeck stone industry flourished in medieval times and Corfe Castle became the centre of stone working. There was a road from there to Ower Quay on the south shore of the Harbour, from which finished products were exported. Ower Quay was also used for importing timber to be used in building work at Corfe Castle in 1286. The planned thirteenth century town of Newton, east of Ower, would have had access roads planned, but, like the town itself, they were probably never built. There were other industries on the Harbour which would have needed road access: salt production from earliest times at many places around the Harbour (Chapter 14), and copperas production at Lilliput in the sixteenth century (Chapter 15).

On the south side of the Harbour, Sharford Bridge on the Corfe River, not far from where it meets the Harbour at Wytch Lake, represents an old route from Wareham to Ower Quay and other places on the Harbour shore. The bridge appears on a map of 1610, which indicates its importance at that time. On the north side of the Harbour, a traveller in 1540 noted that the land route east of Wareham went through the farms of Keysworth and Holton, and a ferry operated across the mouth of Lytchett Bay.

Maps begin to show principal roads in the seventeenth century, by which time Poole was the main focus of roads. The three main routes from Poole were to Christchurch, Ringwood, and Wimborne. Another route towards Wimborne was from Hamworthy, via the old Roman road. There was also a route to Sturminster Marshall and Blandford from Hamworthy. This ran parallel to the later road, the present A350, east of Beacon Hill (Lytchett Beacon), where it is still in use as Beacon Hill Lane and as a bridleway on Upton Heath. A section of this road on the north side of the 1847 railway crossing

Sharford Bridge, on the Corfe River: the remains of an old route between Wareham and Ower Quay.

Upton Heath was abandoned shortly before the railway was built (see below) but it can still be seen in places south of the railway. Palmerston Road, Upton, marks its course.

Eighteenth century maps also show roads radiating from Wareham, to Poole, Blandford, Bere Regis and Dorchester.

Industries such as clay extraction and pottery-making were developing, and their products were exported via quays on the Harbour, served by tracks. Quays

The first Ordnance Survey map of Poole Harbour, 1811, clearly shows the principal roads and tracks between the various quays on the southern side of the Harbour.

ABOVE Poole's first bridge opened in 1834.

BELOW The second bridge between Poole and Hamworthy, with the tollhouse on the Poole side on the right. It opened in 1885, and was replaced by the present bridge in 1927.

The eighteenth century turnpike between Wareham and Poole east of Sandford, now a bridleway. The stone is a boundary marker.

for the export of clay from Purbeck were built on the Arne peninsula (Russel Quay and Hyde's Quay). There were also quays at Wytch Passage and on the Studland peninsula (at Redhorn and South Haven). There was also a good deal of passenger traffic across the Harbour, between Poole and the various settlements and quays on the southern shore, with their own access tracks.

Until the eighteenth century, roads were in theory maintained by the parishes, but the result was that the standard of roads was very poor. The road system was revolutionised in the later eighteenth century with the creation of the turnpike trusts. These trusts built and maintained main roads, raising revenue by charging tolls. They remained responsible for the roads until county councils took them over in the 1880s. In some cases the new roads followed the same courses as the old ones, but many new routes were constructed, leaving the old ones as minor roads or even abandoned altogether.

They were built with stone foundations and surfaced with gravel, and were, as far as possible, straight.

In the years following 1756 the three main routes from Poole (Poole Gate, where Towngate is now) to the east and north were 'turnpiked'; to Christchurch via Bourne Bottom (Bournemouth, as it became); to Ringwood via Longfleet, Constitution Hill, Kinson, and Longham Bridge; and to Wimborne via Gravel Hill. A road branched west from the Wimborne Road to pass through Upton, and this branched to Bere Regis via Lytchett Matravers, and to Wareham via Lytchett Minster. From 1766 turnpike roads were built from Wareham to Creech, Bere Regis, Dorchester via Wool, and Swanage via Corfe Castle.

The eighteenth century turnpike roads have remained the basis of the main road system around the Harbour to this day. There have, of course, been modifications and additions. The original turnpike between Sandford and Kings Bridge (near Lytchett Minster) took a more easterly route than the current one. Part of this road is in use as a bridleway on Sandford Heath where it is known locally as 'The Roman Road.' The current road (A351) was built sometime between 1795 and 1811. In 1834 the first Poole Bridge linking Poole and Hamworthy opened. This meant that traffic between Poole and destinations to the west took the route through Hamworthy rather than the longer one round Holes Bay. The road through Hamworthy was therefore improved and a new straight section was built to Upton. From there it was continued (forming the cross roads at Upton) as a new road to Sturminster Marshall and Blandford. The road took a new route to the west of the former route described above. At this time a plan to build a road between Hamworthy and the Wareham-Poole road in the Organford area was dropped, presumably because the cost of the proposed bridge over the mouth of Lytchett Bay would have been prohibitive.

The expansion of Poole and its suburbs since the middle of the nineteenth century has led to much road building, although the pattern of the main roads remains based on the turnpikes and rural lanes of earlier times. In the 1970s and 1980s various new roads were built to cope with increasing motor traffic. In Poole itself the Towngate flyover opened in 1971. The A35 Lytchett Minster and Upton bypass, and its continuation eastwards, opened in 1975. Holes Bay Road, a new route linking the bypass with the centre of Poole, opened in 1988. It was intended to continue the Lytchett Minster bypass westwards, skirting Sandford, to link up with the proposed Wareham bypass, but this section was never built. The northern section of the Wareham bypass opened in 1980, the southern section eight years later.

The only public roads on the south side of the Harbour lead to Arne, Wytch, and South Haven (Studland). The latter road became more important when the vehicle ferry across the mouth of the Harbour to Sandbanks began operating in 1926. Other roads lead to individual houses and farms. In 1987 the oil company BP built a road from the A351 at Norden to its gathering station at Wytch Farm, and built a network of roads from there to oil wells to the east. One of these roads follows part of the route of the old clay tramway which ran between Norden and Goathorn.

On the north side of the Harbour, between Hamworthy and Wareham, roads to farms at Holton, Keysworth, and Swineham stop short of the shore, which is low-lying and muddy.

RAILWAYS

Numerous mineral and industrial railways (most of them technically tramways, being unfenced) were built to quays on the shores of the Harbour from 1806 onwards, and the main line north of the Harbour developed between 1847 and 1893.

The railways serving the clay industry in Purbeck, the first of which was built in 1806, have been described in Chapter 18. Mineral and industrial lines developed much later on the northern shores of the Harbour, after the arrival of the main line from London in 1847, and in most cases they were connected to it. The first was built by George Jennings in 1867 to transport pipes made at the South Western Pottery Works, Parkstone, to a quay at Salterns,(Chapters 5 and 19). The line was upgraded from narrow gauge to standard gauge in 1874, so that it

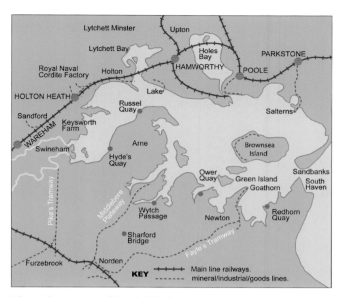

The railways round Poole Harbour.

could link with the newly-built main line at Parkstone. The line later served Salterns Engineering Works which repaired railway wagons during the First World War. The Salterns section closed in about 1925, the Parkstone section in 1963. Another pottery, at Sandford, had a tramway link to the main line. The pottery opened in 1857 but the tramway as probably built to serve the earlier brickworks on the site. The line remained in use until the pottery closed in 1966.

The clay works at Lake (now part of Ham Common) on the west shore of the Hamworthy peninsula were served by a short narrow gauge line from about 1870 to about 1938. Trucks, which latterly were pulled by cable, took the clay to drying sheds and from there to a pier where it was tipped into barges and taken to Poole for transhipment. The works closed before the Second World War, and during the war the pier was used as part of a fuel depot for fuelling RAF flying boats (see Chapter 31).

Even Brownsea Island had its own tramway. It was built in 1855 as part of a pottery, brick, and tile enterprise by the then owner of the Island, Colonel Waugh (see Chapter 19). The line ran for more than a mile from clay pits on the north shore, round the west coast to the works on the south coast. The works closed in 1887.

Two railway developments around the Harbour originated during, and in connection with, the First World War. In 1914-15 the Royal Naval Cordite Factory (see Chapter 16) was built at Holton Heath to the north of the Wareham–Poole main line, and it was served by a network of standard and narrow gauge lines, the latter totalling 14 miles in length. Raw materials were

ABOVE Lake Pier on Ham Common is now popular with anglers and swimmers, but it was originally built to serve the clay works at Lake.

BELOW The tramway along Town Quay opened in 1874 and closed in 1960.

brought in on the main line, and Holton Heath Station was built for the thousands of workers. The highly dangerous cordite was exported via a tramway which ran eastwards on the north side of the main line and then crossed it by a bridge to a massive wooden pier, Rockley Pier, at the mouth of Lytchett Bay. Barges then took the cordite to naval dockyards at Gosport and Chatham. Export via tramway and pier ceased in 1938 when it was feared that the barges could become targets for German submarines, and thereafter the main line was used. The

pier was demolished in about 1980. Another tramway led direct to the shore of the Harbour where waste was dumped. Most of the tramway network in the Holton Heath works closed in 1957 when cordite production ended.

Also in 1914 the Admiralty took over the foreshore of Holes Bay parallel to West Quay Road, Poole, as a stores base. Most existing buildings were demolished to make way for a siding which was built between the Quay and Poole Station. The line was taken up in 1920.

The main line from London arrived in 1847, when the Southampton and Dorchester Railway opened. From Brockenhurst the line meandered westwards through Ringwood and Wimborne, well to the north of the route of the present main line through Bournemouth (which hardly existed then) and Poole. This section was promoted by Charles Castleman, and with its meanders was called Castleman's Corkscrew; the footpath and cycle track which now runs along part of the route also perpetuate the name. From Wimborne it continued to Hamworthy and westwards to Wareham and on to Dorchester. At Hamworthy Station, at first known as Poole Junction and later Hamworthy Junction, a branch left for a station near the end of the Hamworthy peninsula, called Poole Station.

Poole was connected to the main line in 1872 when a branch – the Poole Junction Railway – was built from Broadstone to Poole. The station was built on a site slightly east of the present station (it was demolished in 1969 to make way for the Towngate flyover). Two years later this line was continued eastwards through Parkstone as far as Bournemouth West, and in 1888 it was joined to Bournemouth East – the present

The main line between Weymouth and London where it crosses Lytchett Bay at Rockley. The projection is the beginning of the former Rockley Pier.

Bournemouth Station – which was already connected to Christchurch (and a direct line from Christchurch to Brockenhurst was also built then). The section east of Poole was built out on a causeway across Parkstone Bay, enclosing what is now the boating lake(Chapter 5). Also in 1874 a goods line (tramway) was built along West Quay Road to The Quay. The evolution of the main line was completed with the opening of the causeway and bridge across Holes Bay (the Holes Bay Curve) in 1893.

Inevitably, the decline in traffic on the older routes caused by the opening of the busier and more direct southern route, and the increasing use of the roads, meant that the older routes would close. The original 1847 line from west of Brockenhurst to West Moors closed in 1964 and the section between West Moors (fuel depot) and Wimborne closed in 1974. The section from Broadstone to Hamworthy Junction closed in about 1965, although in the last years the southern section had been used for freight only, by Upton Brick Company. The Poole to Wimborne line closed in 1977, although passenger services on this line had stopped in 1964. The Town Quay tramway closed in 1960.

The Hamworthy branch closed to passenger traffic in 1896 but was extended to wharves at the end of the peninsula and continued in use as a goods line. The line remains open, although it is now very little used. The station building survived until the 1990s.

The Wareham to Swanage branch line, which opened in 1885, closed in 1972, although the first two miles remained open to serve the clay works, and, later, a BP depot at Furzebrook. The section from Swanage to Norden has re-opened as The Swanage Railway, now extended to the main line at Wareham via Furzebrook.

THIRTY-ONE

Flying Boats and Poole Harbour

POOLE FLYING BOATS CELEBRATION

THE BOAC STORAGE FACILITY in the 1950s was at Lake, Hamworthy, on the site of the former RAF Hamworthy, with its tight compound, hard, and slipways. The group of disused aircraft there, and on the foreshore at Lower Hamworthy, were the last obvious remnants of Poole Harbour's era as a flying boat hub for the United Kingdom.

The Fleet of 'British Flying Boats' belonging to Imperial Airways Limited was moved from Hythe to Poole at the outbreak of war in September 1939, to put into effect the carefully formulated plans that had been prepared as early as 1937, when the possibility of hostilities with Nazi Germany seemed increasingly likely.

This decision was taken as it was feared that the Luftwaffe would immediately target Southampton Water for its raids because of the significant number of important installations and facilities based around its shoreline. Poole Harbour had been selected as it was not so busy. The large expanse of water with its islands and inlets offered a good range of options to mark out runways, and might afford some degree of protection. The Royal Navy had been responsible for making the necessary arrangements and putting defences in place. Operational HQs for Imperial Airways were on 2 craft moored at Town Quay, with the Control vessel in Brownsea Roads. The threat passed as Britain entered a period known as 'the phoney war', when little happened. Hythe was again used on occasions whilst Poole was ticking over: this though was the lull before the storm.

Poole again became fully operational from the start of 1940 in dreadful winter weather and atrocious conditions. This time the bulk of the Imperial Airways flying boats were brought over from Hythe which was left as the repair facility. There were no Imperial Airways slipways at Poole so maintenance had to be carried out on the sets of Flying Boat moorings.

A Training School for fliers with the Fleet Air Arm using the seaplanes of 765 Squadron also moved to Poole. This was based at the Royal Motor Yacht Club

A Submarine Walrus of 765 Squadron coming ashore at the Royal Naval Air Station Sandbanks, HMS Daedalus II in about 1942. HMS Daedalus II was established at Sandbanks in 1940 as a Fleet Air Arm Seaplane Training Centre. The Royal Motor Yacht Club clubhouse became its offices, and its boatshed was used for servicing and repairs

at Sandbanks and used its clubhouse, its slipway and boatshed. Another hangar, yard and slip were at the site of the Sandbanks Yacht Co.: other properties were requisitioned. It was called the Royal Naval Air Station Sandbanks HMS Daedalus II, after its former base at Lee-on-Solent. Of the types of seaplane that served there, the Walrus was the most numerous and ideal for the further purpose of Air Sea Rescue.

The civil flying boat operations had also taken over various sites scattered in and around Poole as its facilities. Imperial Airways Limited was incorporated as British Overseas Airways Corporation (BOAC) by April 1940. In June 1940 flying boat services from Poole via the Mediterranean through to Egypt and on to South Africa, or via the Middle East to the Indian Subcontinent, to Asia and onwards to Australasia, were under direct threat. When France fell, and Italy came into the war

ABOVE G-AGBZ *Bristol* off Poole's New Quay illustrates the difference between this US-built Boeing 314A with its 'sponsons' and British flying boats with floats. Two blockships anchored in the Harbour in case it became necessary to scuttle them in the entrance are visible in the background. The tender was bringing ashore a party of Indian politicians for talks with the War Cabinet in September 1942.

BELOW G-AGCB *Bangor* was another of BOAC's three Boeings bought from PanAm. They served here until 1946, and had a much larger capacity than British flying boats. The launch bears the title 'British Airways 49', as the three Boeings, although part of the BOAC Fleet, were actually owned by a subsidiary called 'British Airways (Atlantic)' – an interesting foretaste of the eventual renaming of BOAC as BA!

on the side of Germany, the Mediterranean routes were severed. Covert missions were flown from Poole Harbour into France, and also surveillance over Irish territorial waters. Contingency plans again were enacted where BOAC moved its operational HQs beyond Cairo down to Durban. Flying boats were used to keep these lines of communication open on what is known as the Horseshoe Route. A large consignment of staff, engines, and spare parts to keep these services going was shipped out from the UK.

This left Poole with a selection of longer distance flying boats, including some older types moored here. A significant function was to operate 'Shuttle Services' to Foynes to keep transatlantic links open with America as the US was neutral and could not fly into Poole when the UK was at war, so Eire was the terminus for Pan Am. Two famous C-Class Empire FBs did fly from Poole to New York via Botwood in the autumn of 1940. The four return crossings by G-AFCZ *Clare*, and by one G-AFCX *Clyde* with some VIPs as passengers from Poole, were significant to the nation's morale in the darkest days of the Second World War, and with enormous publicity in the USA.

The long distance flying boats were necessarily switched to the quest of securing a route via Lisbon to West Africa, where the colonies of France were consequently influenced to join in with Free French Forces on the Allies' side. With staging posts along the West African coastline, Lagos became a focal point before moving down to the Congo and inland along the course of the river and its ports, to Port Bell in Uganda, and linking with the Horseshoe Route. This opened the way for four revamped Poole flying boats to reinforce Durban's fleet when the Japanese threat materialised, and the India to Australia section of the Horseshoe Route was broken (though a route from Perth to Ceylon was started).

Another important mission of *Clare* was to open the flying boat route with vital supplies via Gibraltar to Malta. Sadly *Clare* was later lost off West Africa. *Clyde* sank in a storm at Lisbon, and G-AFCK *Golden Horn* crashed there.

On 11th. June 1941, Poole Harbour suffered an air raid as G-ADHK *Maia* was bombed when moored off Salterns. BOAC's Marine Terminal at Poole had been moved from (firstly) the 'Norton Building' just off

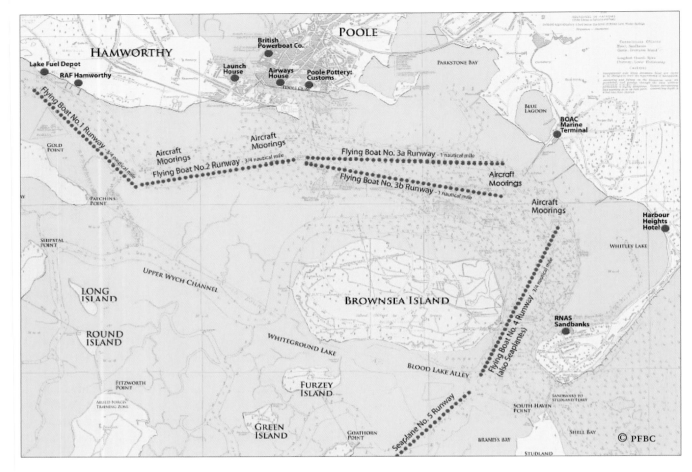

ABOVE Map showing the runways and principal sites used by Flying Boats and Seaplanes in the Harbour between 1939 and 1948 [copyright Poole Flying Boats Celebration (Charity 1123274)].

BELOW This photograph of Speedbird Class G-AGBZ *Bristol* contrasts with the first as it is out of wartime camouflage and is shown in Poole Harbour awaiting a launch to board passengers for New York in 1945.

the High Street, to the former Poole Pottery Buildings (since demolished to make way for the 'Dolphin Quays Development'); then to the Harbour Club at Salterns, later the site of the Poole Harbour Yacht Club, now Salterns Marina Hotel.

Sir Winston Churchill was able to influence the US Government to provide BOAC at Poole Harbour with three Boeing 314As which were ordered for Pan Am but became the 'Speedbird Class' of *Bangor, Berwick,* and *Bristol.* They had good transatlantic capability and with a larger capacity for passengers than the Short Empire C-Class. These were to be significant acquisitions on lend-lease based at Poole (1941-46) for BOAC's Flying Boat Fleet. The summer route to the US from Poole was via Foynes and Botwood, with the new BOAC base at Baltimore; in winter, Lisbon, the Azores and Bermuda lay along a more southerly route which would not be affected by ice; and a third transatlantic passage was from the US to Bermuda, West Indies, Belém in Brazil and over to Lagos, (there connecting with the River Congo routes links from the Horseshoe Route) before heading northwards back to Poole.

American-built flying boats differed in design from

Two BOAC stewardesses carrying flasks to a launch at Customs House steps. Note the seawoman aboard the launch. Poole was unused to women afloat, and their use aboard the launches was regarded as highly radical!

their British counterparts in having 'sponsons' instead of floats and at Poole the three joined BOAC's first Catalina G-AGBJ *Guba* (purchased from an American survey company). Other Catalinas on lend-lease were to follow, including G-AGDA which was lost on a training exercise at Poole. Five were commissioned here by BOAC before then being forwarded to Australia as much-needed reinforcements. When joined by 12 RAF military Cats, various Flying Boats in wartime Poole had a significant American origin.

G-AFCI *Golden Hind* possibly when at Poole and off Salterns. Through adaptations *Golden Hind* was the largest and the last surviving of the Short G-Class UK-built FBs and was left at Poole when BOAC's Fleet departed in April 1948. *Golden Hind* was bought privately and plans were afoot for preservation but were scuppered when she sank by the slipway on the River Swale. Unfortunately the jigs which could have been used for a repair had just been broken up at the Short Bros Works at Rochester!

RAAF Sunderland Mk III EJ 134 UT-N 'N for Nuts' resting upon its beaching wheels at RAF Hamworthy – surrounded and supported by maintenance scaffolding.

RAF Poole was rapidly constructed along the shore at Lake, Hamworthy, as a base for its military Flying Boats. This was then commissioned on the 1st.August 1942. With a change of name to RAF Hamworthy, it became the home to 461 Squadron Royal Australian Air Force which moved from RAF Mount Batten, by Plymouth Sound. This was popularly known as 'The ANZAC Squadron' as it had been formed on 25th. April, ANZAC Day, 1942. Its Sunderland Flying Boats at Hamworthy were under operational control of 19 Group RAF Coastal Command.

The Sunderlands were developed from the design of the Empire C-Class; they were known as Flying Porcupines. (In all 739 were constructed.) Those from Hamworthy saw action in attacking U-Boats in the South Western Approaches and the Bay of Biscay. One of its ten Sunderlands, T9085 was lost on the 21st. January with all 11 crew members. Initially, 300 staff were based here including crews, engineers, ground and support staff, also WAAFs and Wrens. Vital maintenance had to be carried out at the moorings, slipways, or the hard standing as there was no hangar. Facilities were dotted around Lake Estate at Hamworthy, on Parkstone Road, Poole, and the Harbour Heights area.

461 Squadron left by May 1943 in transferring to Pembroke Dock in Wales. Their bravery and exploits when stationed at RAF Hamworthy are remembered today both in Poole and throughout their homeland of Australia. During 1942-1944 83 squadron members died. The squadron motto was: 'They shall not pass unseen'. 210 Squadron arrived as their replacement in late April 1943, becoming known as the 'Catalina

A pair of BOAC converted Sunderland flying-boats at their moorings. This 1947 photograph, which as well as the sailing boats includes the Sandringham Class: G-AHZC *Penzance*, vividly captures the final episode of BOACs years at Poole. *Penzance* was one of a dozen Sandringhams and Solents which were eventually brought back to Poole for 'disposal'.

Squadron' after its 12 American-built flying boats. Fitted with Leigh Lights, they were to continue to fly the vital RAF antisubmarine patrols over the Bay of Biscay. The motto of 210 Squadron had been chosen in Welsh as: 'Yn y nwyfre yn hedfan' (Hovering in the Heavens), There were 46 officers and 235 other ranks, together with 21 WAAF, again billeted throughout Poole. One of these officers was John Alexander Cruickshank, who was later awarded the Victoria Cross for flying his damaged flying boat to the Shetlands from the Arctic when seriously injured after sinking a U-Boat.

At the start of 1944 the Squadron was moved, but not before the tragic loss of its 'FP287' and 8 of the 12 crew after crashing near Round Island in foggy conditions when returning from a training exercise with Leigh Lights. The Catalinas had left Poole as the base was required for the build-up of forces for D-Day on the 6th. June 1944. Some 50 staff remained at RAF Hamworthy which was taken over in February 1944 by the Royal Navy as HMS *Turtle*.

After D-Day, Transport Command then deployed to Poole 24 Sunderland Mark IIIs which had been converted for passenger-carrying as the 'Hythe Class' operating BOAC routes as these gradually opened again. These flew long distance to destinations such as Africa, the Middle East, the Indian subcontinent, Asia and Australia. In the post-war period they took civil aviation registrations and names, with also BOAC's famous Speedbird logo. They were joined (1947) by another set of nine better-converted Sunderlands as the Sandringham 'Plymouth Class', and, just before Flying Boat Control left Poole for Hythe in the spring of 1948, the more comfortable 'Solents'.

From 1946 the American-built presence in Poole Harbour had been from visiting PanAm Clippers, and latterly a tour company's Bermuda Sky Queen (ex

OQZB taking off from Runway No 3 by Salterns. 'B for *Bertie*' appeared in Poole's first post war Town Guide.

G-AHIL *City of Salisbury* beached at Lower Hamworthy in 1954. It was finally dismantled in 1956.

Capetown Clipper) which didn't make it back to the US from Poole: battling against headwinds it ran out of fuel, but everyone was saved by a US Coastguard Cutter, the *George M.Bibb*. All scheduled passenger services from Poole were ended before the end of 1947, and Baltimore in January 1948.

New facilities were based at Southampton's Pier 50, but in 1950 BOAC discontinued flying boat operations. There were extensive airfields worldwide gradually released by the military in peacetime for the Civil Airlines. It was the end of the BOAC Flying Boat era, although a few independent operators struggled on until 1958. The closure of BOAC operations at Poole brought to an end its Marine Section responsible for various launches and work boats. The launches had been brought over from Hythe in 1939, and the work boats recruited locally along with their crews who took the opportunity to be instated as coxswains after training and passing the tests. This had given rise to BOAC Marine School at Poole when most of the original members of the Marine Section enlisted in the Royal Navy, or were called up. Their place was mainly taken by seawomen trained at the Marine School.

After being demobbed, many of the men came back to their duties, and witnessed the return of former prisoners-of-war after the surrender of Japan in August 1945, many in very poor condition and brought in by flying boats. In the immediate post-war years BOAC's Marine Section was at its busiest as passenger numbers increased from 11,500 in 1945, later topping 25,000. After the spring of 1948 some took over watch duties for moored aircraft. They had played their part in a significant record that no passenger departing from Poole had ever been injured!

Of the premises and facilities requisitioned in 1940-42, the Royal Motor Yacht Club recommenced in September 1945, and others were handed back at short notice by the Royal Navy and Royal Air Force, and BOAC Marine Terminal at Salterns in 1948. The markers for the seaplanes' runway had been removed with the departure of the Fleet Air Arm from RNAS Sandbanks, and from the other five remaining runways in 1947, leaving just the stretch of the Wareham Channel for the arrivals and the occasional departure under very strict supervision of the Port Authorities during the 1950s.

With the cessation of its Flying Boat operations, BOAC had upwards of 50 aircraft in service or already laid-up.

When the bulk of its fleet of 'Hythes', 'Sandringhams' and 'Solents' were removed from Poole to Southampton, several surplus flying boats remained on the sets of moorings along the Wareham Channel. These included the last of the Empire Class, G-ACTI *Golden Hind*, which had been earmarked for conservation as all the other 'Empires' in UK waters, which had survived the war years, had been dismantled in 1946 and '47.

During the early 1950s, Poole, with Belfast and Felixstowe, became a storage facility for BOAC's flying boats. These were brought into the Harbour and placed on the moorings, then gradually dispersed to potential purchasers, or in most instances – brought to the hardstanding at the former RAF Hamworthy base for storage and disposal.

The site could accommodate up to a maximum of eleven aircraft brought up from the slipway upon their trolleys. Some of these were virtually new in having been flown from the manufacturer Shorts in Belfast directly to Poole. In 1959 the last Sandringham G-AHZA *Penzance* was scrapped; though beached on the shore at Lower Hamworthy were G-AHIU *Solway* and G-AKNS *City of Liverpool*, moved there from Lake in an attempt to create a coffee bar. The venture subsequently failed, and many people still recall the forlorn sight of these being finally dismantled. From 1954 the Royal Marines had gradually taken over at Lake and the facilities of the Hamworthy base.

With the new millennium a group of friends from Lilliput/Salterns, Sandbanks, and Hamworthy and their contacts came together with the express purpose of Celebrating the History of Flying Boats and Seaplanes based at Poole: in particular, to form a public access archive of all such matters – including the role of the 1,000+ Poole families formerly involved in both the civil and military flying boat operations, and in the provision of the services which supported these, together with recording all the facilities which were used. In 2008 this organisation became the UK Charity 1123274, Poole Flying Boats Celebration (www.pooleflyingboats.com).

THIRTY-TWO

Leisure and Pleasure

PETER BURT

'The general impression abroad amongst yachtsmen who have never visited the Port is that there is an awful lot of mud about. This is quite true. But there is an awful lot of water as well.

Although a strong wind blowing against the tide in the larger channels can knock up quite a nasty sea for a small craft, the motion is kindly to the most squeamish tummy and never takes on that "long, slow gastric heave", which can be so trying [at sea].'

Official Handbook of the Port of Poole
Percy Woodcock, 1960

A quiet read. Poole Quay in the 1920s. Note the steam-driven pile driver and Thames barges in the background.

THE EARLIEST HARBOUR boats, such as the log boat dating to 250 BC and found in the Harbour in 1964, would undoubtedly have been built for the purely practical purpose of ferrying people and goods, and perhaps for fishing. However, on a beautiful day when there might have been a village celebration, or just for the pure delight of being on the Harbour, there must have been some element of enjoyment. With the relatively narrow beam of such boats, they were probably unstable and not handy to use, and would have required a number of paddlers to move them along safely, with the possibility of shared enjoyment.

Such dual usage for Harbour boats probably continued for at least the next two millennia. Even at the end of that period, the main recreational activities were extensions of hunting and fishing, and it was not until the end of the nineteenth century with increasing wealth and leisure time that recreational yachting, as we now know it, really began.

There has been little direct evidence of the types of boat used in the Harbour following the log boat until the archaeological dig carried out by David Watkins of the Poole Museum Services in 1986-7 on the site of the old Poole Iron Foundry, between West Street and Thames Street some 90 metres from present-day Poole Quay (see page 147). Ships' timbers were found lying in a horizontal stratum, which probably formed the fifteenth-century beach. They were for vessels up to thirty feet long, with a beam of ten or twelve feet. Although their primary use would have been for trading, they could equally have been used on occasion, for pleasure.

Poole canoes or punts are first recorded in Georgian times. Often referred to as 'flatties', these local boats were used both for work and for pleasure. They appear to have evolved from the normal run of local small boats that appeared around the coast of the UK. Similar boats could be found at Weymouth, where they are known as Fleet trows or Backwater boats. The basic

John Edward Wills (bearded) and party in Poole canoes up the River Frome near Wareham. Once a year, according to tradition, they netted the river and gave the catch to the townspeople.

size of the Poole canoe is similar to many others, but they have taken a particular shape because of the local topography. The conditions in the Harbour with small winding channels between wide shallow areas of mud caused the local boats to evolve higher topsides and a shallow draught.

Colonel Peter Hawker, the well known field sportsman who left us wonderful diaries of his day-to-day hunting, shooting, and fishing exploits, writes of coming to Poole in January 1818 and his local contact in Sandbanks providing him with a canoe or punt from which he proceeded to shoot large numbers of duck.

A 'leg o' mutton' sail, rigged on a simple mast was often used when the wind was blowing in the right direction. This was a single triangular sail, Gunter rigged, with a loose foot, sometimes on a makeshift boom or with the leech tied by way of a main sheet through a hole in the transom. One oar was used to steer and the other was used to minimise leeway, by pulling the occasional stroke to windward from the leeward side. It is only a few years since these were seen regularly in the Harbour. First-hand reports of conversations with men who used these sails mention returning with a boat full of mullet when the wind was piping up from Round Island and Arne. If the water was choppy with a wind against the tide at Stakes Buoy it required quite a lot of

nerve and some skill to handle it safely and return to the Fisherman's Dock.

From the 1930s most of the later boats had a transom to accommodate an outboard engine. Many canoes were fitted with two positions for thole pins, later replaced by rowlocks, in order that two people could row at once or to balance the boat if it was full of fish. Poole canoes were used as a maid of all work: cockling, netting, punt gunning, and days out with the family. Many families still remember going 'up between Quays', into Holes Bay to Pergin's Island, for glorious picnics and fun on the small sandy beach facing what is now the Holes Bay Relief Road. Peter Hawker used Poole canoes for sport and many others did the same right up until the present. Fibreglass hulls are now the order of the day with powerful outboard engines set into a well, forward of the transom. This gives the modern canoe a great turn of speed but retains its ability to work in very shallow water.

Commercial yacht yards started to appear in mid-

ABOVE Newman's Yard, Hamworthy, in the late 1930s. The bridge of 1927 is visible in the background, but not the power station, which didn't open until 1949.

BELOW The Quay in the 1920s, with a cruising yacht in the foreground, a steam yacht in the centre, and a full rigged ship in the background.

Victorian times. By the 1880s, there were many yards building yachts as well as commercial vessels in Poole. J. Allen, D Lewin, G. Musselwhite, T Musselwhite, E. Pinney, J. Saunders, C.J. Stone, and T. Wanhill were some of the individuals found in the *Lloyds Register of Yachts* of 1889, who were building yachts in Poole. In the twentieth century, Newman's Yard in New Quay Road became one of the top yards in the area. Photographs of the yard in late Victorian times show small craft of all sorts in the yard for repair, on the slipways, and in the water. Sailing cruisers, steam launches and dinghies were all built here and hundreds of craft right up to the 1970s were serviced, repaired and repainted every year. The yard was sold to Southern Ocean Shipyard in the 1970s who built their Gallants, Ocean 60, 70s, and 80s for a number of years until the 1980s, when the yard was sold to Dean and Dyball, who modernised and filled in the slipways. Dean and Dyball sold the yard in 1989 to Sunseeker International, who continue to build fast motor yachts on the site, as well as either side.

On the River Frome below Wareham stood the old and dilapidated wooden quay at Ridge, which was used to ship ball clay from the clay mines in Furzebrook up to the late 1930s. In the mid 1960s a London company, Bason and Arnold, established a small boatyard and repair facility called Ridge Yachting Centre using and improving the old wooden-piled quays. In the 1970s Commander Clarke purchased the Yard. He carried the business forward and established a large area of winter storage, rebuilt the jetties, and put pontoons alongside them. His son, Anthony Clarke, continues the family tradition of running the yard, which is always full and busy.

In Hamworthy, the site of the Dorset Yacht Company was first used as a boatyard before the First World War. During the war it built concrete barges. The site was purchased by the Culpan family in 1938 and built and repaired boats all through the Second World War. Many fine yachts were built there through the 1950s, 60s and early 70s. Now much reduced in size, it is still run by Robin and Russell Culpan. In 1985 the Lake Yard Club was formed, and in 1995 a new marina and dock were constructed.

Cobbs Quay started life as a Nissen hut and slipway on the saltings at the top of Holes Bay, above the Lifting Bridge. Mr Cobb sold the land to a Mr Buckingham, who brought in Eric Scoble to run and expand the place. Buckingham sold the yard to Marina Developments in 1975, by which time it had a large marina with 600 berths, a slipway with a railway capable of carrying 100 ton boats, and storage on the concrete hard for 600 boats during the winter. Now owned by the Iliffe family (who

had previously owned Furzey Island but now own Green Island), it continues to be a successful operation with a yacht club, many local marine businesses, workshops and offices and over a thousand boats ashore and afloat.

Next door, Lloyd Davis purchased a piece of Salting in the 1960s and with the broken tiles from the Carter Tile factory, created a boatyard which has a storage area and a flourishing small marina.

In West Quay Road, by the Lifting Bridge, was Newports Garage. They opened a marine division in 1962 run by Peter Rothwell. Newports Marine sold small motorboats and launches, outboards, and accessories. It lasted until the 1970s

Next door, Harvey's Boatyard, which moved from Sandbanks in the 1950s, carried out repairs and serviced moorings, carried goods to the islands in the Harbour and the daily postal service, as well as carrying on their passenger boat trade from Poole Town Quay and Sandbanks. In their yard for a few years, Frank Clarke built exquisite small wooden boats of high quality. Frank won the 'Lloyds Register, Boat of the Show' award at Earls Court twice in the 1960s and 70s. Owners remember the woodwork and joinery being of 'cabinet making' quality.

Arthur Bray Ltd. was next door, at No. 4 West Quay Road. They had moved from the top of the road by the Hunger Hill roundabout in 1964. Arthur Bray Ltd. had, for many years, been the exclusive importers and distributors of Chris Craft speedboats, Riva sports boats from Italy, and Mercury outboards from the USA. The David Brown Corporation, which also made Aston Martin cars, purchased the company in 1954 from Lt-Commander Arthur Bray. David Brown's Yacht *Astromar* wintered alongside the Quay.

ABOVE Dorset Lake Shipyard in the 1930s. Although Lake Yard is still busy, a large part of the photograph is now housing.

BELOW A sailing dinghy in Holes Bay in the 1920s. Note the scandalised mainsail.

Two yawl rigged private yachts sailing out through the Harbour entrance in the 1930s, probably at the start of the Cherbourg Race.

ABOVE AND TOP Poole Regatta in the 1930s. The swimming race was between the quays.

BELOW The rowing race during a Poole Regatta in the 1950s.

In 1970, Peter Burt purchased the Company and created a repair, mooring, and marine distribution business, leasing out many of the factories in the yard to small marine companies who wanted space on the waterfront. In 2007 as part of a consortium of landowners in West Quay Road, the land was sold for regeneration, with future public access along the waterfront.

To the north-east, up West Quay Road, Poole Boat Park managed to stack a large number of speedboats and sports boats on racks, out of the water with the use of a huge forklift truck. The company was owned and run by George Pittock until 2007. It was a very useful asset, enabling many boats to be stored in a small area.

Continuing up West Quay Road, there was the very successful Sunseeker Sales Company, owned and run by Harry and Pat Dodd. Next door was the head office and marina of Sunseeker International.

On Poole Quay, Burdens was the large yacht chandler in the 1950s and 1960s. Next door, was Piplers, another chandler, family-owned until the 1980s. Both these companies were very traditional chandlers with sail lofts, cover making, and rope work carried out on the premises. Burdens closed in Poole in the 1970s but Piplers continues to thrive and expand on the Quay under new ownership.

2003 saw the opening of the Dolphin Haven, a marina for visiting boats, built by the Poole Harbour Commissioners. Now known as the Poole Quay Boat Haven, it is extremely popular with both visitors and locals alike and shares its protective sea wall with the Poole fishermen, who have a marina and their fish

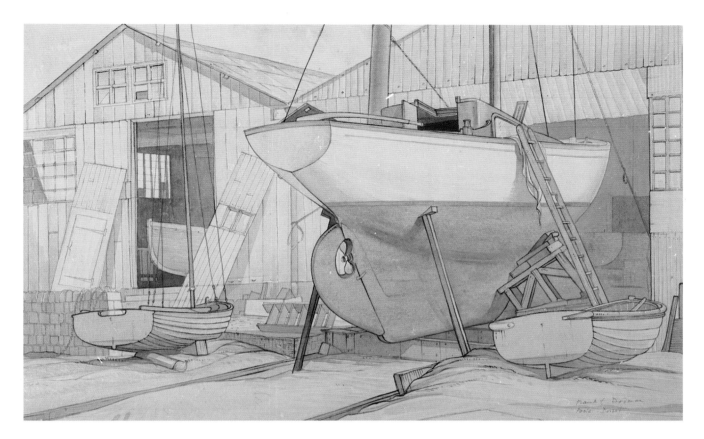

landing area within its sheltered space. Visitors are able to go ashore directly into the Old Town to shop, visit restaurants and watch the crowded Town Quay, with all its summer visitors.

Lathams Boatyard, in Turks Lane, Parkstone, started life as a strip of reeds and mud beside the Harbour, 50 feet wide by 600 feet long, which in 1959 was filled in with gravel and rubble from bomb-damaged properties being rebuilt after the war. Bill (Pop) Latham, transferred his marine engineering business from Parkstone Yacht Club, next door, to the new premises. In 1960, 'Pop's' son Ken Latham took over the yard, and the first of

Mitchell's Boatyard, a watercolour by Frank Dodman, who from 1948 to 1948 was Head of Art Teacher Training Department at Bournemouth and Poole College of Art.

the popular Latham launches was built. These led on to building many fine yachts in timber and fibreglass. Well-known racing boats such as *Breakaway* were built in the 1960s. In 1986 the first of nine X-class One Design racing boats was built. In 2003 the Latham Family sold

Brownsea Island from Sandbanks in the 1930s, showing moored yachts and houseboats.

Inside the Royal Motor Yacht Club's boat shed. A
watercolour by Frank Dodman.

the yard to David Kingsbury. Traditional boat building
and repair work still flourish on the site.

Mitchells Boat Yard, next door in Turks Lane, was
established in the 1930s. Apart from moorings and
storage ashore, Len Mitchell and his team built the
well-liked 'Parkstone Bay' series of 21-foot motor
launches and many yachts. The family sold out to Stuart
Rawlinson in 2003, and the yard continues to operate,
complete with a log cabin café.

John Clark purchased the old BOAC flying boat
terminal at Salterns Way, Lilliput, just after the end
of the Second World War. Poole Harbour Yacht Club
was started on the site in 1949. Clark started South
Coast Yachting Services in 1952. Tom Wills ran SCYS
for many years with members of many local fishing
families involved, including Hayes, Stevens, Davis and
Cartridges. In 1969, the Smith family took over the
ownership and running of the site and brought modern

techniques and equipment to the business, which with
the Salterns Marina and subsidiary companies, is a
flourishing concern stretching from Poole to Chichester.

Throughout the 1950s, 60s and 70s towards Evening
Hill in Lilliput, stood the Lilliput Yacht Station, also
known as Pizey's Yard. With a small amount of storage
for boats, a long timber pier and 80 moorings, it
maintained an old fashioned but popular air. It was sold
in the late 1980s for development.

Sandbanks Yacht Company was a successful small
boatyard in Panorama Road, Sandbanks. Apart from
the usual repairs and engineering, the yard had over 300
moorings and two service piers complete with petrol and
diesel pumps. They also ran a large fleet of popular hire
boats, which could be taken anywhere in the Harbour.
Stories abound of customers being towed back from the
far reaches of the Harbour at all times of the day and
night. The Seaton family sold out for development in the
mid 1990s.

Just down the road in the Royal Motor Yacht Club's
huge boat shed, originally built by Lord Lyle in 1927
for his yacht-building company, Randall and McGregor

ran a boat building company in the 1950s and 60s. Quality motor cruisers and launches were built in timber and, later, fibreglass hulls were fitted out. The business was taken over by Bernard Hiscock and Graham Titterington,who retired in 1989.

Across the Chain Ferry to Studland and Swanage, Lovell's Boatyard grew from small beginnings in the 1950s and 60s. From the 1970s it could boast 150 moorings, a crane and slipway and storage ashore for 30 or more boats and offered a service for those who lived in the Isle of Purbeck but wanted to moor near the entrance of the Harbour.

A host of small marine businesses sheltered under the wings of the bigger, busier yards. Involved in supplying equipment, servicing diesel and petrol inboard engines, outboard engines, electronics, life rafts, inflatable boats and ribs, these companies were the oil that lubricated the fun and pleasure of boating in the Harbour, and made it possible for 4,000 to 5,000 sailing and motor cruisers and the same number of dinghies to enjoy the Harbour in relative peace and safety.

With the rise in interest in the sport of yachting, came the yacht clubs. The earliest boat club in the Harbour according to local history was the Poole Yacht Club, established in 1865. However, its history is not clear and it amalgamated with the Hamworthy and Bournemouth Yacht Club (known as the 'Ham and Bones') in 1948. The Hamworthy had started life in 1889 in a railway coach near Hamworthy Beach. After a time the members

ABOVE Randall and McGregor's boatbuilding works in the Royal Motor Yacht Club boat shed.

BELOW Poole Yacht Club from the air, now the Harbour Commissioners Harbour Office. Starting in 1979, the Harbour Commissioners reclaimed 40 acres of land for the new ferry port, leaving the old Poole Yacht Club clubhouse 300 metres from the water.

ABOVE Parkstone Yacht Club in the 1950s. The original clubhouse shown here is now encased in later extensions.

BELOW A half-decked dinghy flying the Parkstone Sailing Club burgee off Poole Quay in the 1920s.

purchased a local cottage and then built a substantial clubhouse. This survived until the Poole Harbour Commissioners expanded the port in 1984, when a deal was struck with the Club, for the Poole Harbour Commissioners to build the members a new clubhouse and marina. Poole Yacht Club races Cruisers, R19s, Yachting World Day boats, Mirror dinghies, 420s and Lasers on at least two evenings a week in the summer season.

Parkstone Boating and Pier club started in 1895 at

Westons Point on the Elms Estate in Parkstone. By 1905 it had changed its name to Parkstone Sailing Club. It flourished and changed its name to Parkstone Yacht Club in 1948 to reflect the members' boating interests. Mostly involved with dinghy racing in the 1950s and 60s, classes included X One Design, Dolphins, Merlin Rockets, National 12s, Cadets, Porchester Ducks, Fireballs, catamarans, and many other classes. The club runs national and international regatta weeks, and from the end of the Second World War has run Poole Week. The Club built a substantial marina on its foreshore in 1995, and races two evenings and on Saturdays in the season.

East Dorset Sailing Club was started in 1875 at the bottom of Evening Hill. The tin boat shed, which was

The Royal Motor Yacht Club powerboat race, 1936.

ABOVE The first clubhouse of the Royal Motor Yacht Club was the *Florinda*, which was moored on Poole Quay.

The 100 mile Yachting World International Trophy race for powerboats at the start, off Bolson's Yard, Hamworthy, in 1931.

ABOVE The inner basin of Poole Harbour Yacht Club showing the inner basin and the lock gates.

BELOW Poole Harbour Yacht Club. The clubhouse was the old terminal for the BOAC flying boats.

built shortly afterwards survived until 1969, when the current clubhouse was built. With its long pier and moorings near the Club it continues to thrive.

The Royal Motor Yacht club was established in 1905 in Southampton Water. It amalgamated with the British Motor Boat Club in 1933 and moved to Poole to a floating clubhouse the *Florinda*, moored near the Lifting Bridge on Poole Quay. In 1936 the Club moved to a purpose-built clubhouse in Sandbanks. In 1989 the club built and opened a marina on its foreshore. The Club introduced Panther class speedboats between the wars and ran many motorboat races in the Harbour

and between the Quays into Holes Bay, both before the Second World War and afterwards in the 1950s. Its members also raced large and small cruisers and racing boats in offshore powerboat races throughout the 1960s, 70s, and 80s. The X One Design Class yacht was designed for the Club in 1910. During the 1960s, the Club organised The Poole Bay Olympic Sailing Association. Club members ran the Olympic training scheme from moorings in South Deep channel. These national and international regattas went on until 1972. The Club currently races Cruisers, Flying Fifteens, and Shrimpers on a Thursday evening in the season.

In 1956 a group of sailors at Lilliput Yacht Station (Pizey's Yard), decided to join together to create Lilliput Sailing Club. In the 1960s they purchased a piece of land on the side of the Blue Lagoon and in 1966 opened their own clubhouse, built substantially by the members themselves. It continues to thrive as a self-help club.

Rockley Cruising Club was founded in 1979 by a small group of mooring holders on moorings at Rockley. Original members are still involved but new members continue the Club.

Poole Harbour Yacht Club was started in 1949 as a commercially owned yacht club. Based at what is now the Salterns Hotel in Lilliput, 'PH' was a very successful social and boating club, with 'booze cruises' and an enthusiastic waterskiing section. In the early 1960s young members built a waterski jump which was initially moored in the Wych Channel near the fuel barge, before being moved round to Goathorn, where a slalom course was laid. The Club was centred around the bar and the inner basin plus the 'walk-on' moorings alongside the old pier. In 1969 the club and pier were purchased by the Smith family who built a successful marina on the site.

X boats under full sail.

North Haven Yacht Club started life in 1965 as the North Haven Lake Boat-owners Association. An enthusiastic self-help club, which built its own clubhouse in 1972 and rebuilt it in 2008, with floating pontoons and many moorings.

By the 1960s leisure boating, in all its forms, was taking place in the Harbour. Poole, Parkstone, East Dorset, and other clubs were racing regularly, each in their part of the Harbour, on a particular evening. The requirement for moorings in the Wych Channel, Brownsea Roads, Rum Row, off Parkstone, and off Hamworthy from Poole Yacht Club up the Oil Pier, north of Dorset Yacht Co. were increasing year by year. Elsewhere, in other ports and harbours, a new phenomenon was appearing. Sailors were beginning to find it easier to moor their boats in sheltered havens where they could walk aboard without the struggle of launching dinghies, non-starting outboards, and getting wet before even starting to sail.

The idea quickly spread to Poole, and PHYC, later to become Salterns Marina and Boat yard, at Lilliput had a number of berths alongside in the inner basin and along the old pier, where wooden catwalks were rigged between boats. Cobbs Quay at the top of Holes Bay was the next to follow suit, digging into the salt marshes and creating channels out to deep water to create a marina for more than 800 boats.

Poole Yacht Club created their Marina after their deal with Poole Harbour Commissioners in 1984. Next, The Royal Motor Yacht Club felt the need for a Haven and built on their foreshore in 1989, quickly followed by Parkstone Yacht Club, Dorset Yacht Company, now Lake Yard, Moriconium Quay, and finally Poole Quay Boat Haven built by the Poole Harbour Commissioners. Between these marinas and havens it is possible to moor well over two thousand boats in safety and comfort, in a minimum space. The number of swinging moorings in the Harbour was reduced, by a thousand or more.

The moorings, marinas and havens all come under the licensing control of the Poole Harbour Commissioners, who licence moorings, piers, pontoons and other 'works' in the waters of the Harbour. As well as issuing mooring licences, they also collect the revenue for the Crown Estates Commissioners' licences for the seabed, and Harbour dues.

Kite surfers on Whitley Lake.

Numerous boats are moored and kept in the River Frome, which although it is strictly outside the regime of the Harbour, must be included. Leisure boats are moored at Rockley Park, and on Poole Town Quay and the private quays above the Lifting Bridge.

Sailing schools appeared in the 1950s. The first one in the Harbour was started by a group of four ex-soldiers. Major-General A.W.C. Richardson, Colonel Broome, Captain Cox, and Major Stirling. It was successful, until the status of those teaching was challenged, and the question asked, as to whether they were amateurs and could continue to race in yacht-club races. The Sandbanks Sailing School closed after a few years. Harry Poole appeared in the late 1950s and for a good many years until the late '70s ran the Poole School of Sailing from his house in Sandbanks.

In 1976, Jim Gordon, an ex-Naval Officer who became a chartered accountant and finance director, came to Poole to start the Rockley Point Sailing School. A second-hand mobile home was the office and classroom. Then wartime 'prefabs' were brought to the site and rebuilt. They lasted 37 years. Within 5 years there were 32 instructors, mostly students on their long vacation in the summer. Jim and his wife Barbara retired in 1997 leaving Peter, their son and his wife Lis to run the school.

Other Cruising Schools have come and gone, charter companies take groups and individuals for tuition, team building, and for pleasure sailing.

Boats have been moved by road to and from Poole over the period of the 1960s to the present day, by a number of local transport companies. Bolden Boat Transport, started by John Bolden was established in West Quay Road in the 1960s, later taken over by Bill Shakespeare, it continued to flourish through the 1970s and into the 80s. Bugler Transport specialises in moving Powerboats, particularly Sunseeker Boats all over Europe.

From small beginnings in early times, Poole has produced boatbuilders of every size, each specialising in their own type of boat, catering to their own niche market. Leisure sailors have used the Harbour for a hundred and fifty years or more, mostly keeping on good terms with the fishermen and other professionals

Topper racing in the Harbour.

who also use the water. The Harbour has been a nursery for hundreds of sailors who have started in dinghies and moved onto the larger boats. Racing sailing dinghies and yachts has become a major hobby for many people, some going on to achieve great success in the Olympics and in World Class sailing of all sorts. Many others have cruised the north coast of France or ventured to far-flung places across the world. Still others potter happily to Goathorn, Studland, Swanage, or the Isle of Wight during summer weekends. Many boats are used for fishing and sub-aqua diving in Poole Bay.

Waterskiing has taken place from the 1950s; Rockley provided a calm area for the Rockley Water Ski School,

in the 50s and 60s. Jet skiers have their own area in the Harbour within which they can use their craft at speed. Large numbers of sailboarders and kite surfers use the area below Evening Hill, called Whitley Lake, as it is shallow and catches the prevailing wind.

Not only is Poole one of the most sheltered harbours on the south coast, it is also blessed with helpful tides giving long periods of high water and scenery that is that is the equal of any. No wonder pleasure boaters congregate here to enjoy what nature has created and man has nurtured.

Brownsea Island, Arnold Knight (1906-1949)

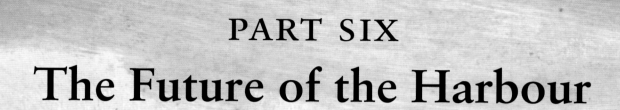

PART SIX
The Future of the Harbour

THIRTY-THREE

Likely Natural Changes

EDWARD COOMBE

As explored in part i, significant positive and negative changes have occurred in the level of water in the Harbour in relation to the land beneath and surrounding it since its dramatic formation following the end of the Ice Age 10,000 years ago.

There have been – and continue to be – two major processes at work, the net effect of which determines the depth of water in the Harbour: (1) a long-term (and continuing) land depression in the south of England that began with the formation of the English Channel, and (2) positive or negative changes in absolute sea level around the British Isles.

Whilst the first of these is localised, the second is determined by global changes in the volume of water in the oceans.

There is considerable difference of opinion as to the causes of changes in global sea levels, or even if these are currently happening at all. Without any such change the depth of water in the Harbour would still be increasing as a result of the land-depression effect. Any increase in global sea levels – which might be caused by global warming if this occurs – would reinforce the land-depression effect. The additional controversy as to whether mankind's activities have any measurable effect on global warming adds to the difficulties of predicting future changes.

Whatever the relative magnitudes of the individual effects might be, the net effect is that currently the depth of water in the Harbour in relation to the land is increasing at the rate of between 3 and 4 mm per year but exponentially rather than linearly. For the reasons given above, very long–term forecasting is impossible but, based on past experience, present trends seem likely to continue for at least the foreseeable future.

Taking an average increase figure of, say, 5mm per year for the next 100 years, the mean level of water in the Harbour in the early years of the twenty-second century would be 500 millimetres or 20 inches above present levels, with a correspondingly major effect on

sea defences at vulnerable places such as Sandbanks, particularly at high spring tides.

But the situation can be even more complicated than the direct result of rising (or falling) water levels in relation to the land, serious though that in itself might be.

Sediment deposited from the rivers flowing into the Harbour can be affected by both changing levels and increased (or reduced) rainfall resulting from climate change. Such changes in rainfall can also affect the floodplains around the Harbour, particularly around the lower reaches of the River Frome and River Piddle.

The growth of flora such as *Spartina* Grass with its ability to retain sediment can be affected by the temperature of water in the Harbour which can itself be caused not only by general atmospheric climate change but also by the increasing 'heat island' caused by developments in the Poole and Bournemouth conurbation. One estimate places the effect of such increasing growth as a reduction in the tidal capacity of the Harbour between eight and ten million cubic metres of water.

Increasing wave energy can have an adverse effect both outside and inside the Harbour, particularly to exposed beaches around Poole Bay and to sites such as Brownsea Island exposed to incoming wave patterns. Such increased waves may be the result (a) of climate change in the Northern Hemisphere if this leads to increasing winds, and (b) to increasing depth of water in the approaches to the Harbour leading to reduced sea-bed drag.

Overall, as was said in the Introduction to this Book, the Harbour is a dynamic place in all senses of the word that continues to respond to the many forces acting upon it. Fortunately, unless some entirely unforeseen catastrophic event occurs, the time-scale and magnitude of likely changes are such that they can be coped with to retain its aesthetic and utilitarian value. What is required is continuing evaluation of potentially adverse changes, with remedial action where necessary.

THIRTY-FOUR

Balancing the Future

PETER BURT

IN THE FUTURE AS IN THE PAST, the fortunes of the Harbour will be shaped by often-competing natural and man-made forces. The previous chapter has shown that whilst changes in water level may well have a significant long-term impact, it is man's use of the Harbour that could have the greater short-term impact.

The port of Poole is a Trust Port. Such ports hold a unique place in the United Kingdom ports industry as there are no shareholders or owners, and any surplus is ploughed back into the harbour and port operations for the benefit of the stakeholders of the Trust.

Responsibility for the well-being of the Harbour in all its forms rests with the Poole Harbour Commissioners. With no Government financial support, they must ensure sufficient income not only to perform their duties of conservation in order to enable the Harbour to operate effectively as a port, but to balance the potentially-conflicting commercial, leisure and environmental considerations of the Harbour as a whole.

Conservancy is, at best, expensive, with channels to be kept dredged, navigation marks to service, licensing works in the Harbour, providing a pilot service, policing the few who always want to break the rules, and keeping up to date with endless legislation from the European Union – to mention just six activities.

In balancing the potentially-conflicting commercial, leisure and ecological considerations of the Harbour, it is clear from what has already been said in previous parts of this book that those responsible are fully aware of the elements involved.

The Harbour has been recognised as an area of international ecological importance. The islands, and still largely-untouched southern and western shores, offer a superb contrast to the built-up northern and eastern shoreline. There are already many controls in place that will continue to curb any possible damaging development on the southern and western sides of the Harbour.

On the northern and eastern shoreline, the wish to build ever larger and more expensive waterfront houses will undoubtedly continue. Although this rarely has an effect on the Harbour, this pressure does change the

Long Island and Round Island from the air. Any future rise in sea levels would have a significant impact on the lower-lying parts of the Harbour.

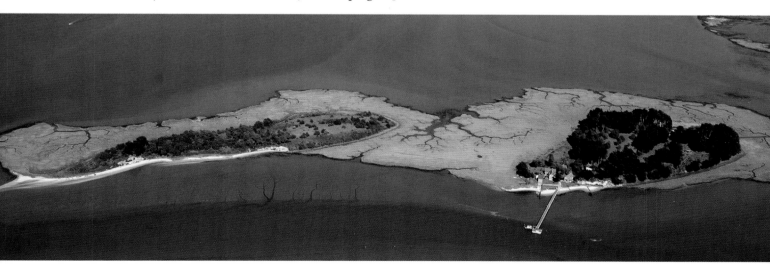

LEFT An artist's impression of the proposed Twin Sails Bridge over Holes Bay.

to lower passenger volumes in every south coast ferry port. Despite reductions in Brittany Ferries services to Cherbourg, Poole continues to play a pioneering role in the development of freight services to Northern Spain. Poole also continues to be the leading fast ferry port east of Dover, with Brittany Ferries and Condor Ferries services racing across to France and the Channel Islands.

The port has for centuries played an important role in moving bulk cargoes in and out of the region. Today we see high quality Purbeck clay regularly shipped to Spanish ceramics companies, and large quantities of timber continue to be shipped to Poole from the Baltic. Grain is both imported and exported through the port, and Poole regularly discharges steel cargoes from all over Europe. Aggregate is also shipped into the port for the construction industry.

Channel Seaways operate liner services between Poole and the Channel Islands three times a week, and the port frequently handles project cargoes such as pipes and special machinery.

The Harbour Commissioners are keen to build on these traditional cargoes whilst recognising that Dorset does not have the industrial hinterlands which drive volumes through other major UK ports.

Smaller coasters are not currently being replaced and consequently short sea vessels are likely to become larger in future years. As a consequence of the Harbour dredging project of 2006 which increased the main channel draft to 7.5 metres, Poole is likely to grow in importance as a key regional port of the South West as other shallower ports find it increasingly difficult to handle the larger vessels.

The Commissioners have been looking at other revenue streams to assist them in completing their statutory duties. The port has handled a number of container vessels in recent years and hopes to develop this trade as the European economy recovers from its recent bruising downturn. It is very likely that the Harbour will see a sharp increase in cruise shipping, as plans are being prepared which would create a cruise ship mooring system adjacent to the main port, enabling Poole to play host to larger cruise ships. The position of Brownsea Island close to the Harbour entrance, however, makes it unlikely that Poole could accommodate vessels much in excess of 200 metres.

The Harbour has proved to be a popular sailing arena for decades, and the Commissioners are keen to help develop the marine leisure reputation of Poole still further. In addition to the commercial marinas at Cobbs

look of the shoreline. Any other developments with a potentially-adverse effect on the Harbour can be monitored in cooperation with the Local Authorities concerned.

The Port of Poole, along with every other major port in the United Kingdom has been tasked by the Government with completing a master plan which looks ahead to 2030 and beyond. The Harbour Commissioners have started a consultation process which will assist them in understanding the views of the different groups of stakeholders within the Harbour and which will help them finalise the plan in early 2011.

The ferry sector will continue to play an important role within the port, despite the changes that the sector has seen over the years. The abolition of duty free shopping, the construction of the Channel Tunnel and the growth of low cost airlines have all contributed

Quay and Salterns, and those associated with the yacht clubs, the Quay Boat Haven currently accommodates approximately 120 leisure boats of varying design, as well as providing welcome shelter for over 100 fishing, angling and dive boats. The spotlight of the 2012 Olympic sailing events will shortly be on Dorset, and the Commissioners are keen to construct a small 55 berth marina within the existing port area.

Plans are also in place to investigate a larger marina to the west of the port which could accommodate over 800 boats. This project will require a great deal of environmental impact research as well as extensive consultation with the people of Poole and the different stakeholder groups within the Harbour. If successful, the marina would greatly enhance Poole Harbour's ability to host major maritime events. The project would also provide an economic boost to the town, generating additional revenues for Poole businesses and restaurants, as well as enabling the numbers of swinging moorings in the Harbour to be reduced.

The port of Poole is also currently in negotiations to provide a support base for a proposed wind farm off the Dorset coast. This project could provide the catalyst for the construction of new quays within the port, which would provide increased opportunities for commercial shipping in Poole.

It is critically important that the port continues to

Poole Harbour's future rests with the young.

evolve. The iconic Twin Sails Bridge linking Poole and Hamworthy is currently being constructed and will be formally opened in 2012. It will greatly improve port traffic flows within Poole, as well as enabling the former Power Station site to be developed, together with the Poole waterfront opposite. This development along with the projects mentioned above will assist the Commissioners in creating a successful future for Poole Harbour. All ports see an ebb and flow in their business as some existing customers disappear whilst new cargo handling opportunities present themselves. The port of Poole cannot afford to stand still if the Harbour Commissioners are to continue to have sufficient revenues to undertake the multitude of important roles involved in the conservancy and management of one of the largest and most beautiful natural harbours on the globe.

Poole Harbour and its surroundings will continue to thrive. The problems and opportunities for the immediate future are well understood, and organisational awareness is well in place to optimise their overall effect. Perhaps equally importantly, those glorious views towards the islands and onwards to the Purbecks, together with its special light and microclimate, will surely continue to make Poole Harbour a favoured and favourite place.

References

PART I

Chapter 1 Introduction

Bird, E.C.F. & Ranwell, D.S., 1964, *Spartina* salt marshes in southern England. IV. The physiography of Poole Harbour, Dorset. *Journal of Ecology*, 52: 355–66.

Caldow, R., McGrorty, S., West, A., Durrell, S.E.A. le V dit., Stillman, R. & Anderson, S., 2005, Macro-invertebrate fauna in the intertidal mudflats. In J. Humphreys & V. May (eds.) *The Ecology of Poole Harbour*. Amsterdam: Elsevier. 91–108.

Gray, A.J., 1985, *Poole Harbour: ecological sensitivity analysis of the shoreline*. Abbots Ripton: Institute of Terrestrial Ecology.

Gray, A.J., Marshall, D.F. & Raybould, A.F., 1991, A century of evolution in *Spartina anglica*. *Advances in ecological research*, 21: 1–62.

Hubbard, J.C.E. & Stebbing, R.E., 1968, *Spartina* marshes in southern England. VII. Stratigraphy of Keysworth Marsh, Poole Harbour. *Journal of Ecology*, 56: 702–22.

Hubbard, J.C.E., 1965, *Spartina* marshes in southern England. VI. Pattern of invasion in Poole Harbour. *Journal of Ecology*, 53: 799–813.

Humphreys, J. & May V. (eds.), 2005, *The ecology of Poole Harbour*. Amsterdam: Elsevier.

Jarvis, K., 1992, An intertidal zone Romano-British site on Brownsea Island. *Proceedings of the Dorset Natural History and Archaeological Society*, 117: 89–95.

Oliver, F.W., 1925, *Spartina townsendii*; its mode of establishment, economic uses and taxonomic status. *Journal of Ecology*, 13: 74–91.

Ranwell, D.S., 1967, World resources of *Spartina townsendii (s.l.)* and economic use of *Spartina* marshland. *Journal of Ecology*, 52: 95–105.

Ranwell, D.S., Bird, E.C.F., Hubbard, J.C.E. & Stebbings, R.E., 1964, Spartina saltmarshes in Southern England: V. Tidal submergence and chlorinity in Poole Harbour. *Journal of Ecology*, 52: 627.

Raybould, A.F., 1997, The history and ecology of *Spartina anglica* in Poole Harbour. *Proceedings of the Dorset Natural History and Archaeological Society*, 119: 147–58.

Stapf , O., 1913, Townsend's grass or rice grass. *Proceedings of the Bournemouth Natural Science Society*, 5: 76–82.

Chapter 2 The Formation of the Harbour

Gupta, S., Collier, J.S., Palmer-Felgate, A. & Potter, G., 2007, Catastrophic flooding origin of shelf valley systems in the English Channel. *Nature*, 448: 342–45.

Nowell, D.A.G., 2000, Discussion on late Quaternary evolution of the upper reaches of the Solent River, southern England, based upon marine geophysical evidence. *Journal of the Geological Society*, 157: 505–7.

Tyhurst, M.K. & Hinton, M.T., 1997, The evolution of Poole and Christchurch Bays: another look at the Flandrian Transgression. Available on-line at www.dorsetforyou.com/media/pdf/o/o/evoluc.pdf. Dorchester: Dorset County Council. Accessed 27 July 2010.

Velegrakis, A.F., 1994, *Aspects of morphology and sedimentology of a transgressional embayment system: Poole and Christchurch bays*. Unpublished PhD thesis, University of Southampton.

Velegrakis, A.F., Dix, J.K. & Collins, M.B., 1999, Late Quaternary evolution of the upper reaches of the Solent River, southern England, based upon marine geophysical evidence. *Journal of the Geological Society*, 156: 73–87.

Chapter 3 Flora & Fauna

Humphreys, J. & May, V. (eds.), 2005, *The ecology of Poole Harbour*. Amsterdam: Elsevier.

Welton, S., 2003, *Coast & Sea*. Wimborne Minster: The Dovecote Press.

PART II

Chapter 5 Boundaries, Quays, Jetties, Slipways and Marinas

Horsey, I.P., 1991, Poole: the medieval waterfront and its usage. In G.H. Good, R.H. Jones, & M.W. Ponsford (eds.), *Waterfront archaeology*. London: Council for British Archaeology Research Report 74. 51–55.

Hutchins, J., 1774, *History and antiquities of the County of Dorset*. London: W. Bowyer & J. Nichols. (Third edition corrected, augmented, and improved by W. Shipp and J.W. Hodson 1861–70, London: Nichols)

Le Pard, G., 2002, The draining of the Fleet. *Proceedings of the Dorset Natural History and Archaeological Society*, 124: 35–43.

Papworth, M., 2008, Maryland, Brownsea Island. *Proceedings of the Dorset Natural History and Archaeological Society*, 129: 127–38.

Rackham, O., 1986, *The history of the countryside*. London: Dent.

Van Raalte, C., 1906, *Brownsea Island*. London: Arthur L. Humphreys.

Watkins, D.R., 1994, *The Foundry: excavations on Poole Waterfront 1986–7*. Dorchester: Dorset Natural History and Archaeological Society Monograph 14.

Chapter 6 Water Quality Changes

Drake, W. (ed.), 2006, *Poole Harbour aquatic management plan*. On-line publication at: www.pooleharbouraqmp.co.uk. Poole: Poole Harbour Steering Group. Accessed 27 July 2010.

Environment Agency, 2005, *The Frome, Piddle, and Purbeck catchment abstraction management strategy*. Exeter: The Environment Agency.

Humphreys, J. & May, V. (eds.), 2005, *The ecology of Poole Harbour*. Amsterdam: Elsevier.

Langston, W.J., Chesman, B.S., Burt, G.R., Hawkins, S.J., Readman, J., & Worsfold, P., 2003, *Site characterization of the south west European sites, Poole Harbour SPA. A study carried out on behalf of the Environment Agency and English Nature by the Plymouth Marine Science Partnership*. Exeter: The Environment Agency.

Robinson, M., 2008, *History report for Poole Sewage Treatment Works*. Bath: Wessex Water.

Sheldrick, W.F., Syers, J. & Lingard, J., 2003. Contribution of livestock excreta to nutrient balances. *Nutrient Cycling in Agroecosystems*, 66: 119–31.

Sheldrick, W.F., Syers, J.K. & Lingard, J., 2002, A conceptual model for conducting nutrient audits at national, regional, and global scales. *Nutrient Cycling in Agroecosystems*, 62: 61–72.

Wessex Water, 1978, *South East Dorset Water Services Study. Consultations and the further appraisal of sewage disposal options*. Bath: Wessex Water.

Wessex Water, 1980, *South East Dorset Water Services – scientific study*. Bath: Wessex Water.

PART III

Chapter 8 Early Inhabitants

Ashbee, P., 1960, *The Bronze Age round barrow in Britain*. London: Phoenix House.

Barton, R.N.E., 1992, *Hengistbury Head, Dorset. Volume 2: The late upper Palaeolithic and early Mesolithic sites*. Oxford: Oxford University Committee for Archaeology Monograph 34.

Bennett, G.J., 1899, The Roman occupation of Wareham. *Proceedings of the Dorset Natural History and Archaeological Society*, 20: 148–60.

Bridgland, D.R., 2001, The Pleistocene evolution and Palaeolithic occupation of the Solent River. In F.F. Wenban-Smith & R.T. Hosfield (eds.), *Palaeolithic archaeology of the Solent River*. London: Lithic Studies Society Occasional Paper 7. 15–25.

Bristow, C.R., Freshney, E.C. & Penn, I.E., 1991, *Geology of the country around Bournemouth: memoir of the Geological Survey of Great Britain Sheet 329*. London: HMSO.

Calkin, J B, 1951, The Bournemouth area in Neolithic and early Bronze Age times. *Proceedings of the Dorset Natural History and Archaeological Society*, 73: 32–70.

Calkin, J.B., & Green, J.F.N., 1949, Palaeoliths and terraces near Bournemouth. *Proceedings of the Prehistoric Society*, 15: 21–37.

Calkin, J.B., & Piggott, S., 1938, A Neolithic 'A' habitation site at Corfe Mullen. *Proceedings of the Dorset Natural History and Archaeological Society*, 60: 73–4.

Calkin, J.B., 1959, A possible avenue to the Rempstone Circle. *Proceedings of the Dorset Natural History and Archaeological Society*, 81: 114–16.

Calkin, J.B., 1962, The Bournemouth area in the middle and late Bronze Age, with the 'Deverel-Rimbury' problem reconsidered. *Archaeological Journal*, 119: 1–65.

Campbell Smith, W., 1963, Jade axes from sites in the British Isles. *Proceedings of the Prehistoric Society*, 29: 133–72.

Cox, P.W., & Hearne, C.M., 1991, *Redeemed from the heath. The archaeology of the Wytch Farm Oilfield (1987–90)*. Dorchester: Dorset Natural History and Archaeological Society Monograph 9.

Darvill, T., 2010, *Prehistoric Britain*. Abingdon: Routledge.

Dimbleby, G.W., 1962, *The development of British heathlands and their soils*. Oxford: Oxford Forestry Memoir 23.

Edwards, R.J., 2001, Mid to late Holocene relative sea-level change in Poole Harbour, southern England. *Journal of Quaternary Science*, 16: 221–35.

Evans, J., 1897, *The ancient stone implements, weapons and ornaments of Great Britain* (Second edition). London: Longmans, Green and Co.

Field, N., Matthews, C.L. & Smith, I.F., 1964, New Neolithic sites in Dorset and Bedfordshire, with a note on the distribution of Neolithic storage-pits in Britain. *Proceedings of the Prehistoric Society*, 30: 352–81.

Grinsell, L.V., 1959, *Dorset Barrows*. Dorchester: Dorset Natural History and Archaeological Society.

Grinsell, L.V., 1982, *Dorset Barrows supplement*. Dorchester: Dorset Natural History and Archaeological Society.

Ladle, L., & Woodward, A., 2003, A middle Bronze Age house and burnt mound at Bestwall, Wareham, Dorset: an interim report. *Proceedings of the Prehistoric Society*, 69: 265–77.

Ladle, L., 2004, *Pits, pots and people: the archaeology of Bestwall Quarry, Wareham, Dorset*. London: English Heritage and Bestwall Archaeology.

Lawson, A.J., 1990, The prehistoric hinterland of Maiden Castle. *Antiquaries Journal*, 70: 271–87.

Long, A.J., Scaife, R.G. & Edwards, R.J., 1999, Pine pollen in intertidal sediments from Poole Harbour, UK; implications for late-Holocene sediment accretion rates and sea-level rise. *Quaternary International*, 55: 3–16.

Maddy, D., 1997, Uplift driven valley incision and river terrace formation in southern England. *Journal of Quaternary Science*, 12: 539–45.

Maynard, D., 1988, Excavations on a pipeline near the River Frome, Worgret, Dorset. *Proceedings of the Dorset Natural History and Archaeological Society*, 110: 77–98.

Momber, G., 2000, Drowned and deserted: a submerged prehistoric landscape in the Solent, England. *International Journal of Nautical Archaeology*, 29: 86–99.

Piggott, C.M., 1945, A flint axe of Scandinavian type from Dorset. *Proceedings of the Dorset Natural History and Archaeological Society*, 67: 28.

Piggott, S. & Piggott, C.M., 1939, Stone and earth circles in Dorset. *Antiquity*, 13: 138–58.

Piggott, S., 1937, The excavation of a long barrow in Holdenhurst Parish, near Christchurch, Hants. *Proceedings of the Prehistoric Society*, 3: 1–14.

RCHME [Royal Commission on the Historical Monuments of England], 1970, *An inventory of historical monuments in the County of Dorset. Volume 2: South-East*. London: HMSO. (3 parts)

Roe, D., 1981, *The lower and middle Palaeolithic periods in Britain*. London: Routledge.

Standing, K. & Smith, J., 1987, Two new prehistoric sites on Canford and Knighton Heaths, Poole. *Proceedings of the Dorset Natural History and Archaeological Society*, 109: 123.

Standing, K., 2002, A new Mesolithic site in Poole. *Proceedings of the Dorset Natural History and Archaeological Society*, 124: 129.

Wainwright, G.J., 1965, The excavation of a round barrow in Worgret Hill, Arne, Dorset. *Proceedings of the Dorset Natural History and Archaeological Society*, 87: 119–25.

Waller, M.P. & Long, A.J., 2003, Holocene coastal evolution and sea-level change on the southern coast of England: a review. *Journal of Quaternary Science*, 18: 351–9.

West, I.M., 2008, *The Sandbanks Sand Spit or Sandbanks Peninsula: geology of the Wessex Coast*. On-line publication at: www.soton.ac.uk/~imw/Sandbanks.htm. Southampton: School of Ocean and Earth Science, National Oceanography Centre, Southampton University. Accessed: 21 April 2008.

Wymer, J. (ed.), 1977, *Gazetteer of Mesolithic sites in England and Wales*. London: Council for British Archaeology Research Report 20.

Wymer, J., 1999, *The lower Palaeolithic occupation of Britain*. Salisbury: Wessex Archaeology. (2 volumes)

Chapter 9 The Growth and Decline of Specific Sites

Introduction

Hearne, C.M. & Smith R.J.C., 1991, A late Iron Age settlement and Black-Burnished ware (BB1) production site at Worgret, near Wareham, Dorset. *Proceedings of the Dorset Natural History and Archaeological Society*, 113: 55–105.

Bestwall

Ladle, L. & Woodward, A., 2009, *Excavations at Bestwall Quarry, Wareham 1992–2005. Volume 1: the prehistoric landscape*. Dorchester: Dorset Natural History and Archaeological Society Monograph 19.

Ladle, L., forthcoming, *Excavations at Bestwall Quarry, Wareham 1992–2005. Volume 2: the Iron Age and later landscape*. Dorchester: Dorset Natural History and Archaeological Society Monograph.

Green Island, and Ower

Bromby, A., 1969, *Site report on excavations on Green Island*. Poole: Poole Museum Manuscript PM62.

Calkin, J., 1955, Kimmeridge coal-money: the Romano-British shale armlet industry. *Proceedings of the Dorset Natural History and Archaeological Society,* 75: 45–71.

Cox, P., 1985, Excavation and survey on Furzey Island, Poole Harbour (SZ011871): an interim note. *Proceedings of the Dorset Natural History and Archaeological Society,* 107: 157–8.

Cox, P., 1988. Excavation and survey on Furzey Island, Poole Harbour, Dorset. *Proceedings of the Dorset Natural History and Archaeological Society,* 110: 49–72.

Cox, P.W., & Hearne, C.M., 1991, *Redeemed from the heath. The archaeology of the Wytch Farm Oilfield (1987–90).* Dorchester: Dorset Natural History and Archaeological Society Monograph 9.

Cunliffe, B., 1978, *Hengistbury Head.* London, Elek.

Cunliffe, B., 1987, *Hengistbury Head, Dorset. Volume 1: the prehistoric and Roman settlement,* 3500 BC – AD 500. Oxford: Oxford University Committee for Archaeology Monograph 13.

Edwards, R., 2001, Mid to late Holocene relative sea-level change in Poole Harbour, southern England. *Journal of Quaternary Science,* 16: 221–35.

Farrar, R., 1964, Iron Age and Roman occupation on Green Island, Poole Harbour. *Proceedings of the Dorset Natural History and Archaeological Society,* 85: 104–5.

Jarvis, K., 1985, Observations for sea-level changes on the south-east side of Furzey Island, Poole Harbour. *Proceedings of the Dorset Natural History and Archaeological Society,* 107: 153–4.

Jarvis, K., 1992, An inter-tidal zone Romano-British site on Brownsea Island. *Proceedings of the Dorset Natural History and Archaeological Society,* 114: 89–95.

Wilkes, E.M., 2004, *Iron Age maritime nodes on the English Channel coast. An investigation into the location, nature and context of early ports and harbours.* Bournemouth: Unpublished PhD thesis, Bournemouth University.

Wilkes, E.M., 2007, Prehistoric sea journeys and port approaches: the south coast and Poole Harbour. In V. Cummings & R. Johnston (eds.), *Prehistoric Journeys.* Oxford: Oxbow Books. 121–30.

Woodward, P., 1987, Excavations of a late Iron Age trading settlement and Romano-British BB1 pottery production site at Ower, Dorset. In N. Sunter & P. Woodward (eds.), *Romano-British Industries in Purbeck.* Dorchester: Dorset Natural History and Archaeological Society Monograph 6. 44–124.

Other Iron Age and Roman Settlements

Bryant, L. & Horner, W., 1990, Dorset. In B. Coles (ed.), *Organic archaeological remains in southwest Britain. A survey of the available evidence.* Exeter: WARP Occasional Paper 4. 35–56.

Cox, P.W., & Hearne, C.M., 1991, *Redeemed from the heath. The archaeology of the Wytch Farm Oilfield (1987–90).* Dorchester: Dorset Natural History and Archaeological Society Monograph 9.

Cunliffe, B., 1972, The late Iron Age metalwork from Bulbury, Dorset. *Antiquaries Journal,* 52: 293–308.

Sunter, N. & Woodward, P. (eds.), *Romano-British industries in Purbeck.* Dorchester: Dorset Natural History and Archaeological Society Monograph 6.

The Roman Occupation of Hamworthy

Jarvis, K., 1993, *Excavations at Hamworthy in 1974.* Proceedings of the Dorset Natural History and Archaeological Society, 115: 101–9.

Smith, H.P., 1930, The occupation of the Hamworthy Peninsula in the late Celtic and Romano British times. *Proceedings of the Dorset Natural History and Archaeological Society,* 52: 96–130.

Newton: a Failed Settlement

Bowen, H.C. & Taylor, C.C., 1964, The site of Newton (*Villa Nova*) Studland, Dorset. *Medieval Archaeology,* 8: 223–6.

Cox, P.W., & Hearne, C.M., 1991, *Redeemed from the heath. The archaeology of the Wytch Farm Oilfield (1987–90).* Dorchester: Dorset Natural History and Archaeological Society Monograph 9.

Widdowson, C., 1998, *Housing tradition in south east Dorset.* Southampton: Unpublished MA thesis, University of Southampton.

Chapter 10 The Islands

Anon. no date. *Brownsea Island. An English gem in an exquisite setting.* Bournemouth: Hankinson & Son.

Battrick, J. (ed. J. Lawson), 1978, *Brownsea Islander.* Poole: Poole Historical Trust.

Bennett, T.,1881, *A sketch of Brownsea Island.* Poole: C.J. Woodford. (Reprinted 1971, Wakefield: S.R. Publishers)

Blomfield, R., 1974, *Poole Harbour, heath and islands.* Sherborne: Dorset Publishing Co..

Brannon, P., 1857, *An illustrated historical and picturesque description of the island and castle of Branksea, Dorsetshire.* Poole: Sydenham.

Bugler, J. & Drew, G., 1995, *A history of Brownsea Island.* Dorchester: Dorset County Library.

Drayton, M. (ed. J.W. Habel), 1933, *Poly-olbion.* Oxford: Blackwell Works of Michael Drayton 4.

Drivers, 1859, *Sale catalogue. Branksea Island. Auction sale specification August 5, 1859.* Bournemouth: Drivers Auctioneers.

Hankinson & Sons, 1927, *Sale catalogue. Brownsea Island: catalogue of the contents of the mansion. Sold by auction June 1927*. Bournemouth: Messrs Hankinson and Son.

Humphreys, J. & May, V. (eds.), 2005, *The ecology of Poole Harbour*. Amsterdam: Elsevier.

Hutchins, J., 1774, *History and antiquities of the County of Dorset*. London: W. Bowyer & J. Nichols. (Third edition corrected, augmented, and improved by W. Shipp and J.W. Hodson 1861–70, London: Nichols)

Legg, R., 1986, *Brownsea – Dorset's fantasy island*. Sherborne: Dorset Publishing Company.

Moore, P. 2003, *For nature, not humans: recollections of Brownsea Island under the ownership of Mrs. Bonham Christie*. Poole: Poole Historical Trust.

Moore, P., 2009, A winsome place. Poole: Poole Historical Trust.

National Trust, 1963, *The antiquities of Brownsea Island*. London: The National Trust.

Short, B.C., 1963, *A short history of Brownsea Island*. Poole: Looker.

Sutton, J. & Bromby, A., 1981, *Brownsea Island. A history*. London: The National Trust.

Van Raalte, C., 1906, *Brownsea Island*. London: Arthur L. Humphreys.

Chapter 11 Development of Wareham and Poole

Wareham

Davis T., 1984, *Wareham, gateway to Purbeck*. Sherborne: Dorset Publishing Company

Hinton, D., 1998, *Discover Dorset: Saxons and Vikings*. Wimborne Minster: The Dovecote Press.

Ladle L., 1994, *Wareham: a pictorial history*. Chichester: Phillimore.

Poole

Andrews, I.K.D. (trans.), 1992, *Poole Census 1574*. Poole: Poole Borough Council Borough Archives 1.

Cochrane, C., 1970, *Poole Bay and Purbeck 300 BC to AD 1600*. Dorchester: Privately published. (Available at the Dorset History Centre 942.336)

Horsey, I.P., 1992, *Excavations in Poole 1973–1983*. Dorchester: Dorset Natural History and Archaeological Society Monograph 10.

Markey, M., Wilkes, E., & Darvill, T., 2002, Poole Harbour. An Iron Age port. *Current Archaeology*, 181, 7–11.

Penn, K.J., 1980, *Historic towns in Dorset*. Dorchester: Dorset Natural History and Archaeological Society Monograph 1.

Short, B., 1932, *Poole – the romance of its early history*. London & Aylesbury: Hunt, Barnard & Co..

Smith, H.P., 1948, *The history of the Borough and County of the Town of Poole. Volume I: origins and early development*. Poole: Looker.

Smith, L.T. (ed.), 1964, *The itinerary of John Leland in or about the years 1535-1543*. London: Centaur Press (5 volumes)

Sydenham, J., 1839, *History of the Town and County of Poole*. Poole: Privately published. (Reprinted 1986, Poole: Poole Historical Trust)

Watkins, D.R., 1994, *The Foundry: excavations on Poole waterfront 1986–7*. Dorchester: Dorset Natural History and Archaeological Society Monograph 14.

Chapter 12 Defence of the Harbour

Beamish, D. & Andrews, I., 1993, *D-Day Poole*. Poole: Poole Historical Trust.

Beamish, D., Bennet, H., & Hillier, J. 1980, *Poole and World War II*. Poole: Poole Historical Trust.

Brown, R.A., Colvin, H.M & Taylor, A.J., 1963, *History of the Kings Works. Volume 2. The Middle Ages*. London: HMSO.

Dobinson, C., 2000, *Fields of deception: Britain's bombing decoys of World War II*. London: Methuen.

Edgington, M.A., 1999, *Bournemouth and the Second World War*. Bournemouth: Bournemouth Local Studies.

Harrington, P. 2007, *The castles of Henry VIII*. Oxford: Osprey.

Hodges, M.A., 2004, *Prepared for battle some details of forts and fights in and near Christchurch over the last three millennia*. Christchurch: Privately published. (Available at the Dorset History Centre 942.339)

Lowry, B., 2004, *British home defences 1940-45*. Oxford: Osprey.

Moore, P. 2003, *For nature, not humans: recollections of Brownsea Island under the ownership of Mrs. Bonham Christie*. Poole: Poole Historical Trust.

Saunders, A., 1997, *Channel Defences*. London: Batsford & English Heritage.

Smith, H.P. 1951, *The history of the Borough and County of the Town of Poole. Volume 2: County corporate status*. Poole: Looker.

PART IV

Chapter 14 Salt Production

Barker, K., 2005, *Salis ad ripam maris aet Lim*: of salt and the Dorset coast at Lyme. *Proceedings of the Dorset Natural History and Archaeological Society*, 127: 43–51.

Bowen, H.C. & Fowler, P.J., 1965, Earthwork circles and mounds on Studland Heath, Dorset. *Antiquity*, 37: 220–30.

Calkin, J.B., 1948, The Isle of Purbeck in the Iron Age. *Proceedings of the Dorset Natural History and Archaeological Society*, 70: 29–59.

Cox, P.W. & Hearne, C.M., 1991, *Redeemed from the heath. The archaeology of the Wytch Farm Oilfield (1987–90)*. Dorchester: Dorset Natural History and Archaeological Society Monograph 9.

Farrar, R.A.H., 1975, Prehistoric and Roman saltworks in Dorset. In K.W. De Brisay & K.A. Evans (eds.), *Salt: the study of an ancient industry*. Colchester: Colchester Archaeological Group. 14–20.

Fawn, A.J., Evans, K.A., McMaster, I. & Davis, G.M.R., 1990, *The Red Hills of Essex: salt-making in antiquity*. Colchester: Colchester Archaeological Group.

Fielding, A. & Fielding, A., 2006, *The Salt Industry*. Risborough: Shire Publications.

Gilman, P., Barford, P., Fielding, A. & Penney, S., 1998, *Monuments Protection Programme. The salt industry*. Chelmsford: Essex County Council, Unpublished printed report for English Heritage.

Gouletquer, P. L., 1974, The development of salt-making in prehistoric Europe. *Essex Journal*, 9: 2–14.

Hathaway, S.J.E., 2005, Poole Harbour: a review of early and more recent archaeological investigations with evidence for Iron Age and Romano-British salt production. *Proceedings of the Dorset Natural History and Archaeological Society*, 127: 53–7.

Holden, E. & Hudson, T., 1981, Salt-making in the Adur Valley, Sussex. *Sussex Archaeological Collections*, 119: 117–48.

Maltby, M., 2006, Salt and animal products: linking production and use in Iron Age Britain. In M. Maltby (ed.), *Integrating zooarchaeology. Proceedings of the 9th Conference of the International Council of Archaeozoology*. Oxford: Oxbow. 117–22.

Olivier, L. & Kovacik, J., 2006, The 'Briquetage de la Seille' (Lorraine, France): proto-industrial salt production in the European Iron Age. *Antiquity*, 80: 558–66.

Rapp, G., 2002, *Archaeomineralogy*. London: Springer.

Smith, H.P., 1931, The occupation of the Hamworthy Peninsula in the late Keltic and Romano-British periods. *Proceedings of the Dorset Natural History and Archaeological Society*, 52: 96–130.

Woodward, P.J., 1987, The excavation of a late Iron Age trading settlement and Romano-British BB1 pottery production site at Ower, Dorset. In N. Sunter & P.J. Woodward (eds.), *Romano-British industries in Purbeck*. Dorchester: Dorset Natural History and Archaeological Society, Monograph 6. 44–124.

Chapter 15 Alum and Copperas

Agricola, G. (trans. H.C. Hoover & L.C. Hoover), 1556 / 1950, *De re metallica*. New York: Dover.

Allen, T., Cotterill M., Pike, G. & Miller, I. (ed.), 2004, *Copperas. An account of the Whitstable Works and the first industrial-scale chemical production in England*. Canterbury: Canterbury Archaeological Trust Occasional Paper 2.

Bettey, J.H., 1982, The production of alum and copperas in southern England. *Textile History*. 13: 91–8.

Bettey, J.H., 2001, A fruitless quest for wealth: the mining of alum and copperas in Dorset *c.1568–1617*. *Southern History*, 23: 1–9.

Bright, M.J., 1961, *Brownsea Island*. Poole: Oriole Publishing Co..

Cross, C., 1996, *The Puritan Earl: the life of Henry Hastings, third Earl of Huntingdon, 1536–1595*. London: Macmillan.

Gough, J.W., 1969, *The rise of the entrepreneur*. London: Batsford.

Jenkins, R., 1914, *The alum trade in the 15th and 16th centuries, and the beginning of the alum industry in England*. London: South-Eastern Union of Scientific Societies.

Miller, I., (ed.), 2002, *Steeped in history. The alum and copperas industry of north-east Yorkshire*. Hemsley: North York Moors National Park Authority.

Morris, C. (ed.), 1949, *The journeys of Celia Fiennes (1685–1703)*. London: Cresset Press.

Sheldrick, W.F., 2007, *Project design submission to English Heritage by Poole Harbour Heritage Project for the Poole Alum and Copperas Industries Project*. Poole: Poole Harbour Heritage project, unpublished printed report 26 February 2007.

Smith, H.P., 1948, *The history of the Borough and County of the Town of Poole. Volume I: origins and early development*. Poole: Looker.

Chapter 16 Other Chemicals

Bowditch, M.R., 1983, *Cordite, Poole*. Poole: Privately published. (Available at the Dorset History Centre 662.26)

Bowditch, M.R. & Hayward, L., 1997, *A pictorial record of*

the *Royal Naval Cordite Factory, Holton Heath*. Wareham: Finial Press.

Cocroft, W.D., 2000, *Dangerous energy: the archaeology of gunpowder and military explosives manufacture*. Swindon: English Heritage.

Chapter 17 Oil and Gas

British Petroleum, 2008, *Asset portfolio 2008 BP Exploration*. Aberdeen: British Petroleum.

British Petroleum, no date, *Landscape on loan*. Poole: BP Public Affairs Department.

Dorset Coast Forum, 1998, T*owards policy for Dorset's Coast: oil and gas*. On-line publication at: http://www.dorsetforyou.com/media.jsp?mediaid=8830&filetype=pdf . Dorchester: Dorset Coast Forum. Accessed 27 July 2010.

IPIECA [The International Petroleum Industry Environmental Conservation Association], 2003, *The oil industry operating in sensitive environments. BP in Dorset, southern England*. On-line publication at: http://www.ipieca.org/sites/default/files/system/BP_WytchFarm.pdf . London: IPIECA. Accessed 27 July 2010.

Webb, P., 1986, *A short guide to the Wytch Farm oilfield development*. London: British Petroleum.

Chapter 18 The Clay Industry

Cooksey A.J.A., 1980, *The Poole clay tobacco pipes*. Bournemouth: Bournemouth Local Studies Publication 644.

Cousins, D.R., no date, *The Purbeck clay trade in the seventeenth and eighteenth centuries*. Winchester: unpublished MA thesis, University of Winchester.

Cox, P.W., & Hearne, C.M., 1991, *Redeemed from the heath. The archaeology of the Wytch Farm Oilfield (1987–90)*. Dorchester: Dorset Natural History and Archaeological Society Monograph 9.

Davies, D.J., 1982, Tobacco pipe clay in Poole's coastal trade. *Somerset and Dorset Notes and Queries*, 31: 235–38.

Green, C., 1999, *John Dwight's Fulham Pottery: excavations 1971–79*. London: English Heritage Archaeological Report 6.

Lyne, M., 2002, The late Iron Age and Romano-British pottery production sites at Redcliffe, Arne, and Stoborough. *Proceedings of the Dorset Natural History and Archaeological Society*, 124: 45–100.

Messenger, M.J., 1982, *North Devon clay: the history of an industry and its transport*. Truro: Twelvehead Press.

Spoerry, P.S., Ceramic production in medieval Dorset and the surrounding region. *Medieval Ceramics*, 14: 3–17.

Terry, J.A., 1987, East Holme pottery. *Proceedings of the Dorset Natural History and Archaeological Society*, 109: 39–46.

Weatherill, L.M., 1983, The growth of the pottery industry in England, 1660-1815. Some new evidence and estimates. *Post-Medieval Archaeology*, 1: 15–46.

Willan, T.S.,1967, *The English coasting trade 1600–1750*. Manchester: Manchester University Press.

Chapter 19 Pottery

Blakeston, M., 1999, *History of Sanford*. Sanford: Sanford Millennium Committee.

Brannon, P., 1857, The illustrated historical and picturesque guide to Poole and Bournemouth, and the surrounding country. Poole: Sydenham.

Carter, H., 1949, *I call to mind*. Poole: Looker.

Chimes. M., 2001, *Historic concrete: background to appraisal*. London: Thomas Telford.

Haywood, L. (ed. P Atterbury), 1998, *Poole Pottery, Carter & Company and their successors 1973–1998*. Shepton Beauchamp: Richard Dennis.

Legg, R., 1986, *Dorset's fantasy island*. Sherborne: Dorset Publishing.

Papworth, M., 1992, *Archaeological survey, Brownsea Island*. Trowbridge: The National Trust Wessex Region.

Stone, C., 2007, *Rails to Poole Harbour*. Usk: The Oakwood Press.

Stout, V., 1992, *Around Kinson Pottery*. Over Wallop: Privately published. (Available at the Dorset History Centre 666.394233)

Waters, J., 2009, Lilliput's industrial past. *Dorset Life*, 367 (October 2009). Available on-line at: http://www.dorsetlife.co.uk/2009/10/lilliput%e2%80%99s-industrial-past/. Wareham: Dorset Life. Accessed 28 July 2010.

Wilnecker, P.M., 1991, *A history of Upper Parkstone (beginning to 1939)*. Bournemouth: Bourne Press.

Young, D., 1971, Brickmaking in Dorset. *Proceedings of the Dorset Natural History and Archaeological Society*, 93: 213–42.

Chapter 20 Mechanical Engineering

British Seagull, 2010, *Just how many British Seagull outboard engines are in sheds, garages and outhouses?* On-line publication at: www.britishseagull.co.uk/history.php. Moulsford: British Seagull. Accessed 27 July 2010.

David Brown Hydraulics, 2008, *The heritage of David Brown Hydraulics*. On-line publication at: http://www.davidbrownhydraulics.com/aboutus.aspx . Poole: David Brown Hydraulic Systems Ltd. Accessed 27 July 2010.

Hillier, J., 1990, *Victorian Poole*. Poole: Poole Historical Trust.

Wear, R. & Lees, E., 1978, *Stephen Lewin and the Poole Foundry*. London: Industrial Railway Society & Industrial Locomotive Society.

Chapter 21 Brewing

Hillier, J., 1990, *Victorian Poole*. Poole: Poole Historical Trust.

Page, W. (ed.), 1908, *A history of the County of Dorset. Volume 2*. London: Constable, Victoria History of the Counties of England.

Chapter 22 Ship and Boatbuilding

Anon., 1954, Bolson's of Poole: a man and his war. *Ship and Boat Builder*, July 1954.

Armstrong, J., 1978, *The Poole Ship of 1325*. Poole: Poole Maritime Trust.

Beamish, D. & Andrews, I, 1993, *D-Day Poole*. Poole: Poole Historical Trust.

Beamish, D., Bennett, H. & Hillier, J., 1980, *Poole and World War II*. Poole: Poole Historical Trust.

Cocksedge, A.E., no date, *Ships built in Poole*. Poole: Privately published. (Available at the Dorset History Centre 387.2025)

Cullingford, C.N., 1988, *A history of Poole*. Chichester: Phillimore.

Law, C.A., RCN, 1989, *White plumes astern: The Short Daring Life of Canada's MTB Flotilla*.

Leather, J., 2002, Family fortunes: Wanhill of Hamworthy. *Classic Boat*, March 2002.

Watkins, D.R., 1994, *The Foundry: excavations on Poole Waterfront 1986–7*. Dorchester: Dorset Natural History and Archaeological Society Monograph 14.

Chapter 23 Fishing

Humphreys, J. & May, V. (eds.), 2005, *The ecology of Poole Harbour*. Amsterdam: Elsevier.

Page, W. (ed.), 1908, *A history of the County of Dorset. Volume 2*. London: Constable, Victoria History of the Counties of England.

Poole Harbour Steering Group, 2006, *Poole Harbour Aquatic Management Plan: Chapter 8: Fisheries*. Available on-line at: http://www.pooleharbouraqmp.co.uk/pdf/ph_amp2006_Chapter_8.pdf. Poole: Poole Harbour Steering Group. Accessed 29 July 2010.

PART V

Chapter 26 Shipping

Andrews, I.K.D., forthcoming, *Poole and Newfoundland*.

Bannister, J., 2003, *Rule of the Admirals: law, custom, and naval government in Newfoundland, 1699-1832*. London & Toronto: University of Toronto Press.

Beamish, D., Dockerill, J. & Hillier, J., 1988, *Pride of Poole 1688–1851*. Poole: Poole Historical Trust.

Beamish, D., Hillier, J. & Johnstone, H.F.V., 1976, *Mansions and merchants of Poole and Dorset*. Poole: Poole Historical Trust.

Cell, G.T., 1969, *English enterprise in Newfoundland 1577–1660*. Toronto: University of Toronto Press.

Cochrane, C., 1970, *Poole Bay and Purbeck 300 BC to AD 1600*. Dorchester: Privately published. (Available at the Dorset History Centre 942.336)

Cook, J., 1768, *Directions for navigating the west coast of Newfoundland*. London: J. Mount & T. Page.

Davis, R., 1962, *The rise of the English shipping industry in the seventeenth and eighteenth centuries*. London: HMSO for the National Maritime Museum.

Handcock, W.G. 1997, *The story of Trinity*. Trinity (Newfoundland): Trinity Historical Society.

Handcock, W.G., 1980, *A biographical profile of the 18th and early 19th century merchant families and entrepreneurs in Trinity, Trinity Bay*. Unpublished manuscript. (Available at Memorial University of Newfoundland, Centre for Newfoundland Studies FF 1036 T82 H3)

Handcock, W.G., 1981, *The merchant families and entrepreneurs of Trinity in the nineteenth century*. Unpublished manuscript. (Available at Memorial University of Newfoundland, Centre for Newfoundland Studies FF 1036 T82 H316)

Handcock, W.G., 1981, *The origin and development of Trinity up to 1900*. Unpublished manuscript. (Available at Memorial University of Newfoundland, Centre for Newfoundland Studies FF 1036 T82 H32)

Handcock, W.G., 2003, *Soe longe as there comes noe women: origins of English settlement in Newfoundland*. Milton (Ont.): Global Heritage Press.

Mannion, J. (ed.), 1977, *The peopling of Newfoundland: essays in historical geography*. St. John's: Memorial University of Newfoundland, Institute of Social and Economic Research Social and Economic Papers 8.

Mathews, E.F.J., 1934, *Gallant neighbours: being the story of the relationship of the Port of Poole with France*. Poole: Looker.

Mathews, F., 1936, *Poole and Newfoundland*. Unpublished manuscript. (Available at Memorial University of

Newfoundland, Centre for Newfoundland Studies DA 690 P78 M3 1936)

Matthews, K., 1968, *A history of the west of England-Newfoundland fishery*. Oxford: Unpublished DPhil thesis, University of Oxford.

Matthews, L., 1988, *Lectures on the history of Newfoundland 1500–1830*. St. John's: Memorial University of Newfoundland, Maritime History Group.

Neary, P., 1983, *Part of the main: an illustrated history of Newfoundland and Labrador*. St. John's: Breakwater Books.

O'Flaherty, P., 1999, *Old Newfoundland. A history to 1843*. St. John's: Long Beach Press.

Perry, P., 1968, The Newfoundland trade. *The American Neptune*, 28. (Available at the Dorset History Centre 381.094337)

Prowse, D.W., 1896, *A history of Newfoundland* (Second edition). London. (Reprinted 2002, Portugal Cove: Boulder Publications Ltd.)

Seary, E.R. (ed. W.J. Kirwin), 1998, *Family names of the island of Newfoundland* (Corrected edition). London: McGill-Queen's University Press.

Short, B., 1932, *Poole – the romance of its later history*. London: Barnard Hunt.

Thomas, A. (ed. J.M. Murray), 1968, *The Newfoundland journal of Aaron Thomas: able seaman in HMS*. London: Longmans.

Thwaite, A., 2002, *Glimpses of the wonderful: the life of Philip Henry Gosse, 1810-1888*. London: Faber.

Williams, A. (ed. A.G. Macpherson), 1987, *Father Baudoin's War: D'Iberville's campaigns in Acadia and Newfoundland, 1696 and 1697*. St. John's: Memorial University of Newfoundland, Department of Geography.

Yonge, J. (ed. F.N.L. Poynter), 1963, *The journal of James Yonge, 1647 – 1721: Plymouth surgeon*. Hamden (Conn): Archon Books.

Chapter 28 Unofficial Trade

Angel, M.V., 2008, *In search of Isaac Gulliver: legendary Dorset smuggler*. Wild Geese Publishing.

Anon., 1338–1403, *Calendar of Patent Rolls preserved in the Public Record Office*. [See esp. Edward III, Sept 1338; Henry IV, July 1402; and Henry IV. May 1403].

Atton, H., 1908–1910, *The King's Customs: an account of maritime revenue and contraband traffic in England, Scotland and Ireland*. London: John Murray. (2 volumes)

Bell, N., 1916, *From harbour to harbour*. London: G. Bell.

Capgrave, J. (ed. F.C. Hingeston), 1858, *The Chronicle of England*. London: Rerum Britannicarum medii aevi scriptores.

Carson, E., 1972, *The ancient and rightful Customs: a history of the English Customs Service*. Hamden (Conn.): Archon Books.

Chacksfield, K.M., 1978, *Smuggling heritage around Bournemouth: the romantic history of 'the gentlemen of the night'*. Bournemouth: Bournemouth Tourist Information Centre.

Chacksfield, K.M., 1984, *Smuggling days* (Third edition). Sherborne: Dorset Publishing.

Cochrane, C., 1971, *Poole Bay and Purbeck 2: 1660–1920*. Dorchester: Longmans.

Crombie, Sir J., 1962, *Her Majesty's Customs and Excise*. London: G. Allen & Unwin.

Farquharson-Coe, A., 1975, *Hants and Dorset's smugglers*. St Ives: James Pike.

Foster, D.A., 1936, *At war with the smugglers*. London: Ward Lock.

Guttridge, R., 1987, *Dorset smugglers* (Second edition). Sherborne: Dorset Publishing.

Hardy, E., 1955, *Thomas Hardy's notebooks*. London: Hogarth Press.

Hardy, W. M., 1978, *Smuggling days in Purbeck*. Swanage: Purbeck Press.

Marsden, R.G. (ed.), 1916, *Documents relating to law and custom of the sea*. London: Naval Record Society 50. (2 volumes)

Mathews, E.F.J., 1934, *Gallant neighbours: being the story of the relationship of the port of Poole with France*. Poole: Looker.

Morley, G., 1983, *Smuggling in Hampshire and Dorset 1700-1850*. Newbury: Countryside Books.

Morley, G., 1994, *The smuggling war: the government's fight against smuggling in the 18th and 19th centuries*. Stroud: Sutton.

Oakley, R., 1944, *Smugglers of Christchurch, Bourne Heath and the New Forest*. London: Hutchinson.

Paxton, J. & Wroughton, J., 1971, *Smuggling*. London: Macmillan.

Pitts, J., 1965, *The Gentle Smuggler: a play in three acts*. Bournemouth: Borough of Bournemouth Art Gallery and Museums.

Short, B.C., 1969, *Smugglers of Poole and Bournemouth*. Bournemouth: Dorset Publishing Co.

Smith, G., 1983, *Kings cutters*. London: Conway Maritime Press.

Wood, G.B., 1966, *Smugglers' Britain*. London: Cassell.

Chapter 30 Road and Rail.

Beaton, D., 2001, *Dorset maps*. Wimborne Minster: The Dovecote Press.

Cochrane, C., 1970, *Poole Bay and Purbeck 300 BC to AD 1600*. Dorchester: Privately published. (Available at the Dorset History Centre 942.336)

Cochrane, C., 1971, *Poole Bay and Purbeck 2: 1660–1920*. Dorchester: Longmans.

Cox, P.W., & Hearne, C.M., 1991, *Redeemed from the heath. The Archaeology of the Wytch Farm Oilfield (1987–90)*. Dorchester: Dorset Natural History and Archaeological Society Monograph 9.

Cullingford, C.N., 2003, *A history of Poole* (Second edition). Chichester: Phillimore.

Good, R., 1966, *The old roads of Dorset* (Second edition). Bournemouth: Commin.

Hutchins, J., 1774, *History and antiquities of the County of Dorset*. London: W. Bowyer & J. Nichols (Third edition corrected, augmented, and improved by W. Shipp and J.W. Hodson 1861–70, London: Nichols)

Chapter 31 Flying Boats and Poole Harbour

PFBC [Poole Flying Boat Celebration], 2009, *About us*. On-line publication at: http://www.pooleflyingboats.com/about.html. Poole: Poole Flying Boat Celebration. Accessed 27 July 2010.

Trautmann, J, 2007, *Pan American clippers: the golden age of the flying boats*. Poole: Chris Lloyd.

Chapter 32 Leisure and Pleasure

Cuthell, Lieut-Col. T.G., 1893, *A sailing guide to the Solent and Poole harbour: with practical hints as to living and cooking on and working a small yacht*. London: Gill.

Lloyds, 1889, *Register of Yachts 1889*. London: Lloyds.

McKee, E., 1983, *Working boats of Britain*. London: Conway Maritime Press and National Maritime Museum.

Smith, H.P., 1948–51, *The history of the Borough and County of the Town of Poole*. Poole: Looker. (2 volumes)

Watkins, D.R., 1994, *The Foundry: excavations on Poole Waterfront 1986–7*. Dorchester: Dorset Natural History and Archaeological Society Monograph 14.

Index

town gas 113–5
trade and industry
    alum and copperas production 109–12, 138
    brewing 141–5
    brick 135
    chemicals 109–17
    clay 122–8
    fishing 147–8, 158–63, 191
    marble 40, 73, 173
    mechanical engineering 136–40
    metalworking, pre-Roman 64, 66, 67
    oil and gas 118–21
    pottery 64, 67, 70, 129–35
    salt 68, 70, 72, 74, 92, 106–8
    ship and boatbuilding 146–57
    town gas 113–5
turnpikes trusts 212

Van Raalte, Charles 79–80

Wanhill family 148, 155, 224
Wareham
    brewing 141–2, 145
    fishing industry 159
    harbour scheme abandoned 44
    history 86–9, 93
    oil production 119–20
    Saxon quay 40
    transport links 213, 214, 215
water levels and tides
    geography and geology 10, 20–1, 75, 158, 238
    pre-Roman occupation 39–40, 58–9, 61, 66, 82
water quality 48–53, 239
waterskiing 235
Watkins, David 147, 222
Waugh, Colonel William 37, 79, 112, 129, 213
Wessex Water 49–52
'West of Corfe River' settlement 61, 70
Wheeler, Sir Arthur 81
White family 193, 196
Whitley Lake 28, 235
wildlife 29–31
Wildman, John 112
Wytch Farm 118–21